# Sermons

## of the

# 𝔆𝔬𝔫𝔣𝔢𝔡𝔢𝔯𝔞𝔠𝔶

## 1861-1862

edited by

## Dr. William G. Peters

CHATTANOOGA:
C. S. Printing Office
2014

Originally published separately in various forms
during the War for Independence
in the
CONFEDERATE STATES OF AMERICA.

Edited by

DR. WILLIAM G. PETERS
PRESIDENT
THE CONFEDERATE STATES OF AMERICA, INC.

Copyright © 2014, Dr. William G. Peters, President, THE CONFEDERATE STATES OF AMERICA, INC. — All rights reserved in all media formats under Berne Convention for U.S. and International Copyrights.

Published by the CONFEDERATE STATES PRINTING OFFICE[1], CONFEDERATE STATES OF AMERICA, INC.

---

[1] A division of the Confederate States of America, Inc. Also designated the C.S. PRINTING OFFICE.

# CONTENTS

Foreword ........................................................................................... i

## 1861

God's Presence with the Confederate States ........................... 1

A Sermon by Rev. Daniel Dreher ........................................... 21

God Our Refuge and Strength in this War ............................ 37

God's Presence with Our Army at Manassas ....................... 59

God in the War ......................................................................... 79

Christian Duty in the Present Time of Trouble ................. 105

A Tract for the Times — Slavery & Abolitionism ............. 117

The Silver Trumpets of the Sanctuary ................................ 151

A Sermon for the Confederate Cadets ................................ 163

## 1862

New Wine Not to be Put in Old Bottles ............................. 185

God, the Giver of Victory and Peace .................................. 203

Our Cause in Harmony with the Purposes of God .......... 217

God's Providence in War ...................................................... 239

A Fast Day Sermon ................................................................ 251

Shiloh ....................................................................................... 271

The Word of God a Nation's Life ........................................ 281

Our Danger and Our Duty ................................................... 301

## Afterword

Correspondence between Lord Acton and R.E. Lee ....... 317

# Foreword

The South has traditionally been a bastion of the Christian Faith. This was true before Lincoln's War against the South as much as today. At the time of the War, the North had become largely Unitarian, agnostic, or otherwise unbelieving as its Puritanism morphed into Yankee self-righteousness with a veneer of religion.

Indeed, at the time the South had the majority of Catholics in North America, and its hierarchy in the Southern States was pro-Confederate — recognizing that the Confederate government was more in line with Christian principles.

Protestantism was strong in the South, particularly among the evangelical churches, although these churches were organized as national churches usually governed in the North.

These Protestant churches split into Northern and Southern branches as secession became a reality. Hence, the Protestant Episcopal Church became the Protestant Episcopal Church in the Confederate States. The Southern Baptists, the Southern Methodists, etc. date from this time.

These separations of North from Southern Church were done peacefully, though perhaps with some sadness as long time relationships were sundered. Catholic dioceses simply became dioceses of the Confederate States rather than the United States.

The Southern States as a whole left the political bonds of the United States peacefully and without rancor, although enthusiastically, as THE CONFEDERATE STATES OF AMERICA began her life as a new country. But peace was not to be, because of Abraham Lincoln and his "Republicans."

Lincoln's War against THE CONFEDERACY was the first to break with the commonly recognized rules of warfare which had been in place for a thousand years. These rules, authored by the Church in Medieval times, required Christian States to limit warfare among Christians except for just causes. Many practices were proscribed to Christians. Weapons which caused high losses of life and property were forbidden, for example. Warfare against the citizenry was also forbidden, etc.

Lincoln, in union with his fellow Radical Republicans, and Marxist allies from Europe, who had fled to the United States following their failed revolutions in 1848, introduced a new barbarism, or a return to pagan norms if you will, in the conduct of Lincoln's war. Some may be scandalized that I mention Marxists, but Lincoln himself engaged in a continuing correspondence with Karl Marx, who gave him advice on the conduct of the war.

In this horrific war the United States, ostensibly fighting to "restore the Union", disregarded the recognized rules of war and determined to destroy THE CONFEDERATE STATES by any and all means possible.

This included the destruction of houses and farms, of cities, the raping of women, starving of the populace, deliberately desecrating Southern churches, the killing of prisoners of war through starvation in Yankee concentration camps and withholding of medicines, etc.

THE CONFEDERATE STATES were above all Christian, and sought to fight a Christian, chivalrous defensive "JUST WAR" even in the face of brutal Yankee barbarism. The Confederate Clergy were a bulwark in the face of this onslaught.

Winston Churchill said, "History is written by the victors." And so it was for Lincoln's War. But the truth cannot be hidden forever. This work is one that allows you to peek into the truth of THE CONFEDERATE STATES.

This book is a collection of sermons by priests, ministers, bishops, and a rabbi, from 1861 to 1862[2] as they explained to their congregations the Southern understanding of the causes

---

[2] Another volume will continue from 1863-1865.

of the War, their obligations as Confederate citizens, and invoked God's blessings upon the Confederate cause.

The welfare of the negro was not neglected in these sermons. Negroes, both free and slave, were regarded as part of the Southern culture and civilization. Indeed, negroes both free and slave fought for THE CONFEDERATE STATES.

One will find much to ponder within this work upon our ancestors' drive for freedom from Yankee bigotry and greed. The great war of the Confederacy for freedom and independence will take on new lights and understanding as you read these sermons.

For these are not the rantings of bigots, rednecks, and hate mongers — as Yankees are prone to call Southerners. They are the reasoned exposition of Southern Clergymen upon Southern culture, civilization and hope for a real, permanent Republic in North America — THE CONFEDERATE STATES OF AMERICA.

Lord Acton, writing to Gen. Robert E. Lee stated: "secession filled me with hope, not as the destruction but as the redemption of Democracy....I deemed that you were fighting the battles of our liberty, our progress, and our civilization; and I mourn for the stake which was lost at Richmond more deeply than I rejoice over that which was saved at Waterloo."[3]

That the United States invaded a peaceful country, THE CONFEDERATE STATES, in order to force them against their will to become second class U.S. citizens, which invasion resulted in the devastation of Confederate cities, the countless rape of Confederate women, wanton murder of Confederate civilians, and the destruction of the Confederate economy is undeniable.

It is estimated by experts that over 200,000 Southern civilians lost their lives, including 56,000 Slaves, and over 350,000 Confederate Soldiers and Sailors. The losses for Southern men between the age of 20-24 in 1860 alone is

---

[3] See the Afterword for the correspondence between Lord Acton and Gen. Lee.

almost 25%. The conclusion is unmistakable that the South was devastated beyond our modern comprehension.

And, certainly, in reading these sermons you will find that the problems that beset the United States today, as the U.S. government becomes more despotic and belligerent, are largely the very same problems that the South recognized, sought to separate herself from, and fought so valiantly against.

We must always remember that our Southern ancestors were Christians who fought to defend their homes, families and Faith against the bigotry of Yankee Puritanism that still afflicts us to this day in the "social gospel", "desegregation", political correctness, and other crimes against the Southern people.

The sermons in these two work are by Confederate Clergy of all types, Catholic, Episcopal, Lutheran, Methodist, Presbyterian, Baptist, and Jewish. They represent men of God looking upon the War and giving their thoughts, prayers and guidance to the citizenry of THE CONFEDERATE STATES OF AMERICA.

May we, the descendants and citizens of this proud and upright country, which never surrendered, remain the custodians of truth, and speak for our ancestors.

## DEO VINDICE!

Dr. William G. Peters
President

THE CONFEDERATE STATES OF AMERICA, INC.

Anno Domini 2014

1861

# God's Presence with the Confederate States

PREACHED IN

## CHRIST CHURCH, SAVANNAH

ON THURSDAY, THE 13TH JUNE.

BEING THE DAY APPOINTED

AT THE REQUEST OF CONGRESS

BY THE

### President of the Confederate States

AS A DAY OF

## Solemn Humiliation, Fasting and Prayer

RT. REV. STEPHEN ELLIOTT
RECTOR OF CHRIST CHURCH

SAVANNAH
1861

## Sermon

PSALMS 115: 1, 2, 8.

Not unto us, O Lord, not unto us, but unto thy name give glory, for thy mercy and for thy truth's sake.

Wherefore should the heathen say, Where is now their God

But our God is in the Heavens: be hath done whatsoever he pleased.

The devout Proclamation of our President invites us to give, today, a public manifestation of our gratitude for the clear proofs of the Divine blessing hitherto extended to the people of the Confederate States in their efforts to maintain and perpetuate public liberty, individual rights and national independence.

At the same time it calls upon us to humble ourselves before God in this our time of peril and difficulty, to recognize His righteous government, to acknowledge His goodness in times past, and to supplicate His merciful protection for the future. It is a day to be devoted to mingled gratitude and humiliation — to thanksgiving for great mercies and to a confession of our unworthiness of them — to acknowledgment that unto Him alone belongs the glory of our present condition, and to supplication that he will continue to be our shield and strong tower of defense.

This direction which the Proclamation of our Chief Magistrate has given to the devotions of the day will require a review of our civil affairs from the commencement of our constitutional struggle, in order to point out to you the overruling and directing hand of God in all our movements. May His Holy Spirit rest upon me and preserve my pen from bitterness and my tongue from evil speaking, and may that same Spirit enlighten your minds to perceive His presence in all that is past, and sanctify your hearts to keep it there through all that is before us.

For many years past, God has permitted us, as a people, to be deeply humiliated. While we have enjoyed great material prosperity and have, in a certain sense, maintained our position under the forms of the Constitution, we have been systematically slandered and traduced, in public and in private, at home and abroad, in a way such as no free and independent people has ever before so quietly submitted to, because of the maintenance of an institution inherited from our fathers, which the rest of the world was pleased to consider as incompatible with civilization and with Christianity, we have been made, thro' every form of literature, a by-word among the nations of the earth.

The lecture room, the forum, the senate chamber, the pulpit, have all been used as the instruments of our denunciation. The newspapers of the Northern States and or Europe have vied to express their abhorrence of our social life and their contempt for ourselves. The grave statesman, the flippant poet, the sentimental novelist, the critical reviewer, the witty satirist, has each, in turn, singled out our homes as the targets of his falsehood, and our mothers, and wives, and daughters, as the objects of his insult.

In many of the religious bodies of the United States, their communicants from the slaveholding States were excluded from the participation of the sacrament of the Lord's Supper, and the Southern ministers from brotherly interchange of services. We had committed an unpardonable sin in doing what Abraham, the friend of God, had done, what Philemon, the dearly beloved fellow laborer of Paul the aged, had not been ashamed to do.

All this abuse and misrepresentation was borne according to the temper of men, by some with the patience of Christians, leaving their justification in the hands of God, by others with contempt for an hypocrisy which could see the mote in a brother's eye, but not the beam in his own eye; by not a few with arrogant defiance and words of bitter scorn.

So far it had been a war of ideas, but leaving, nevertheless, rankling wounds behind. Gradually it passed from literature to politics, and we were soon made aware that a deep laid scheme, resting upon the double basis of fanaticism and interest, was closing in upon us, which was to reduce to overt acts the ideas which had been so assiduously impressed not only upon the minds but upon the feelings of a whole generation.

We were to be humbled, not simply by being held up to the scorn of the noble and generous all the world over, but by being virtually disfranchised, even while retaining the forms of constitutional liberty, and being permitted to keep up the appearances of equality. This scheme was devised by a far-seeing statesman, now occupying a position of commanding influence, who laid his plans with consummate skill and has pursued them, for twenty years, with undeviating firmness, alto' good report and thro' evil report.

He advanced from point to point with the steady pace of inevitable destiny, drawing his lines closer and closer around his fluttering yet unresisting victim. He educated through the Press and through the Pulpit, a whole generation, and the two ideas which he has made the ideas of the times, are the irrepressible conflict, under democratic institutions between freedom and slavery, and the utter inability of slavery to maintain itself in the face of freedom.

The one idea combined into a great party of the fanatic, the laborer, the foreigner, the farmer, the manufacturer — the other idea gave confidence and fearlessness to his followers. When this powerful and ever growing host was thoroughly prepared for its work, he decided, after a calm survey of all the chances of the conflict which he was about to inaugurate, that success was inevitable.

He perceived that there was but one movement that could defeat his plans — a dissolution of the Union — and he maintained that to be an impossibility. He believed that party divisions could keep the South so distracted — could separate her statesmen by such lines of bitterness — that no combined resistance to his sure but stealthy advances, could ever be brought about.

Had all his followers been as prudent as himself, and had not God been on our side, nothing could have saved us from slow but inevitable destruction, for it was not his purpose to strike any blow that might alarm or arouse the South, but to achieve all his purposes thro' seemingly constitutional movements. He well knew that the rapid growth of free territory, filling up with a foreign population of the most radical description, would surely give him what he aimed at, and that gradual changes in the Constitution or plausible interpretations of it would cover all his advances with the forms of law, and render any opposition difficult which proceeded beyond the limits of legislative or judicial resistance, of which he had no fear.

And then he looked upon the section he was devoting to ruin and perceived that she was engaged in a fierce Presidential strife even while he was closing his coils around her, well might he have supposed that his game was a sure one and that time only was needed to make his triumph complete. At this moment, in the confidence of his heart, he might well have asked "Where is now their God?" and our answer could only have been "Our God is in the Heavens: he hath done whatsoever he pleased."

But just at that moment, when he considered us deserted and doomed, commenced a series of events which has brought us this day to the altar of the living God to ascribe the glory of our deliverance not to ourselves but to Him, to confess our unworthiness of all this unmerited goodness and to pray him to continue to bless the work which he has thus far so graciously favored — "Not unto us, O Lord, not unto us, but unto thy name give glory, for thy mercy and for thy truth's sake."

By that mercy of God our greatest difficulties have been successfully passed through, I do not say our greatest privations or our keenest sufferings. We may yet have before us years of self-denial and of self-discipline — we may be called to suffer in our fortunes and in our homes — our chambers may be clothed in mourning and our hearts may be lacerated with sorrow, and yet, with all this it may be true that our greatest difficulties as a nation have been already met and overcome.

The severest trials through which a movement, such as ours, is forced to wade, are those which arise in its inception and in its organization. The work which we had undertaken to accomplish was in many respects a novel one. It was not a revolution against intolerable ills — it was not the casting off of a foreign tyranny which had ground us to the dust — it was not even rebellion against the forms of the government under which we had lived, that we might substitute for them other forms, but it was the withdrawal from an Union, which had given us, in spite of its abuse and corrupt administration, a large share of material prosperity and social happiness, and which was associated with all our anticipations of national greatness.

The love of the Union was deeply ingrained into the hearts of the nation, and into no part of it more deeply than our own Southern section. We were proud of it as that which gave us dignity abroad and advancement at home. The people considered its freedom to be the envy of the world, its constitution the "ne plus ultra" of political wisdom. Our most prominent statesmen had held it up before the nation as the bond of our greatness and as the hope of the human race.

Webster had consecrated it, in the Northern mind, by that master piece of eloquence which, as a rhetorical effort, has not been surpassed in ancient or modern times. CLAY had surrounded it with all the charms of his fascinating personal popularity, and had identified it, all through the West, with his wide-spread political opinions. Jackson had added to the influence of this idol of the West, the idea that the Union had been once preserved by him and that he had left its continued preservation as a sacred legacy to his followers. Even Calhoun, while advocating the doctrines of State sovereignty, had pressed them most earnestly as the means whereby alone the Union could be maintained. But above all, Washington, the personification of American constitutional liberty — had committed it, in his dying words, to the people, as the central idea around which the future should forever revolve.

It seemed impossible ever to overcome this idea, and yet the question had become one, in the minds of many, no one knew how many, between the Union and a passive subjection to the yoke which had been so skillfully preparing for our necks. Again and again had disunion been attempted and had failed in some cases, with ignominy, with hopelessness in others.

The Union was fast absorbing every thing in the popular mind and becoming the devouring idol of the nation. Before it the constitution had changed its whole scope and meaning — before it liberty was fast becoming a mere word — under its sanction an irresponsible majority was transferring power, prosperity and wealth from one section of the country to the other. The cry of Union had become a sanction for every irresponsible decree, a war-cry against all opposition that promised to be effectual.

The greatest danger of the South was, lest her people should permit this idea to overlay every other consideration and to rise superior to every constitutional infraction. There was no overt act of tyranny to arouse the people to madness — no action on the part of the government to render resistance immediately necessary — nay, the government had, in a certain way, been in the hands of those who were willing to concede to the South her constitutional rights.

It was necessary to meet the deeply laid and far reaching scheme of which we spoke just now, by an equally far-seeing and prospective opposition, and the difficulty was lest the people should not see, with any degree of unanimity, the necessity for immediate action. All saw that the time was coming — all looked shudderingly at the prospect of civil convulsion which seemed drawing nearer and nearer — but hope was strong in many of our most devoted Southern hearts — men who are now standing with their swords in their hands and their shields clasped over the bosom of their mother in the very front rank of battle — that God might yet avert the evil and postpone if not defer forever the stern necessity.

Secession was urged more upon what was before us in the future, than upon what had actually taken place. Coming events had, to be sure, cast their ominous shadows before, but as yet there was no act which had come directly home to the cottage and fireside. The raid into Virginia in 1859, had, at the time, produced a deep sensation, but as that Mother of

States had treated it lightly herself, having been satisfied with the punishment of the wrong-doers, it had died away.

Under these circumstances, the most sanguine feared the issue of the question between Secession and the Union. They believed that a majority in certain States would sanction an act of separation, but they dreaded such an opposition in each State as might neutralize the action and impair its whole moral effect. Anything like a nearly equal vote in the States would have created a nucleus of opposition which would have rendered the whole proceeding inefficient. But thanks be to God he gave us among ourselves a more remarkable unanimity than any had dared to hope for, and what was lacking in ourselves, was supplied by the blunders of our adversaries.

Instead of supporting those who were not prepared for separation, by granting their moderate demands of constitutional amendment, they struck blow after blow upon an already over excited country, with a folly that was inconceivable. Every plank upon which the Union men of the South desired to stand, was successively struck from under them, and the unanimity which the merits of the question failed to produce, their stubborn obstinacy rendered inevitable.

Instead of meeting the advances of the Union men of the South with a lofty magnanimity — a magnanimity which a victorious party can always afford to exhibit — they met them with a defiant arrogance. They showed evidently by all their actions that they considered the struggle as at an end, and that they were commissioned to walk as conquerors over a subjugated territory.

One by one, all their friends were driven from them, and thus has been produced an union of The South which was scarcely hoped for when the struggle first began. And thanks be to God their folly still continues, and if, with humble hearts, we bow ourselves before God and ascribe this important result not to ourselves but to His overruling and protecting Providence, we shall see still greater wonders worked for us, and new stars rising to take their place in our constellation, and nations coming to our aid who were supposed to be bound to the North by strong bonds of sympathy and fanaticism. "Not unto us, O Lord, not unto us, but unto thy name give glory, for thy mercy and for thy truth's sake."

Another danger which threatened us and which is the "experimentum crucis" of all new nationalities, was the adoption of the permanent constitution under which we were to live. It is always a moment of critical peril. It was the rock upon which Cromwell's successful usurpation crumbled to the dust. So long as he lived, his genius sustained the civil arrangements which he had substituted for the English constitution, but with his death things flowed back into their ancient channel and the nation returned joyfully to the monarchical government even of the Stuarts. It was the rock upon which the European revolutions of 1848 all split.

Theorists took up the question of government and inexperienced professors and fantastic poets were deputed to arrange constitutions and to mold the necessities of a practical world. It ended just as any man of common sense might have foreseen that it would end, in the usurpation of a clear-headed man of practical experience.

In the formation of the constitution of 1789, that which we have just amended, there was large diversity of opinion, and much time was consumed ere it could be made satisfactory to the thirteen States. The leading men of the country were forced to exert all their influence to secure its adoption.

Washington talked for it — Madison and Hamilton and Jay wrote for it — the heroes who had illustrated the war of the Revolution, prayed for it as the seal to their bloody triumph. And yet, with all this array of influence, it was very reluctantly adopted by several of the States, and one distinguished gentleman of South Carolina said, during the debates upon its adoption in the Convention of that State, "I desire no other epitaph to be written upon my tomb than this: 'Here lies the man who voted against the adoption of the Federal Constitution.'"

How wonderful then, that in a few weeks a Congress of gentlemen, who had differed all their lives upon questions of national policy, who were just warm from heated discussions of principles as well as men, who were yet reeking with the sweat of one of the bitterest Presidential elections which had ever distracted the country, should have submitted to the people of the Confederate States a constitution of the most conservative character in which many grave errors of the old constitution had been amended and new features introduced of the highest moral and religious import.

They entered that Congress with several questions ominous of evil pressing upon them — questions upon which, if they had erred, their cause must have been shaken to its center. Among these were the re-opening of the African slave trade, the change in the value of slave representation, and that question which had once before disturbed the Union, the proper scale of duties upon imports and exports.

A false step upon any one of these three questions would have been, in our then condition, almost irretrievable. The reopening of the African slave trade would have disgusted Europe and produced great dissatisfaction at home. A change in the value of slave representation would have disaffected that large population of our mountains and pine barrens who own no slaves, and would have thrown them at once into the hands of demagogue. Too high a tariff would have checked the sympathy of England and France, and too low a tariff would have forced us to resort to direct taxation, which a people must be educated to bear.

Marvelous then was it in our eyes that these gentlemen should have laid upon the altar of their country all their private views and all their public differences, and should have adjusted every point with such nice discrimination, with such wise and Christian moderation, with such a happy conception of the necessities which surrounded their States, that an almost unanimous shout of applause should have arisen from a delighted constituency. And afterwards, that seven conventions, composed in a like manner of men of every shade of opinion and of every party in politics, should have so quietly and so unanimously accepted their work, can be attributed to nothing else but the overruling spirit of God.

All these bodies entered upon their duties with fasting and prayer — they all acknowledged God every day in prayer — they placed him in the forefront of their constitution, and they recognized him as the supreme ruler of the universe, and we therefore can truly say again "Not unto us, O Lord, not unto us, but unto thy name give glory, for thy mercy and for thy truth's sake."

The next trial, through which the Confederate States were called upon to pass, arose out of the regulation of its financial affairs. Napoleon is reported to have said, blasphemously enough, that battles were decided by the heaviest artillery, and the world is fast corning to the conclusion that the longest purse is the arbiter of war. Granting this to be in some measure true, we yet acknowledge most humbly the presence of God with our Government in this most important matter.

The most arrogant boast of the North was of its own abounding wealth and of our exceeding poverty, and so long had this assertion been made and so persistently had it been adhered to, that both sides were fast becoming to believe it. The North and the South were both losing sight of the unalterable principles of political economy and had become confused amid the complications of commerce and trade and exchange.

In a conflict like this, wealth must be looked at from a different stand point from that in which it is viewed in a time of peace. At its commencement, the North has the most accumulated money, because its great cities have been the converging centers from all parts of this widely extended country, but accumulated money is very soon expended in a war like this, and the ability to continue it will depend far more upon the available income of each section than upon its money capital at the outset.

The wealth of the North depends upon manufactures, upon trade, upon commerce, and the North West furnishes a very abundant supply of food. Analyze this wealth and you will perceive that its results depend upon the ability to find consumers and to furnish an exchangeable value upon which to trade. Unless manufactures find a market, they remain a drug upon the hands of the manufacturers and are a loss instead of a gain. Unless trade finds purchasers as well as sellers, it very soon becomes bankrupt in the face of rents and living and the taxation of a war such as this will be, if it goes on.

Unless commerce has something to export as well as to import, it must necessarily come to an end, for one cannot buy, as the world goes on now, unless he has something to sell. The North has no great export of its own which is a necessity to the world. Now and then the failure of a grain crop in England or upon the Continent, creates a demand for corn, and then, for a season, the West can furnish a value that is exchangeable. But this is an exceptional case, and the commercial men of the North have never placed any permanent dependence upon it.

It has rested its exchanges upon the cotton and tobacco of the South, and it has obtained possession of these by flooding our States with its manufactures and knickknacks of every description, and by acting as the commercial broker of the South. And besides selling our valuable staple for trifles like these, which we could as well make for ourselves, we have annually distributed much that remained of these staples upon hotels and watering places, in steamboats and railroads, in shops of luxury and temples of fashion and upon what is facetiously called education and accomplishments.

And by the time that the cotton and the tobacco were made, it no more belonged to us than did the manufactures of England, and we were compelled in common honesty to let it go where it was really owned. At a very moderate calculation, the exchangeable value thus furnished the North in return for its manufactures and its climate and its fashion, amounted annually to between one and two hundred millions of dollars.

But all this is now changed; we have seen the last of it, at least during the war, and a year or two will soon show that the subtraction of this amount from the one side, and the addition of it to the other, will make a marvelous difference in the aggregate of wealth. And while the withholding of this immense sum of money from the North will cripple its resources, it will be put in circulation among ourselves and add to the income and resources of our own citizens. For there is no truer principle in political economy than this, that the distribution of money has as much to do with the wealth of a country as its production.

God seems to have endowed our financial officers with the wisdom to seize the strong point of our economical position and our people with the patriotism to receive and adopt it. They have made our great staple to supply for them the place which gold and silver supply for the Banks. As they issue paper money upon the coin which they possess, so will the Confederate States issue paper upon the cotton which it will accumulate by the exchange for it of Confederate bonds, and thus, instead of a currency depreciating continually like the old continental money, we shall have a currency always at par, because the cotton which is its basis, is always wanted and receives no injury of any material consequence from being piled up during a blockade.

If a currency keeps at par, and it will always keep at par when it is known to represent an actual value, nobody will care to have it redeemed, especially so long as he may be hemmed in from intercourse with any except those whose currency it is. And besides furnishing a Bank capital for the Confederate States, it becomes in the hands of the government an instrument of great power for the regulation and control of foreign alliances.

Refusing to permit its export except through our own seaports, it will soon bring all the nations who use our cotton, face to face, with the question between us and our enemies. It is not that cotton is King, but that God has given our statesmen wisdom to use a great advantage aright, and the people self-denial to acquiesce in the arrangement, and to stand manfully by it. "Not unto us, O Lord, not unto us, but unto thy name give glory, for thy mercy and for thy truth's sake."

And in this very matter our God does seem to have smitten our enemies with judicial blindness. Just when they most needed sound wisdom, they have inaugurated a financial system which must cripple their resources. A prohibitory tariff, and one which they will find it difficult to repeal, because it was given as a sop to particular States, just when a nation needs both friends and money, is the very height of folly, and a system of borrowing, at a heavy discount, is a poor beginning for a people boasting of its wealth and arrogant about its resources.

The commercial men of the North perceive this weakness and therefore it is that they cry out for quick measures and a short war. They know that they cannot bear a long one, and very soon will they begin to murmur at any Commander-in-chief who desires to move slowly and surely, and will either hurry him into measures which will ensure his defeat or force him to yield his marshal's baton into bolder because more ignorant hands. Truly does God seem to have ordered every thing for us and to have made every thing work for the security of our cause. How can any one distrust him or be faithless enough to ask with our enemies, "Where is now their God?"

If we turn from the financial to the military affairs of the Confederate States, we perceive the same visible presence of God in our concerns. In the beginning of this movement we appeared to have no resources wherewith to meet the immense preponderance of power that was against us. They had armies, navies, armories, manufactories, every thing that could conduce to their strength — fortresses bristled in our midst and aimed their guns against the people they had been built to protect — a large, well ordered army, stood upon our Texan frontier quite in a condition to have invaded and embarrassed us — a large armament was fitted out to strike at the heart of South Carolina, which was considered the soul of the rebellion — a navy yard of immense resources, filled with arms and ammunition and ordnance, supported by the strongest fortress in the Union and defended by men of war armed with guns of the heaviest caliber, lay upon our North eastern frontier.

# GOD'S PRESENCE WITH THE CONFEDERATE STATES   17

A hastily raised militia was all we had to depend upon in the conflict. But in a moment every thing seemed, changed in a way more than natural. Skilful officers sprang from every direction into the arena. Armed men arose as if from the dragons teeth which the abolitionists had been sowing for years. And fear seemed to fall upon our enemies — unaccountable fear.

Officers who had never quailed before any living man — soldiers who had borne the old flag to victory wherever it had waved over them — navies which had moved defiant over the world, all, all seemed paralyzed. That large border army surrendered to militia without a blow — that gallant armament, made up of the same fleet which had run in the revolution into the Thames, which had defied the Algerine batteries, which had brought Austria to terms in the Levant, which had spit its fire into the face of the almost impregnable fortress of St. Juan d'Ulloa stood inert and saw a gallant soldier, who was upholding their own flag, beaten out of his fortress by sand batteries and volunteers.

That immense nary yard, with its vast resources, with its great power of resistance, with its huge fortress at its back, with its magnificent men-of-war all armed and shotted, was deserted in an unaccountable panic because of the threats of a few almost unarmed citizens and the rolling during the night of well managed locomotives. And nowhere could this panic have occurred more seasonably for us, because it gave us just what we most needed, arms and ammunition and heavy ordnance in great abundance.

All this is unaccountable upon any ordinary grounds. But two days before a naval officer of very high rank had reported to headquarters at Washington that this navy yard was impregnable. Is not this very like the noise of chariots and the noise of horses, even the noise of a great host which the Syrians were made to hear when the Lord would deliver Israel? "And they said one to another, Lo, the King of Israel hath hired against us the King of the Hittites and the Kings of the Egyptians, to come upon us. Wherefore they arose and fled in the twilight and left their tents and their horses and their asses, even the camp as it was, and fled for their life. "Not unto us, O Lord, not unto us, but unto thy name give glory, for thy mercy and for thy truth's sake."

And now, my beloved people, after such tokens of God's presence with us in all the departments of our civil affairs, need we be afraid of man's revilings, and man's threats? If God be with us, who can be against us? Shimei's cursings did not hurt David: they only returned upon his own head. And if any be presumptuous enough, in the arrogance of their wealth and in the pride of their numbers, and in the presumption of their Pharisaism to ask "Where is now their God?" we can humbly answer "Our God is in the Heavens: he hath done whatsoever he pleased." Nay, more, we can tremblingly rejoice and point to His presence with us upon earth.

He is too manifestly with our people, giving them unanimity and patriotism — with our rulers, giving them wisdom and moderation and a proper sense of their dependence upon him — with our armies, shielding them in the hour of conflict, for us not to acknowledge it. We should be as brute beasts before him if we did not perceive his presence and humble ourselves before him.

God loves to be honored in the assemblies of the Saints, and he delights in the praises and thanksgivings of his people. There is no surer mode of driving Him from us than by refusing to acknowledge His presence among us. It is not humility to be blind to the tokens of God's goodness towards us, it is faithlessness — it is not vain boasting to enumerate his glorious acts in our behalf, it is giving Him the honor due unto His holy name.

Read the Psalms of David and note how frequently he enumerates in long and elaborate verse the wondrous acts of the Lord, closing each stanza with the triumphant refrain, "For his mercy endureth forever." And surely he knew how God loved to be praised. Let us not be afraid or ashamed to see the hand of the Lord in every thing, to believe firmly that He does manifest himself for the right, and to be a praying and a thanksgiving people, as well as a fighting people. "Some trust in horses and chariots, but we will trust in the Lord our God."

But while we render thanks unto the Lord for all His benefits towards us, how deeply should their reception humble us! For we have been utterly undeserving of them. They are the tokens of unmerited mercy, if God was only strict to mark iniquity, which of us could stand? As a people, how little have we done for his cause! how poorly have we fulfilled the great mission entrusted to our hands!

What wretched stewards have we been of the treasures committed to our keeping! How polluted our land has been with profaneness, with blasphemy, with Sabbath breaking, with the shedding of blood! What violence and recklessness, what extravagance and waste have manifested themselves as the normal condition of our people! what an idolatry to fashion has disfigured the ancient simplicity of our people! What a high value has been put among us upon all those qualities which are the very opposites of the graces of the gospel, upon pride, upon self-reliance, upon animal courage!

How inordinately has wealth been sought after and valued! How honor, falsely so called, has been exalted and almost deified! And if with all these hateful sins cleaving to our national skirts, God can yet manifest His presence with us, what might we not hope for, if we would lay down those iniquities at the foot of Jesus' Cross and cry for mercy? Let us begin today and with deep humility of spirit, confess our unworthiness and pray the Lord that He will not turn His face from us, but will still enable us to say, "Our Lord is in the heavens."

We are engaged, my people, in one of the grandest struggles which ever nerved the hearts or strengthened the hands of a heroic race. We are fighting for great principles, for sacred objects — principles which must not be compromised objects which must not be abandoned. We are fighting to prevent ourselves from being transferred from American republicanism to French democracy.

We are fighting to rescue the fair name of our social life from the dishonor which has been cast upon it. We are fighting to protect and preserve a race who form a part of our household, and stand with us next to our children. We are fighting to drive away from our sanctuaries the infidel and rationalistic principles which are sweeping over the land and substituting a gospel of the stars and stripes for the gospel of Jesus Christ.

These objects are far more important even than liberty, for they concern the inner life, the soul and eternity. Let us be strong and quit ourselves as men — strong in the strength of Jesus, strong in the presence of the Lord of Hosts. Let us, in all our efforts in all our successes, say unceasingly "Not unto us, not unto us, O Lord, be the glory." Let us in all our reverses still praise the Lord and in all humility reply "Our God is in the Heavens: He hath done whatsoever he pleased."

# A Sermon

DELIVERED BY

## REV. DANIEL I. DREHER

PASTOR OF ST. JAMES' CHURCH, CONCORD, N. C.

JUNE 13, 1861

### Day of Humiliation and Prayer,

AS PER APPOINTMENT

OF

### The President of the Confederate States of America

1861

# SERMON

"And Abraham said unto Lot, let there be no strife, I pray thee, between me and thee, and between my herdsmen and thy herdsmen, for we are brethren. Is not the whole land before thee? Separate thyself, I pray thee, from me." Gen. 13:8-9.

In obedience to a Proclamation of THE PRESIDENT OF THE SOUTHERN CONFEDERACY, setting apart this day, as one of humiliation and prayer, we are assembled to humble ourselves before Almighty God. The clarion of war has been sounded in our once peaceful land, and the cry now is — to arms, to arms! Every where may be seen troops marshaling themselves, and making ready for the conflict. It is now meet for us to call upon Him who presides over nations as well as individuals, and devoutly ask Him to guide us through the coming struggle — for, "If God be for us who can be against us."

There are but two means, in human power, to prevent strife between individuals and nations, when either feet aggrieved and dissensions have arisen — concession and separation. If concessions cannot be made, then separation must take place, or a collision will inevitably follow. Human nature is so constituted that it will resent a real or supposed wrong.

The text affords us an illustration how men acted many years ago in order to preserve peace. The characters brought to our notice are by no means insignificant, one of them in holy writ, bears the significant appellation of "Father of the faithful," who said to his nephew, "separate thyself I pray thee, from me." From this, we see that when concession was not practicable, he sought peace in separation. We see nor hear nothing here of sustaining "the Union" and of wild devotion to the "stars and stripes" — surely a word from Abram would have quelled the strife of the herdsmen, but we hear not a word beyond that of "separate."

From the principal laid down in the text, I proceed to the following reflections:

I. The separation of the slave from the free States should have been done in peace.

So far as the separation itself is concerned, I look upon that as inevitable, independent of our present troubles — for it is not conceivable that a people so differently educated, and with such antagonistic interests to be served, could, for any considerable time, remain united. We are two people in education and interests, and must be so in government in order to live happy.

The protecting aegis of the same government can never preside over such a heterogeneous mass, without showing partiality to one party or the other; then, of course, strife must follow. Nature and nature's God has marked us out for two nations. The people of New England differ from the people of the South as much as do the inhabitants of Old England, with the exception of their being accustomed to monarchy. With these and other considerations:

1. The present war is, of all things, the most unnatural. Reason would direct one of these sections to go to "the right" and the other to "the left" and make themselves as happy as they could, rather than go to war, and after spending an immense sum of money, and after loosing many valuable lives, and suffering great deterioration in morals — have to separate in the end. Better do so now — no good can result from this war that might not have been secured without it; and upon some one rests the responsibility of having inaugurated it — a fearful retribution awaits some one for this unnatural strife.

No sane man would make war upon his own family, and he who does so, is a madman, and fit only for bedlam. And yet, such is the nature of the present war, declared by Mr. Lincoln against the South. It is said that the mother of the wife of his own bosom is in, and in favor of the South, and that he has a brother-in-law serving in the Southern army.

The condition of this man is only the exponent of the condition of thousands involved in this unhappy contest, and after the fury of battle is over, and the smoke driven away by the winds of heaven, may be seen brother, son or father weltering in his own blood — before such a picture, humanity grows pale and turns away in horror. The strife inaugurated by the government, at Washington, is only a repetition of the conduct of Cain on an enlarged scale, and may we not expect God to put His mark upon it, as He did on Cain.

2. Civilization and Christianity demand a peaceful separation. In the latter half of the nineteenth century — after the human mind has made so many brilliant achievements, and thrown an inextinguishable glory and luster over the arts and sciences unknown to the ancients — how humiliating to see one of the most enlightened nations of the world engage in the hellish purpose of a fratricidal war. Were it not for the deep corruption of the human heart, the present unnatural conflict must remain an enigma forever; that, and that only, affords a satisfactory solution of this fiendish war — and of the appearance of this hydra monster in mid day splendor of civilization.

With what consternation would, the intelligence of a war breaking out between England and France, fall upon our ears, and how much greater the alarm, should we hear that one half of England had proclaimed war against the other — we would then conclude the foundation stone of intelligence was giving way, and that the fair tree of knowledge affords no remedy for human grievances. But stop, it is not the one half of England that has proclaimed war against the other — it is war declared against one part of the once United States by the other — how must this intelligence fall upon the ears of enlightened Europe?

Will they not ask, if a nation so renowned for inventive genius — if the land of Washington, Fulton, Morse and Mills, could not have devised a plan of adjusting their national grievances? How all our vaunted pride and boasting of our free institutions must be humbled in the estimation of Europe — the hopes of all true lovers of liberty must begin to wane as they look at the unhappy condition of that country, once known as the home of the oppressed of every land. They may well conclude that the protecting aegis of liberty is about taking its final flight from our once happy country.

If the South falls in this struggle, with her fall will go down the cause of liberty on the American continent, and a military despotism take the place of popular government — the most wretched of all governments. Shall we not hope that the nation, claiming the intelligence and the high regard for the Christian religion ours does, will yet fall upon some plan, by which peace may be restored, and the hopes of mankind be revived?

If wild fanaticism would give way to sober reason, this could be done — though separated, the olive branch of peace might wave over us. But as it is, the North is frantic with rage — with an apology of a man to occupy the chair of Washington. From this medley no one could expect a rational solution and adjustment of our present troubles. At this moment, I would hail as a God-send the mediation of some of the great European Powers — the North is contending for a shadow — her sceptre has departed from the South, never to return — perhaps if told so by France or England, reason would return to her.

The claims of Christianity certainly are very powerful, and should have great bearing in determining our present troubles. This nation is neither Pagan nor Mohammedan — we are a Christian people — our enemies make loud pretensions of love for the Christian religion — let them now prove their "faith by their works," and as they first proclaimed war, be first to offer peace.

The prosperity of all our religious operations demand a course of this kind — how melancholy to see the cause of Christ crushed by the iron heel of war — the church must bleed at every pore, as this unholy war progresses — congregation be stripped of their members and made food for war — ministers driven front their pulpits for want of support — Colleges and Theological Seminaries shut for want of students, and should this unhappy contest continue long, no human mind can conceive the injury done to religion. This above all other considerations, should lead our enemies to offer us peace, and us to accept it when offered. We are under no obligations whatever to offer peace, as we only have declared war in self-defense, all the South wants is to be "let alone."

3. Humanity demands a peaceful separation. From the immense armies that are gathering at different points, and from the scientific improvement in all the implements of warfare, as well as the implacable hatred of one party for the other, should a collision of arms occur we may naturally look for great destruction of life.

Would it not be well for our enemies to begin to count the cost before any more blood should flow — before this nation is converted into one vast slaughter house. True, we are threatened with "subjugation and extermination," but when the work shall begin, our antagonists will find the business of extermination rather fatiguing, and very bloody.

What folly! what madness to talk so. To subjugate and exterminate ten or eleven millions, when Great Britain could not conquer three millions — remember our enemies have but very little better advantages than Britain had in the Revolution. Still, if this war continues, it must be very bloody — all history proves a civil war the most desperate and destructive to human life. Hence, humanity requires a peaceful separation in order to prevent a waste of blood.

4. The South has given the North no just reason to make war upon her.

The North says the election of Abraham Lincoln, as President of the United States, on the 6th day of November, 1860, by a fanatical party in the North, upon a certain political platform inimical to the South, was not sufficient cause for the South to secede. In answer to this, I say, that the secession of the South, or any part of it — the bombardment of Fort Sumter, under the circumstances, was no just cause for Abraham Lincoln to declare war upon her. I leave the North to settle this question upon the principle of justice to God and man.

To say nothing of ethics, prudence should have induced the North to have made some effort at conciliating the South after the election in last November; but to the everlasting disgrace of the Republican party, when applied to for some guarantee, respecting the rights of the South, they sternly refused all efforts at conciliation.

The South then had but one alternative left for safety, and that was in secession, for which act, the North very piously declared war upon her. Now, "we shall see what we shall see." Had the North, at the proper time, made suitable efforts, this whole trouble might have been avoided — the North still has peace or war in her own power.

I repeat, that the South has not given the North sufficient cause to declare war against her, to leave a Union whose articles of agreement had been violated again and again, without either shame or remorse, and for which there was no redress, surely these violations of the original compact, annulled the agreement, and opened the way for the several States to resume their sovereignty as independent communities, whenever they might think proper to do so.

5. Whenever any contracting party fails to comply with the articles of agreement, the contract becomes null and void, and the contracting parties absolved from their obligations to the agreement. This is precisely the condition of the old government. Because the South wishes to enter into another Confederation with such States as may feel inclined to join for mutual protection — this act, the North considers a causus belli — a cause for war. Now

II. A peaceable separation of the South from the North would be productive of good to both sections.

1. The North could carry on her commercial and manufacturing interests. These, in case of a peaceful separation, need suffer no material change, from the fact that they have the cotton mills, and other mechanical establishments for carrying on the various manufacturing purposes. This would be greatly in their favor in case they had consented to a peaceable separation. But, if they persist in this war, the South will manage to take care of herself and

of her own interest. They will lose more than they will gain, placing the war upon a commercial footing.

In the event of a peaceable separation, the North would be free from the trouble of slavery, and their pious consciences would be free from the sin of slavery. Does not any man know, who knows any thing at all, that if the North was sincere in her negro philanthropy, she would bid the slave States Godspeed in their separation, instead of making war upon them. Then, the North would have a homogeneous government, and in her Congress only have the interests of free States to consult, which would very materially lessen the burthen of legislation.

2. The South, in the meantime, could have carried on her agricultural pursuits. With a government of her own, conscious of being permitted to manage her own institution in her own way — every resource she could command would be developed — new life and energy would be diffused through all her pursuits. Having a homogeneous government also, which would lessen the burthen of legislation. And another important consideration, a matter known to every man in business, the country would be spared a financial crisis every four years, in the event the slave and free States had a government of their own.

For years past, every Presidential election has been attended with tightness in money matters. This would be removed in case of separate governments, and confidence secured.

If we have been correct in the foregoing remarks, (and we think we have,) what can be the cause of the present policy of the Northern government? We have considered the subject in all its possible bearings; for want of time, confining ourself to the most prominent thoughts, and all indicate a peaceable separation as the best course.

But the secret of all this obstinacy must be looked for in the peculiar character of the people of the North. If you turn to history, you will find that the New England States were originally settled by a peculiar people from England, Scotland and Holland, a rebellious and restless people, always fond of liberty, but most intolerable masters when they had the power.

Poor Charles the I, fell a victim to the fury of their ancestors, &c. In America, they raised the hand of religious persecution among the colonies. Strange as it may seem, they who fled from persecution were first to persecute.

They have been people of one idea for many years. This, in connection with the annual influx of foreigners, who knew nothing of our institutions, are the causes of our present troubles. And hence the unwillingness to let the South go in peace; rather than do so, they prefer forcing a war upon us with a view of our subjugation.

Our enemies disregard the voice of reason, religion and humanity, and with frenzied madness, threaten to bring ruin upon us. And for what? just because we have ventured to resist the fanatical aggressions of the North — borne by us with remarkable patience for the last thirty years.

Like Abram of old, loving peace, and wishing to remain loyal to God, we have taken the only course recognized by Him for the accomplishment of this object — separation. We wish to leave them for the sake of peace, and for the quiet pursuit of happiness.

Since we have sought peace in separation, war has been declared against us by our enemies. Mighty and terrible armies are being marshaled into the service of the Federal and Confederate governments. With great propriety it may be asked,

III. Why is this war, and for what are we contending?

1. The North says it is to maintain the integrity of the government in the preservation of the Union and protection of the American flag. In the inaugural of Mr. Lincoln, he declared his purpose to protect the public property, collect the revenue, and preserve the Union, a policy of all things the most foolhardy, a determination fraught with ruin, and ruin only.

From the time of the delivery of his inaugural, Lincoln has seen his cause growing more desperate in the South, but with steady purpose he still pursues his phantom. Immediately after the reduction of Fort Sumter, in Charleston Harbor, war was declared against seven States in the South. This remarkable and arrogant production, induced four more Southern States to withdraw from the Federal compact; in fact the entire South is nearly a unit. This act of the South has exasperated the North beyond measure, who, inflated with pride, and burning with rage, wish and labor for our ruin.

This feeling, no doubt, has been inflamed from the false conception of the true nature of the Constitution of the United States, viewing it as a law consolidating the several States into an inseparable Union; whereas, it is only a mutual compact or covenant, and each State an integral member, having separate laws for its internal regulation.

Having violated the constitution again and again without the least compunction of conscience, the North with pious modesty tells us fidelity to the Union requires us to submit to their domination. The Union! the Union! is all that call be heard. The North is now in arms against the South, with a view of coercing her back into an unnatural Union.

Ministers of the Gospel are proclaiming loudly for the Union in their sermons — men and women, under the garb of religion, either pure or hypocritical, are lifting their hands in prayer that God may prosper their cause in our reduction and acquiescence to the tyrannical rule of those with whom we have no common sympathy. On the other hand, when we turn to the

2. South, it is her violated rights for which she is contending, as expressed in her separation from the old government. Her policy, as declared by her chief Executive in his inaugural, at Montgomery, is that of peaceable separation, simply "to be let alone;" but if war was forced upon her she would defend herself, nothing more nor less could reasonably be asked or given. Blind and infatuated zeal for the Union, "the whole Union," has forced her to take up arms against her unnatural enemies in self-defense.

Here we find the same religious regime as in the North: ministers pray and preach in favor of the South; pious men and women pray that God may prosper our cause, and protect us from the hand of the destroyer. Now the question naturally arises, who is right in this contest? I unhesitatingly say the South.

When aggrieved, and no redress was afforded her under the constitution of the old government for her injured rights, she quietly turned aside without bravadoing any one; and had she been permitted to remain unmolested, the garlands of peace would still hang from her temples. But these garlands have been torn from her brow by rude hands, and civil war with all its fury and devastation, forced upon her, in order to weaken, intimidate, and force her back into the Union.

3. Force can never unite the two sections; this is out of the question. A union to be worth any thing, must be a union of love and mutual affection, and not one of force and mutual hatred. We have gone too for a conciliation, even if conciliation was practicable.

The bitter feeling engendered from past wrongs, inflamed by the military display of the present hour and for months past, render it impossible for us to fall upon any satisfactory plan of adjusting our present national troubles. We must separate, there is no human power that can unite us now, our union is forever broken; between the North and South there is a "great gulf fixed." The known laws of the operations of the human mind forbid any hope of the re-construction of the Federal government in its original integrity.

A popular government, to be perpetual, must respect all sections, and protect the interests of all its citizens. There must be no sectional partiality, for in that case confidence would be lost, bitter feelings excited, and a separation ensue.

The machinery of a popular government is very delicate, and requires to be handled with great care; the least disaffection throws the whole business into confusion, and the damage done beyond repair.

The government of the United States was a popular Government, but her legislation was partial, and that produced disaffection, which resulted in separation. This rupture can never be healed, and it is worse than folly to think so. The evil done is immense and past all hope of recovery. Violated confidence and alienated feeling will never return and be as they once were. Our separation is complete. "Come weal or come woe, sink or swim, live or die," the thing is an unalterable fact.

## REFLECTIONS

1. The war has been forced upon us, and from past and present indications, we have reason to believe that it will be conducted with great cruelty. The enemy is now on Southern soil, perpetrating the most heartless barbarities — men have been shot down because they have dared to defend their own property in their own dwellings. The lamented Jackson is one of this number.

Unoffending women are subjected to a fate worse than death. The rebellion in India, and the massacre of the Christians in Syria by the Druses, alone afford a parallel to the atrocities perpetrated by the soldiers of the North, now in and on the coast of Virginia. The only harm the South has ever done the North, is that of giving the North her trade and shipping, from which they have grown rich, proud and insolent.

Now the worst the base ingrates can do is too good for us. The soil of the South has already been stained with the blood of Southern patriots in defense of their rights; this may only be the prelude of that carnage that must follow a collision between the great armies that slowly and cautiously approach each other.

The man that inaugurated this war has shown himself devoid of all principle, of veracity — having violated the most sacred promises. Under the specious and alluring pretense of protecting the public property, he called out military troops. Some of these same troops are now menacing Virginia, and outraging her citizens. The fact is, from the conduct of the Federal soldiers, one would judge them sent to destroy, rather than protect the property of the government.

From the unhappy conduct of Major Anderson, on Sullivan's Island to the present time, we have been given to understand that destruction, as well as protection, is a part of their policy.

As this war has been forced upon us, we should be united in the defense of our homes, property, liberty and all that men count dear in this life. The South is the soil upon which most of us were born; in that same soil rest the bodies of our parents and friends, let us be a unit in defense of these precious relics, and preserve them from the polluting touch of the Northern vandals, from whom every spark of humanity appears to have departed; for those who are guilty of plunder arson, murder and rape, cannot be very humane.

The Union and the American Flag should no longer be possessed with charms for any Southerner, but all should hold them as objects of disgust, because they are polluted by Northern fanaticism, mingled with cruel wrongs. The days of Washington and his compeers are gone forever; still the South may yet fill a bright page in history.

2. There should be but one mind and one voice in the South on this great question, either as our adopted or natural home. Unanimity among those who occupy her soil is absolutely required, in order to secure triumph. We may differ in the manner of resistance, but agree on the subject of resistance itself — that is the great question. A man who would turn against the South now, would deserve the fate of Benedict Arnold, from the fact that opposition can do no good, and would result in harm, and only harm.

In God's name let us meet our opposing foe with a steady arm and determined blow. They proclaimed the war, now let them first offer peace, which they can have by returning to their homes. We will not follow them in the event they leave us in the possession of our rights.

Let us this day lift our hearts devoutly to Almighty God, Who presides over men and nations, and pray him to prosper our arms in defense of our rights — that our enemies may be put to confusion, and driven back from our Southern soil.

War is what we may expect in this world — men will trample upon the rights of one another, and human nature will resent a wrong. These are circumstances as certain as cause and effect. When war comes, some one is in the wrong, and a just God will hold the offender responsible for the injury done — an awful retribution must await an ambitious man, who, for selfish purposes, makes war upon an innocent people.

I have no hesitation in saying, that the present incumbent of the chair at Washington, has been influenced from motives of ambition and vain glory, and if this country is to be drenched with the blood of human beings, slain in civil war, their blood will be required at his hands and the hands of his party.

We should be prepared to meet those who are determined on our subjugation and extermination, and whose motto is "Booty and Beauty," (if not inscribed upon their banners, is shown by their actions) a more iniquitous and hellish sentiment could not have originated in Pandemonium itself. Before they run over and fulfill this program, they will find the work of subjugation a herculean task. May we not expect vengeance to fall upon the base violators of innocence and shameless insulters of purity.

The long-suffering of God may cause the sulphurous smoke to linger, already exhaling from the fires prepared to consume this modern Sodom, yet the judgment will, and must come; an awful retribution is in store to be dealt out in God's own way at his own time for these vile inhumans.

It may be that the North is given over by Heaven to judicial blindness in order that they may be severely scourged. Upon moral and rational principles, I can see no just reason for the North to make war upon us — reason will forbid the war, if she would be permitted to do her perfect work.

No sane man can think seriously of subjugating the South. That is physically impossible. Religion forbids the prosecution of the war — her mission is one of peace. What must be the condition of those who profess to be wise and religious, yet against reason and religion, persist in an unnatural war. God must intend a scourge for them in this contest, and for that purpose, permits the North to rush madly on to her own destruction.

In this strife, the North has all to loose, and nothing to gain. An immense debt must necessarily be incurred, and in the end fail to bring back the slave States, and be forced to acknowledge their independence. A people determined, as are those of the South, will not be conquered. Our enemies should remember the warning of lord Chatham to the British Parliament: "My lords, you cannot conquer America."

The sequel declared the truth of the assertion of the noble Lord. In the name of God, with our trust in Him for the protection of our cause, we will bear our arms and meet our foes with such means of defense as He has been pleased to give us. At the same time let us pray for our enemies, and do nothing that may unnecessarily provoke them — it may be that reason will return to them, and that they will desist from their unholy purpose.

Something may turn up yet, in a way we think not, under the directing hand of God, by which a speedy termination may be put to the war, and the vast armies now met for mutual slaughter, disband and return to their homes.

Should a conflict ensue and this war last — how many brave ones may fall, and how many hearts made sorrowful, and streams of tears, warm with affection, flow, no one can tell. This picture Is too affecting to dwell upon — would to God the degenerate, and I must say, cruel and despotic Abram, of Illinois, would say, as the good and benignant Abram of Ur of Chaldea said to his kinsman: "Let there be no strife, I pray thee, between me and thee, between my herdsmen and thy herdsmen, For we are brethren. Is not the whole land before thee? Separate thyself, I pray thee, from me."

Such a declaration Might not fill a page in history of bloody deeds, but it would send the murderous and licentious troops of the North to their own homes, to gain a living in some way other than that of waging a cruel war upon the South, while a the same time, it would permit the soldiers of the South to return home and enjoy, with their friends, the sweets of peace and the honest pursuits of life.

Shall we not lift up our hands and hearts to God in devout prayer, that a successful and speedy end may be put to this unnatural war. Surely it is a cause deserving our prayers. God is a hearer of prayer. He can do wonders in a way we know not. O! that the Prince of Peace may interpose and dispel the dark clouds gathering over our land, soon to burst in one mighty crash, so loud and terrible, that the thrill will be felt throughout the civilized world, and the shock of which will be felt by unborn millions for years to come.

He that said to the stormy winds and raging waves, "Peace, be still," can calm the passions of men. He that sent His angel, and in one night destroyed the powerful army of Senacherib for the deliverance of His people, can rescue us from the hand of the destroyer, if it seem good for Him to do so. Into thy hands O! God, we commit our cause — deliver us from the hand of our enemies.

# God Our Refuge And Strength In This War

A DISCOURSE BEFORE THE

Congregations Of The First And Second Presbyterian Churches,

On The Day Of

## Humiliation, Fasting And Prayer

APPOINTED BY

### President Davis

FRIDAY, NOV. 15, 1861

BY

REV. T. V. MOORE, D. D.

RICHMOND, VA

1861

# A PROCLAMATION

## BY THE PRESIDENT

WHEREAS, it hath pleased Almighty God, the Sovereign Dispenser of events, to protect and defend THE CONFEDERATE STATES hitherto, in their conflict with their enemies, and to be unto there a shield:

And, whereas, with grateful thanks we recognize His hand, and acknowledge that not unto us, but unto Him belongeth the victory; and in humble dependence upon His Almighty strength, and trusting in the justness of our cause, we appeal to Him that He may set at naught the efforts of our enemies and put them to confusion and shame:

Now, therefore, I, JEFFERSON DAVIS, President of THE CONFEDERATE STATES, in view of the impending conflict, do hereby set apart "Friday," the 15th day of November, as a day of Fasting, Humiliation and Prayer; and I do hereby invite the Reverend Clergy and the people of these CONFEDERATE STATES to repair on that day, to their usual places of public worship, and to implore the blessing of Almighty God upon our arms, that He may give us victory over our enemies, preserve our homes and altars from pollution, and secure to us the restoration of peace and prosperity.

Given under my hand and the seal of THE CONFEDERATE STATES, at Richmond, this thirty-first day of October, in the year of OUR LORD one thousand eight hundred and sixty-one.

JEFFERSON DAVIS.

By the President:
R. M. T. HUNTER,
Secretary of State.

## DISCOURSE

"If thy people go out to war against their enemies by the way that thou shalt send them, and they pray unto thee toward this city which thou hast chosen, and the house which I have built for thy name; then hear thou from the heavens their prayer and their supplication, and maintain their cause." — 2 Chron. 6:34-35.

Four times since the autumn leaves of last year began to fall, have we been summoned to come before God in humiliation, fasting and prayer. First, by the Synod of Virginia, in November, before that fatal election which opened Pandora's box in our land; then, by the President of the United States, in January, that the cup of wrath which was slowly filling up, might, if it were possible, pass away; then, by THE PRESIDENT OF THE CONFEDERATE STATES, in June, that we might be girded for the terrible conflict that was forced upon us; and now, by the same authority, after we have tasted of that cup, and felt the first shock of that conflict.

And surely it has been good for us thus to draw near to God; for hardly had the voice of our supplication in June died on the air, when we were summoned by our Congress, among its earliest official acts in our menaced Capital, to return thanks to Almighty God for that wonderful triumph of Manassas, where the destinies of our young Republic hung trembling in the balance until God gave us the victory, and when His arm was made bare for our deliverance, so that the most wicked were compelled to acknowledge it.

And now, as we look daily for other and heavier blows upon our assailed and outraged country, assaults by land and by sea, it surely becomes us to approach the mercy seat again, and ask that God would still give wisdom to our councils and success to our arms; that He would grant unto us, that we, being delivered out of the hand of our enemies, and all that hate us, might serve Him without fear, in holiness and righteousness before Him, all the days of our life.

And we are encouraged thus to pray by the implied promise of the text, that when war comes upon a people who have consecrated themselves to God, if they shall penitently pray towards His high and holy sanctuary, He will hear from heaven their supplication, and maintain their cause. Your prayerful attention is, therefore, asked to three leading thoughts implied in this text.

## I. WAR IS A PART OF THE AGENCY BY WHICH GOD DISCIPLINES NATIONS

That war is an evil, and often, a sore and terrible evil, and a thing at variance with the spirit of the Gospel, is what no Christian can for a moment doubt. But these facts do not place it beyond the employment of God, as a means of working out His purposes on earth.

Sickness, suffering, famine and pestilence, are also evils, yet God employs them in this way, and having declared that "the wrath of man shall praise Him," He may also use war to effect His designs among nations. Had there been no sin, there would have been no war, as there would have been no suffering of any other kind; but as long as there is sin in the world, so long may we expect to find this huge, colossal scourge — this Moloch of evils — among men.

Indeed, our Lord expressly declares that wars and rumors of wars shall be among the signs that shall herald the end, so that our fond dreams of a universal peace, when in millennial blessedness, men shall "beat their swords into plough-shares, and their spears into pruning-hooks," may be realized only in those final scenes that lie beyond the great day, and not on this side of it, "in the new heavens and new earth, wherein dwelleth righteousness."

But war is not an unmitigated evil, terrible as its ravages are. It is like the hurricane and the flood in Nature, desolating and terrific, yet accomplishing ends in the physical world that can be accomplished by no other agencies. The brooding miasma, the tainted air and the poisoned water are swept away, and there are left behind a purer air and a richer soil than could have existed without this purgation of tempest and flood. Similar services are rendered by the hurricane of war, in spite of its evils.

A long course of peace and prosperity, acting on our depraved nature, tends to emasculate and corrupt a people. As wealth increases, unless religion advances with it, luxury grows apace. Mammon-worship soon becomes supreme, everything assumes a money standard, and corruption creeps slowly into the very heart of a people.

The refined and intelligent withdraw from political life, either to amass wealth in business, or to enjoy it in scholarly ease, leaving the direction of public affairs in the hands of brawling demagogues; and the fiery energy of youth is expended in revelry and dissipation.

There grows gradually up a worldly and Epicurean expediency that sneers at lofty heroism and high principle as mere Quixotic romance; a hard and brassy materialism that measures everything by the standard of dollars and cents and rejects all that will not pay in this coin; and a secret, but potent skepticism as to the very existence of anything like virtue, honor, unselfishness or truth, believing that every man at last has his price.

The general prevalence of this feeling will at last sap the very foundations of public and private morality, enthrone a shameless selfishness in the high places of life, which in the end will be guilty of some outrages on common justice and right so flagrant as to provoke resistance, the recoil of whose violence may lay the whole fabric of society in ruin.

War tends to break up this mammon-worship, effeminacy and selfish expediency, to show that there are nobler things to be contended for in life than mere material advancement; that the chief end of man is not to make money; that there are great principles of belief, and great elements of moral character which underlie all human prosperity, and the sacrifice of which will, in the end, undermine even material greatness; and that heroism, daring, unselfishness, and a sacrificing patriotism, are living realities, and not mere poetic romances.

As men contend for great political or religious rights, they have a clearer perception of the nature and value of all human rights; and as they endure hardship, hunger, cold and danger, in defense of these rights, there is generated a sturdier manliness, and a loftier tone of character that will descend in kindling memories of noble deeds, at once a heritage and a model to coming generations, inspiring them with a generous ambition to emulate the bright example of their worthy sires.

It is thus that national character is formed. It is thus that vigor, enterprise and honor are breathed into the heart of a people, and that the hardy, simple and manly virtues are worked into the very sources of national life. It was thus that the Hebrew Commonwealth gathered its enduring strength after the effeminacy of its Egyptian life, by battling with the Canaanites, and purchasing their God-given homes and fields with their swords and spears.

It was thus that the Greek republics attained their athletic sinew and symmetry, and quickened into its beautiful life their immortal genius. It was thus that the wolf-nursed colony of the Tiber became at last imperial Rome, stamping in lines of iron her mighty image on all nations and on all time. And it has been thus that God has caused the roots of every enduring nationality to strike deep, and grow strong, as its branches have wrestled with the storms of war.

As no nation has ever risen to greatness without this stern tutorage, it seems but a simple induction from the facts of universal history, that in a fallen world like ours, war is a necessary part of the agency by which God disciplines nations.

These views furnish no apology for an offensive war, which is a crime as well as an evil, but they do furnish an encouragement to those on whom a defensive war is forced; for they show that what is an undoubted evil may be, and has been, overruled by God to good results. Man means it for evil, God controls it for good. It comes as a chastening for sins, and becomes a blessing by extirpating those sins, and bringing to a hardier life the corresponding virtues. We can thus see some of the reasons for that general fact alluded to by Solomon in the text, when he assumes that God's people will go forth to war by "a way in which God shall send them," as if war was one of the inevitable incidents in the history even of a people belonging to God, and under His special protection, and an incident arranged by His special and foreordaining providence.

In the war now upon us there are special considerations bearing on this point.

(1.) One of the sins of the Southern country has been a lazy dependence on the industry of the North for what we might have done, and ought to have done for ourselves. We have looked to them to manufacture everything — from a man-of-war to a lucifer match; allowing them to come and carry away our cotton, wool, iron, lead, copper, coal, hemp, and our very cord-wood, to return them in manufactured forms, whilst we paid not only for the manufacture, but for this double transportation, and brokerage, commission, percentage, exchange, insurance, discount, storage, and a list of charges whose name was legion, for the privilege of being dependent on them for the very necessaries of life, as we are now learning to our cost.

Add to these the tribute that was paid for papers, periodicals and books, boarding schools, seminaries and colleges, that molded our opinions, and the enormous expenditures of travel to watering places, hotels, cities, and other resorts, that molded our fashions and manners, and we have but a faint conception of that condition of provincial dependence to which half a century of fishery-bounty, navigation, tariff, revenue and commercial laws, written and unwritten, had reduced this broad and opulent region.

So enormous was the tribute paid in this way for things wholly unnecessary, that we shall save probably the entire expense of the war by simply keeping at home the wealth that would otherwise have been sent to build up the prosperity of those who would use that very prosperity as an argument to prove the superiority of their institutions to ours.

Now, had a peaceable separation been effected, this dependence would have continued, until with overgrown wealth on one side, and exhausted poverty on the other, that very separation would have been our ruin. But separated by the convulsive throes of war, all these ties must be broken, all these channels filled up; domestic industry must spring up to meet the very necessities of life; manufacturing and commercial independence be firmly established, without which political independence would be a sceptre without a kingdom, a sword without a hand to wield it.

Thus the very blockade, cruel as it is designed to be, will be a blessing; and should another war come upon us, it will not find us, as this one did, without a mill or a manufactory to furnish powder and caps for the muskets of our soldiers.

And in nothing does the suicidal folly of this war on the part of the United States Government appear more vividly than in the light of this fact. It proposes to make us friends by hunting us down as enemies; to restore our love and loyalty by means that must naturally produce the most undying hate; to drag us back, all bleeding and crushed, to the iron embrace of a huge enginery of coercive power, to illustrate the theory of free government; to ravage our coasts, and slaughter our sons, and distress our households, in order to restore our allegiance to those who have thus cruelly, wantonly and bitterly oppressed us.

It professes to regard slave territory as an unmitigated curse, and yet, rather than allow this alleged curse to be separated from it, will raise half a million of men and half a billion of money that it may grasp this accursed soil with a hand of iron, even though it thus makes it but one vast field of blood. Surely the lessons of all past history have been in vain if such means do not engender a hate, a deep, burning and deathless memory of wrong and cruelty, that shall remain in its engendered animosities a wide and yawning gulf for generations to come. These two sections, however this war may end, shall

> "Stand aloof, the scars remaining
> Like cliffs that have been rent asunder,
> A dreary sea shall roll between,

> But neither heat, nor frost, nor thunder,
> Can wholly do away I ween,
> The marks of which once hath been."

The sword may cut apart, but can never unite.

(2.) But there is another effect of the war, not less important than this one. The deep, original cause of that mighty disruption that is now going forward was the diversity of interests that were included in a single government, interests so vast, and connected with other diversities, social, historical and political, themselves so important, that all could not be harmonized under a single organization, without an amount of wisdom, justice and statesmanship but rarely found in any administration.

Similar diversities remain in the separated section, which in time must have produced the same result unless prevented by some powerful agency. The jealousies even now exhibited, which every good man should frown down as the worst kind of treason; and the unkind detractions that have been uttered against our own great old Commonwealth, without whose aid, whatever may be said about her, the success of this struggle would have been a hopeless impossibility, all prove that these divisive tendencies are at work, and that one of our greatest dangers was in the diversities that existed between border, and cotton, and gulf, and western States, producing undue friction in the working of government.

What our young Republic needed was a feeling of oneness, a broad, deep national unity, binding together the separate sovereignties of the Confederacy, so that whilst, politically, they shall be "distinct as the billows," yet, nationally, they shall be "one as the sea." Although the common institution of domestic slavery is a powerful bond of union, especially in view of the mighty hostility against it that compresses its adherents together, yet even this could not have created this national unity, as we had it, under a peaceful separation.

Had the original thirteen colonies separated peacefully from Great Britain they would never have made that e pluribus unum under which they advanced to such peerless greatness, until the spirit of that Revolutionary struggle became extinct in a generation "that knew not Joseph."

In the same way it was necessary that these CONFEDERATE STATES should be put into the furnace of war, that they might be welded into one great, united and loving people, fused together by common weakness common suffering, and common triumphs; having a common heritage of grief, and a common heritage of glory; mingling the blood of the border States with that of the gulf and the great valley on the same battle-fields; garnering their precious dust in the same graves; mingling their tears over the same hallowed sods; and thus creating for all future time, memories so deep and so enduring as to mould into one warm, living and enduring whole, this new birth into the great sisterhood of nationalities.

(3.) There is another result of this war, which as far as it exists, is a yet higher one than that just stated. War is usually a vast demoralizer, and all religious feeling withers under its baleful breath. And, to some extent, this is true of this war, as we mournfully know. And in this aspect the act of our Congress in virtually degrading the office of Chaplain, by making it the only one in the army whose rank and pay were cut down, and after two reductions, fixing it at a rate that excludes from it any man with a family, who has not private means of his own, a thing not very common with clergymen — this marked and seemingly invidious distinction of this office, I feel bound to say kindly, but plainly, was at least an unfortunate act, if not more blameable.

In an army of volunteers, like ours, a good Chaplain is just as important as a good Captain or a good Surgeon, for he is adapted to meet those moral evils arising from inaction, discontent, weariness and home-sickness that are often far more injurious than the dangers of the battle-field. And we know of no reason arising from incompetency or dereliction of duty in those who have filled the one office for any such stigma, which does not exist in a twofold, if not a tenfold degree with the occupants of the others.

It is a false economy that starves the soul to feed the body, even in an army. The eagle that robbed the altar of its sacrificial flesh fired her own nest by the living coals that adhered to it, and so will it ever be in depriving religion of its honest rights in any human organization. Hence we feel bound to say plainly, that this was a wrong, a short-sighted and suicidal wrong, although we also believe an undesigned and inadvertent wrong, which we hope will be remedied as soon as it can be reached by competent authority.

If the finances of the government will not warrant the employment of men of experience and mature age in this office, it were better to abolish it, and leave the spiritual wants of the soldier entirely to the voluntary action of the people. But if the office is to be retained at all, it ought to be put on an equality with other offices of the same importance.

But in spite of all these things, I believe, that there has never been an army since the time of Cromwell, in which there was a more pervading sense of the power of God than our own. A brave, but irreligious officer remarked to me a few days ago, we may well adopt the language of the good book, "If it had not been the Lord who was on our side, now may Israel say, when men rose up against us, they had swallowed us up quick." And this is the solemn conviction of thousands, even the most wicked.

The resources of the mighty organization, whose stupendous gage of battle we fearlessly took up, were so vast in men, money, munitions of war, forts, fleets and armies, that unless God had been with us we must have been crushed.

When we saw the bloodless achievements of Sumter, Gosport, Harper's Ferry, and the river batteries; when we saw an unprotected woman sent forth as it would seem by a Divine impulse to venture alone in imminent peril to give the information that led to the first victory on our soil, which struck the key-note to all the rest; when we saw boys yet warm from their mother's hearts stand like veterans in the iron sleet of Bethel, and college lads from our quiet lowland homes make the gorges of Rich Mountain a very Thermopylae; where we saw squadrons of volunteers stand, "like a stone wall," a sweep like an avenging hurricane over the red plains of Manassas and Springfield, or the green hills of Carnifax Ferry, Belmont, and Leesburg; when we saw the very winds and waves, the very "stars in their courses" conspiring to bring disaster on our enemies; when all human calculation must have predicted the exact opposite; we cannot wonder that even ungodly men have been compelled to pause and say, "this is the finger of God."

And we cannot wonder that many a brave man, as he saw these seeming tokens of the ascending and descending angels, and the protecting presence of God, has found these battle-fields to be Bethels, and said: "Surely the Lord was in this place, and I knew it not;" that many a dear child, while pacing his lonely round as sentinel, or standing on his perilous post as picket, beneath the silent stars, has found his place to be a Manassah, "a forgetting" of the wild delusions of sin, and a solemn rising to his memory of words that he has heard, amid the sweet scenes of home, from lips, some of which are silent in the grave, and others of which may be even then, in the deep silence of midnight, moving in wakeful prayer for the brave and beloved boy who is far, far away.

The many conversions in camp, the prayer-meetings in soldiers' tents, of which we have heard, and the letters we have seen breathing emotions of piety that have been awaked by the exposures and sufferings of the army, induce us to believe that this war will lead many a soul to the Cross that might otherwise have perished in impenitency.

## II. THE PROPER RESORT OF A PEOPLE IN TIME OF WAR IS TO GOD

All history proves, from Abraham and his armed servants, and Gideon's three hundred men, through Marathon, to the Spanish armada, and later struggles of heroic people for their rights, that "the race is not to the swift, nor the battle to the strong." God gives victory as He pleases to carry out His great and holy purposes in human history. Hence the instinctive resort of every right-hearted people at such a time is to that High and Mighty One, "who doeth his will in the armies of heaven and among the inhabitants of earth." This resort is proper for several reasons.

(1.) That the sins which have caused the chastening may be removed.

As these sins have been set forth on former occasions, we will not repeat the enumeration, but only say that, until they are repented of and forsaken, God will continue to smite us. Hence we should come today with honest penitence, and, taking words of truth and sincerity upon our lips, should cry to him, "Turn us, O God of our salvation, and cause thine anger against us to cease, and bear us from thy holy heavens."

(2.) That we may be delivered from evils that must weaken us.

There are evils inevitable to war from which we cannot expect to escape. We must expect to find personal ambition in the guise of patriotism; itch for office, with its horse-leech cry of "give, give;" favoritism and nepotism, by which the sons, relations and friends of those in office will be placed over the heads of better and older men who are unable to command this kind of patronage, and must, therefore, drudge in humbler and harder positions. Wastefullness in the use of public funds and the granting of public contracts; blunders in movements, both civil and military, that are hard to explain; provoking circumlocutions and red-tape delays in the transaction of public business; insolence and petty tyranny in men raised from obscurity and dressed in a little brief authority, who lord it with arrogance and sometimes with cruelty over braver and better men placed under their command. Heartless brutality in drunken surgeons and drunken nurses allowing sick men to pine and suffer, and even to die from sheer and inexcusable neglect; drunkenness in the ranks, as well as among the officers, preparing many a gallant man for disgrace and defeat in battle, and a drunkard's grave when the war is ended. Profanity; gambling, pillage and speculation at least in small matters; all these evils are well nigh inevitable in a time of war, with our poor fallen nature as it is, and can only be diminished by looking to that God before whom we bow this day in reverent supplication.

But there are some evils that we had no right to expect, and that, therefore, as far as they do exist, are the more difficult to bear. We had no right to expect that flaming and furious patriots of twelve months ago, whose voice was then for war, denouncing all who could not go as fast and far as they, should now be as meek and as mute as mice, leaving to others the burdens, sacrifices and dangers of this contest when it has really come.

We had no right to expect that they who have been so long sneering at Yankee greed and Yankee meanness, should emulate this ignoble example by filching the funds that the hard taxation of a burdened people have generously given to their governments, by usurious contracts, and exorbitant charges for supplies which the poor soldier often finds to his cost were made to sell and not to use; buying up the very necessaries of life to pile enormous profits on them.

So that whilst brave men are driving off the hungry invader abroad, at the point of the sword, their straitened families find the wolf at the door in the form of the hungry speculator, who spares not even medicine for the sick, and will wring his percentage out of the very agonies of the suffering; trafficking in the hunger, cold and nakedness of the soldier while living, and speculating upon his very shroud and coffin and grave when dead; blockading our homes by land as really, as wickedly, and as heartlessly as our enemies are blockading them by sea; bribing officials to act as accomplices with them in their schemes to obtain undisputed control of a market; creating needless panics and needless pressures, that they may wring from a groaning and helpless community the hard earnings of the poor on whom these exactions must fall most heavily.

And whilst a struggling country is bleeding at every pore, instead of seeking to staunch that blood, virtually gathering it up drop by drop to sell like butcher's meat in the shambles, and coin it into gold; acting a treason more deadly than an armed aid to our enemies, by compelling many a poor man who once calculated the value of the Union, to begin to calculate the value of disunion, and ask what have we gained by escaping the leeches and blood-suckers of one Confederacy, only to fall into the fangs of the sharks and cormorants of another.

Surely, surely, we had a right to expect that in a struggle so sublime, so tremendous, and so desperate as this, we should have been safe from the cruel greed of such hungry Shylocks, such human vultures as these. And if in any cases we have been disappointed in this reasonable expectation, it but creates another reason for coming before Him whose blood was sold by his own chosen companion for thirty pieces of silver, to pray that He would not only deliver us from the Ahithopels abroad, but also, and even more earnestly, from the Iscariots at home.

(3.) That we may have direct strength from on High for this conflict.

Did time permit, it would be easy to show that the religion which fits men for any duty, suffering and danger, must fit them for the duties, sufferings and dangers of war; and that he who believes that God is with him, and that the field of death will be to him only the vestibule of heaven, must move down to the dread ordeal of battle with a heart all the stronger for this faith and hope.

That the religion which breathed such heroism into the battalions of Gustavus; that made feeble Holland an overmatch for the proud chivalry of Spain; that nerved the iron men of Cromwell to such deeds of daring prowess; that has inscribed the name of Huguenot and Covenanter among the world's heroes; that nerved the hearts of so many brave men in our first Revolutionary struggle; that has written upon her spiritual muster-roll such heroic names as Vicars and Havelock; that has adorned the character of some in our own army, whose glorious work is not yet completed, and whose names our children will utter with enthusiastic love; that such a religion as this should be a yet loftier spring of action than even that wild fanaticism whose religious faith made the Moslem arms resistless for so many centuries.

For such strength then as it gives to suffer and wait at home, as well as to suffer and strike in the field, we should come this day, saying, in the words of the old Hebrew battle-cry, "Some trust in chariots and some in horses, but we will remember the name of the Lord our God; and in the name of our God will we set up our banners."

## III. WE SHOULD THEN GIRD OURSELVES FOR THIS CONFLICT IN THE HOPE THAT GOD WILL MAINTAIN OUR CAUSE

Had we far less to excite our hopes in this struggle than we have, there is a stern necessity upon us to go forward to it which we cannot escape. There is nothing now left us but a death-grapple for very existence. An institution has been planted on our soil, the ethical nature of which, as a relation in human society, it is too late to argue, for God has recognized it twice in the Decalogue, and devoted an entire epistle to an incident connected with it in the New Testament, without hinting at its unlawfullness.

Like all, human institutions, it has its evils, evils which the ceaseless assaults of its enemies give no opportunity to correct, and yet under its influence more members of Christian Churches have been enrolled from a race whose ancestors were heathen, than has been done in the same length of time by all the missionary societies on earth, much good as they have done; and under it there has been secured more temporal comfort to the slaves than has been reached by any corresponding class of laborers on earth.

There is one fact that speaks volumes on this point, that in this bitter struggle, whilst every possible agency has been used upon them, for one colored man who has been unfaithful to the South there have been ten whites; that whilst a Washington was fighting and dying in Western Virginia against white traitors born on her soil, his servants were faithfully tending the fields of Mount Vernon, and trying to secure for him their proceeds from the pillaging vandals, within the sound of whose drums Old Gabriel and his follow-servants remained faithful to their master; and that, in one of the hottest battles on the Kanawha, a servant begged and obtained the privilege of fighting by the side of his master, whilst that master's own blood relations were fighting on the other side.

Nor are these cases few or far between, but enough to show that we have often more reason to trust the black face of the honest servant who fears God and loves his master, than the black heart of many a sniveling white man, whose god is a dollar, and who would sell not only his country, but his very soul, if need be, for a fat office and a bloated salary. Let this be recorded to the honor of the black man, and let it be remembered to his advantage when the struggle is over, as we believe it will be, and let it stand as an answer to some of the slanders that have been heaped on this institution.

Against this institution, and thus both the races that are connected with it, has been waged a hostility whose steady course has never faltered nor turned aside. There is something portentous in the rise and growth of this antislavery Hydra with which we are now struggling.

Spawned in the huge Serbonian bog of French infidelity and radicalism, it was a fitting coincidence that the same year which witnessed the first development of the one in the French Revolution, should have witnessed the first development of the other in the seizure of that magnificent North-Western territory, which the credulous generosity of Virginia bestowed as a free gift to the Federal Government, to rear up on her border a deadly enemy, by the Ordinance of 1787.

Again did the Hydra demand and receive a fresh accession to its bulk in the Missouri Compromise, where rights that were solemnly guaranteed by the Louisiana treaty were ruthlessly disregarded, and yielded to the clamors of this voracious and growing monster. Again and again was it swollen by new gorges of new territory, purchased by the common blood and treasure of all the States, and, therefore, rightfully belonging to the whole, and not to any of its parts.

Grown by these enormous meals, and stimulated by the secret working of foreign emissaries, who saw in this agent the serpent that might strangle this mighty Republic in its infancy, it planned a more deadly assault on the object of its hate. Suborning every avenue to the creation of public opinion, it was able at last to inoculate vast masses of men with its envenomed feeling, until having nullified the Constitution of the United States; divided churches; broken up benevolent agencies; embroiled States; stirred up Kansas and John Brown raids; bespattered the very Bible with its virus; breathed its poison into the very Gospel of the Son of God, and filled its pulpits with a religion of hate

Hissing its venom from a million heads and through a million tongues, from the Senate of the United States to the penny pamphlet, it then proposed, as its coup-de-main, to coil itself in one huge, stifling cordon of hostile settlements around the territory of the Confederate States, so that having crushed this hated institution to death by its tightening folds, these States might be left to the terrible doom of the ancient criminal when a living body was chained to a dead corpse to perish by a slow, loathsome and inevitable death.

Against this dreadful doom these States remonstrated with the most supplicating entreaties, but in vain, for the Hydra was, in contemptuous disregard of them, exalted to the sacred seat that had been filled by the form of Washington. Even then they sought in fraternal conference for some guarantee against this hideous policy, until their entreaties were taken as confessions of cowardice and weakness, their humblest proposals received with sneers of derisive scorn, and they commanded to furnish men and money to murder and crush their own flesh and blood.

Then, and not until then, did an outraged and long-suffering people rise in their indignant might, and, appealing to the God of Justice, resolve to cut with the sword the coils of this mighty constrictor, and crush his beads of venom beneath their feet. And this Herculean task must be done, or we must perish, miserably perish.

There was a time when submission and compromise might have postponed this fate, though perhaps never have finally averted it, but that time has forever gone by, and now they would only make it more abject and complete, adding dishonor to defeat, and degradation to destruction. Never since the terrible scenes of La Vendee, under the ravaging hordes of Republican France, has the old heathen war-cry, Voe Victis, (woe! to the conquered!) been more unmistakably sounded by an army of invaders.

Let this tremendous crusade become successful, either by mismanagement in the army, or cowardice and greediness at home, and history furnishes no page so dark and bloody as that which would record the result.

Our best and bravest men would be slaughtered like bullocks in the shambles; our wives and daughters dishonored before our eyes; our cities sacked; our fields laid waste; our homes pillaged and burned; our property, which we are perhaps selfishly hoarding, wrested from us by fines and confiscations; our grand old Commonwealth degraded from her proud historic place of "Ancient Dominion," to be the vassal province of a huge central despotism, which, having wasted her with fire and sword, would compel her by military force to pay the enormous expense of her own subjugation.

Or, in default of this, parcel out her broad lands to insulting emigrants as a feudal reward for the rapine and murder of this new Norman conquest: whilst the owners of these lands must either remain as cowering factors for insolent conquerors and oppressive lords, or wander as penniless and homeless fugitives in a land of strangers.

Is this picture overdrawn? Does it exceed the avowed designs of the great invasion as proclaimed not only by partisan journals, but by those who profess to be ministers of the gospel of peace? Did not their leading journals, at the outset of this war, exult with gloating delight over the terrible fate that their avenging armies were to inflict on us, our suffering wives and our hunger-bitten children, until all Europe cried out shame on such fiendish barbarity? And has not the work already begun?

Has not a gallant sister State been trodden under foot by an insolent military despotism — some of her best citizens banished to our own borders, (may God bless them, and enable them soon to return to a home untainted by tyranny and outrage,) others imprisoned in loathsome dungeons without even the farce of a legal process; her Legislature and Judiciary insulted, defied and overawed; her houses searched and pillaged; her women subjected by the reeking ruffians of New York stews to those outrages "that turn a coward's heart to steel, a sluggard's blood to flame," whilst rights of the common law, as old as the fields of Runnymede; rights which the Queen of England dare not violate without imperilling her crown, have been scornfully trampled under foot by these lawless miscreants?

Have they not repeated these atrocities as far as they dared in our own State; in Alexandria and Hampton, and elsewhere, where the gray hairs of age, the feebleness of disease, and the helplessness of womanhood have been no protection against insult, robbery and murder? Have they not made war on the sick, the aged and the dying, on childhood and helplessness, by making medicines, and even the Holy Bible itself, contraband of war, thus by a kind of Italian revenge, carrying their warfare to the very interests of the soul, and the very destinies of eternity?

Have not their most magnanimous men-of-war bravely bombarded helpless houses and unprotected villages that two British wars had spared, houses and villages containing the sick and feeble, who had no other notice of their danger, and whose sole attraction to these marauders seems to have been their weakness? Have they not kidnapped hundreds of servants and then made them beasts of burden; and is not their mighty armada now prowling along our coast, intending to arm the rest for another St. Domingo massacre?

Have not sovereign States, whose spindles were turned by Southern staples, and whose coffers were filled by Southern gold, who refused to give a man to the war of 1812, waged to protect their own shipping, and the war with Mexico, to vindicate the honor of that flag which they now so idolatrously worship; yet, now, when their own flesh and blood, their own brothers to whom they were bound by interest and gratitude as well as affection, were to be coerced and trampled under foot, send hordes of men, many of them blood-thirsty braggarts, who fly like sheep when the meet men fighting for their firesides and altars?

And, although we believe that many an honest heart in the North is indignant at these outrages, yet, have not all who have dared to remonstrate against them been muzzled by the bayonet or silenced by the Bastile? And if "they have done these things in the green tree, what will they do in the dry?"

If good men of the North in private life, and good officers in public, have been powerless to prevent these things hitherto, when they were impolitic as well as cruel, how can they prevent their most intense aggravation, when an infuriated and conquering army shall have crushed all opposition? Must not our fate be all the more terrible the more prolonged and determined our resistance? Then, if we must perish, is it not better to die the death of a man on the field of honor, than to die the death of a dog on the gibbet?

Is it not better to meet this huge barbaric invasion with one flaming front of defiant resistance, than to sit hugging our treasures until the grip of the invader is at our throats, his manacles on our wrists, and we bound helpless at his feet?

But no such fate as this awaits us, if we are true to ourselves and true to God. If we are worthy to take our place among the nations of the earth, no human power may hinder us; for eight millions of brave, united and determined people can never be conquered. Battles may be lost, cities may be taken, many a gallant man and many a gentle woman may sleep in a premature grave, and many a home be shrouded with mournful memories, and yet we shall be unconquered still; for

> "Freedom's battles once begun,
> Descend from bleeding sire to son,
> Though often lost are surely won."

The swamps that sheltered Marion's men, the rugged hills that blazed with the deadly fire of Morgan's riflemen, the blue mountains of West Augusta where Washington meant to make a last stand for liberty, and the storied heights of Yorktown, where he did make it, are still standing to tell us, that from the invading hordes of Xerxes, of Varus, of Farnese, and of Napoleon, down to the vanquished columns on the plains of Manassas, a people who are fighting for their altars and their firesides, in the fear of God, can never, never, never be conquered.

God will maintain our cause! He has maintained it. Starting in this conflict as unfurnished for battle as the stripling boy of Bethlehem going forth to meet the gigantic Philistine, nothing but the power of Jehovah could have made the arms of our beardless boys to vanquish again and again the stupendous preparations of our enemies. In that God we will continue to trust.

These brave heroic boys may fall; and though many a weeping parent may not be able to say with the noble stoic of England, "I would not give my dead son for any living son in Christendom," they will say with an humbler, and yet a loftier spirit, "if God has willed that I should lay him as a sacrifice on the altar of my country, I bow to His will with unrepining submission, rejoicing that though he has perished, the cause has not, will not, and cannot perish, for God will maintain it to the end."

Hence, to every prophet of evil, every croaking Cassandra, who tells us we are too weak, and must perish at last before our powerful enemies, we reply, trusting, not in our own might, but in the strength of our covenant God —

> "Down, soothless insulter, I trust not the tale,
> For ne'er shall our brave men a destiny meet
> So black with dishonor, so foul with defeat,
> Though their perishing ranks should be strewed in their gore,
> Like ocean weeds heaped on the surf-beaten shore,
> They still, untainted by flight or by chains,
> While the kindling of life in their bosom remains,
> Shall as victors exult or in death be laid low
> With their back to the field and their feet to the foe,
> And leaving in battle no blot on their name,
> Look calmly to Heaven from the death-bed of fame."

# God's Presence with our Army at Manassas

## A SERMON
## PREACHED IN
## CHRIST CHURCH, SAVANNAH,

On Sunday, July 28th,

BEING THE DAY RECOMMENDED BY THE

### Congress of the Confederate States

TO BE OBSERVED AS

## A DAY OF THANKSGIVING,

IN COMMEMORATION OF THE
VICTORY AT MANASSAS JUNCTION,

On Sunday, 21st of July, 1861.

BY THE

## RT. REV. STEPHEN ELLIOTT, D. D.
### RECTOR OF CHRIST CHURCH.

And Joseph called the name of the first born Manasseh: For God, said he, hath made me forget all my toil, and all my Father's house. — Gen. 41:51.

SAVANNAH
1861

## To the Clergy of the Diocese of Georgia

The Congress of THE CONFEDERATE STATES, on the day after the signal victory at Manassas Junction, adopted the following resolution:

> Resolved, That we recognize the hand of the Most High God, the King of Kings, and Lord of Lords, in the glorious victory with which He has crowned our armies at Manassas; and that the people of these Confederate States are invited, by appropriate services on the ensuing Sabbath, to offer up their united thanksgiving and praise for this mighty deliverance.

Now, therefore, I, Stephen Elliott, Bishop of the Protestant Episcopal Church in the Diocese of Georgia, sympathizing fully with this resolution of THE CONGRESS OF THE CONFEDERATE STATES, and feeling, even amid the sorrow which weighs down our State, because of the many gallant sons whom she has been called upon to offer up as a sacrifice upon the altar of their country, that we should "rejoice evermore and in every thing give thanks," do direct the Clergy of said Diocese to use on Sunday, the 28th July, the following service of Thanksgiving and Praise, in place of the regular service of the day:

### SERVICE

Open with the following sentences:

Deut. 33:27. Psalm 115:12,13. Psalm 107:21.

Instead of the "Venite Exultemus" say or sing the "Psalm of Praise and Thanksgiving after Victory," to he found in the "Forms of prayer to be used at sea," beginning "If the Lord had not been on our side," &c.

Psalter for the day — Psalm 68.

I Lesson, 2 Samuel 22:1-37.

### THE TE DEUM.

2 Lesson 1 Thessalonians 5:1-19.

Add to the Prayers for the day, the Collect to be found in the "Forms of Prayer to be used at Sea," beginning: "Oh Almighty God, the Commander of all the World," &c., and the following

## PRAYER

O merciful God and Heavenly Father, who hast taught us in thy holy word that thou dost not willingly afflict or grieve the children of men: look with pity, we beseech thee, upon the sorrows of thy servants, who, in the midst of our national rejoicing, have been called to mingle the bitterness of tears with the voice of thanksgiving.

In thy wisdom thou hast seen fit to visit them with trouble and to bring distress upon them. Remember them, O Lord in mercy; pour the oil of consolation into their wounded spirits; endue their souls with patience under their affliction, and with resignation to thy blessed will; lift up thy countenance upon them, and give them peace, through Jesus Christ, our Lord. AMEN.

## COLLECT FOR THE DAY

Almighty God, who hast in all ages showed forth thy power and mercy in the wonderful preservation of thy Church and in the protection of every nation and people professing thy Holy and Eternal Truth, and putting their sure trust in Thee; we yield Thee our unfeigned thanks and praise for all thy public mercies, and more especially for that signal and wonderful manifestation of thy Providence, which we commemorate this day; wherefore, not unto us, O Lord, not unto us, but unto Thy name be ascribed all honor and glory from generation to generation, through Jesus Christ, our Lord. AMEN.

## EPISTLE FOR THE DAY

Phil. 4: 4-9.

## GOSPEL FOR THE DAY

St. John, 8:31-37.

Given under my hand this July 24th, 1861.

STEPHEN ELLIOTT

Bishop of the Diocese of Georgia

## A Sermon

EXODUS 15:1-2.

Then sang Moses and the children of Israel this song unto the Lord, and spake, saying, I will sing unto the Lord, for he bath triumphed gloriously; the horse and his rider hath he thrown into the sea.

The Lord is my strength and song, and he is become my salvation: he is my God, and I will prepare him an habitation; my Father's God, and I will exalt him.

No words could express more entirely our feelings upon this day of National Thanksgiving for an almost unparalleled victory, than these opening verses of the song which Moses and the children of Israel sang when God had delivered them from the cruel hands of Pharaoh.

They embody all the ideas which are most appropriate to an occasion like this, and indicate all the acts which we should be glad to perform out of gratitude for so glorious a triumph. They place God in the foreground of the picture, and ascribe all the glory to him, "I will sing unto the Lord, for He hath triumphed gloriously, the horse and his rider hath he thrown into the sea."

They arrange in proper order our past and our present relations to that supreme Ruler of the Universe, "The Lord is my strength and song, and he is become my salvation." They announce the willing gratitude of hearts overflowing with thanksgiving for an unspeakable mercy, "He is my God and I will prepare him an habitation; my father's God, and I will exalt him;" and together they form the key-note of the song of exultation which was poured out over the discomfited Egyptians.

And these words are signally the words for this occasion, because God himself, through the Spirit which guides the Church, placed them in our mouths at the very moment when our victorious hosts were driving before them their vanquished enemies.

Sunday last was the day of battle and of victory, and from all the Episcopal Churches of THE CONFEDERATE STATES were read — as if God was speaking to us from the very altar of the sanctuary and cheering us on with words of prophecy — the chapters of Exodus which contain a detailed account of the preparations of the haughty Pharaoh, which describe the hardening of his heart as shown by that insolent question, "Why have we done this, that we have let Israel go from serving us?" and which wind up with this magnificent hymn of exultant praise, which Moses and the children of Israel sang, and which Miriam and the women answered with timbrels and with dances.

At the very moment when these chapters were reading in the Churches of the living God, parallel scenes were enacting upon, the banks of the Potomac, and God was singing for us, before man knew the result, our song of triumph and of praise. It is the crowning token of his love — the most wonderful of all the manifestations of his divine presence with us. Let us repeat, today, with our imperfect echo, God's own song of victory and thanksgiving.

And it will be none the less welcome, my beloved people, because it is interrupted by grief and broken by tears. Was our thanksgiving one of unalloyed joy, there would be no sacrifice in its oblation, and it might lack the faith which, in God's view, alone consecrates any offering. The most sublime thanksgiving which man offers to God, is that sacrifice of praise which accompanies, in the Christian church, the commemoration of the death of our Lord and Saviour Jesus Christ.

That is the model of all thanksgiving, and it is red with the blood of him who came from Edom, with dyed garments from Bozrah, travelling in the greatness of his strength, and it has been, for centuries, bedewed with the tears of repentance. And so with the sacrifice of praise which we lay today upon the altar of the Church. It will be sanctified by the heavy grief which weighs upon all our hearts, and will ascend into the presence of God consecrated by the tears which have been wrung from the souls of sisters sorrowing for the loved companions of their youth, of wives mourning over the desolation of their homes, of parents refusing to be comforted because they have been bereaved of their children.

In our deep sorrow we kiss the rod, and humbly receive his mercies as he thinks best to dispense them. It is the sorest trial of the heart when it is asked for its first born, and the most vivid imagination of the prophet could conceive no stronger picture of a nation's sacrifice than that her young men were dead in her streets.

Thanksgiving and grief are not incongruous, for all the highest gratitude of man is associated with him who was the man of sorrows and acquainted with grief, and is developed through acts of repentance and humiliation which demand from us the streaming eye and the smitten heart.

A little more than a month since, and the people of the Confederate States humbled themselves before God and mingled together, as became a nation who had received mercies which were altogether undeserved, thanksgiving and humiliation.

We then prayed, as a nation, that God would accept our confessions, would hear our supplications, and would continue towards us His merciful favor and protection. We truly believed that our cause was his cause, that we were defending a condition of society which He had established as one of the links in the chain of his Providence, and that we should be successful, not because of any merits or righteousness of our own — for God knows that we have sins enough to bring upon us any chastisement — but because we were instruments in his hands for the fulfillment of an important part of the economy of his grace.

We maintained that this conflict was not one of the ordinary and ever recurring struggles for independence, but that it wore many of the features of a sacred war, involving in its issues not human rights only, but sound religion, and the maintenance of the truth in philosophy, in morals and in government. It had been forced upon us most unwillingly and we had been compelled to break many long cherished associations and to crush many of our noblest feelings, ere we would engage in it.

As it went on, we had perceived, more and more clearly, its necessity and its righteousness, and such wonderful manifestations of God's presence with us had accompanied it, that we felt satisfied he was acting as our counselor and leader. If any doubt remained upon the mind of any man — if any faithlessness still lingered around the heart and the spirit — God has now so signally displayed himself to our wondering eyes, that the pillar of cloud by day and of fire by night was not more plain to the children of Israel. Putting man altogether aside, truly may we sing today the song of Moses — "He hath triumphed gloriously; the horse and his rider hath He thrown into the sea."

The more in detail that we receive the accounts of this victory, the more that the smoke clears away from the scene of slaughter and of triumph, the more clearly do we perceive that this is God's victory.

There are circumstances connected with it which mark His immediate interposition and which indicate a spiritual meaning too plain to be misunderstood. God has a purpose in every thing he does and He permits his children, when the event is over, when the blow has fallen, to read that purpose and to learn from it lessons which shall discipline the heart and regulate the conduct.

Man learns but little so long as he is rushing forward in the pursuit of objects which fill his eye and absorb his soul. It is only when some great stroke has descended upon him from God's hand, that he is sufficiently sobered to consider his ways and to understand the dealings of the Lord. Such a stroke has come, like a bolt from Heaven, from the hand of the Almighty, filling the one army and the one nation with defeat and humiliation, and the other army and the other nation with sorrow and lamentation.

He has smitten our enemies in their most tender and sensitive point, their invincible power, and he has taken from us the pride of our victory by giving it to us wrapped up in the funeral shroud of the brave and of the young.

For three long and weary months had the North been gathering and marshalling its hosts for our defeat and subjugation. The most experienced warrior of our land had been engaged, night and day, in organizing an army which should ensure victory and which should make a triumphant and uninterrupted march over the ruins of our social life.

The most veteran troops which our late army afforded were collected from distant fortresses, and all our historical and far-famed batteries were concentrated under officers who had given them their names upon hard fought fields and amid the blood and dust of terrific conflicts. Every appliance which mechanical ingenuity could suggest and which a lavish expenditure could supply, was brought to bear upon the perfection of this armament.

Regiments picked from every State; foreign troops who had seen every kind of European and even Asiatic warfare; volunteers selected from the hardy, enduring, active mechanics of our large cities, were brought together and clustered around the veterans of the army, so that they might receive from them, as quickly as possible, the discipline and steadiness which they needed for operations in the field.

The whole North resounded with the preparation of this mighty host, and Europe was bid to suspend her judgment and her action until this army should make its forward movement, and see whether there would be any further need for her anxiety and her intervention. The newspapers from Washington to Maine on the one hand. and to Minnesota on the other, held, with one or two honorable exceptions, one unchanging tone of exultation, boasting of the power, the strength and the invincibility of the North, and saying, in the very language of Pharaoh "We will pursue, we will overtake, we will divide the spoil; our hands shall destroy them."

Not a word about God and His justice and power that we could hear; not a moment's distrust of themselves and reliance upon God! When their Churches were entered, it was to desecrate their altars with star-spangled banners, and to spread over the very communion table, the symbol, not of Christ's sacrifice, but of their national pride.

When the pulpits spoke, they spoke not the words of humiliation and of peace, but the war-cry of destruction issued from them, as if madness had taken hold of this Christian people.

All this stimulated the government at Washington and swelled the pride of the great chieftain who had never known defeat and whom WELLINGTON had called the greatest Captain of the age. His reputation gave him power to hold that host in hand until his preparations had been fully made, so that he chose his time and his occasion for the commencement of his long announced campaign And they were well chosen to give his movements their very best effect.

He waited until the meeting of the Northern Congress had called together at Washington all the great leaders of his party, until he could have the most illustrious eyes of his chosen people fastened upon his every movement, until expectation had been excited to its utmost stretch, and the nation was standing upon tip-toe to witness his strategetical skill and his successive triumphs.

When these dramatic effects had been all arranged, and in the very midst of the exultation which had been occasioned by the victory at Laurel hill, the order was issued to advance upon the rebel crew which pretended to impede the way of the imperial march to Richmond. And great was the parade of that movement! Division after division was poured out of Washington with all the pomp and circumstance of war.

Everything was accumulated to produce a brilliant and an imposing array. Flaunting banners, exultant music, officers surrounded by brilliant staffs, dashing columns of cavalry, heavy masses of infantry, parks of artillery of unrivalled fame, all inspired an assurance of victory which knew no doubt and would conceive of no defeat.

The loyal city turned out "en masse" to witness this unusual display and to cheer on the army to triumph and to glory. Grave senators accompanied these gallant warriors upon their first day's march and returned to dream only of victory and of conquest. Even women forgot their delicacy and went forth to witness what they were told would be another battle of the spurs. And when the sun went down upon that haughty host, there was probably not a single man in that immense army, who did not anticipate a complete and easy triumph.

And well might they have done it, for they were marching with picked veterans upon untried soldiers; with vastly superior numbers of well armed troops upon youths who had never seen a battle-field and who had picked up their weapons here and there as they could soonest find them, with batteries of the most efficient light and heavy artillery, upon troops whose experience had been confined to a holiday parade in the streets and squares of a city.

What was to hinder a complete and decisive victory? Is it possible that those beardless boys can stand the well directed fire of those terrific batteries, which have so often scattered, under like circumstances, the veterans of other armies? Is it within the bounds of possibility that those young men, trained up in the lap of luxury and known at home, many of them, only as the idlers of fashion, can turn back, even with their undoubted valor, the onset of those stalwart men, who, having labored all their days with the hammer and the axe and every tool of iron, amid furnaces and forges, have made their muscles like brass and their sinews as cords of steel?

Can it be that those backwoodsmen, who have rushed so gallantly to the war with no preparation save the few weeks drilling of a disorderly camp, can roll the tide of battle back upon that haughty host whose movements were but yesterday the admiration of the Capital, satisfying even the critical eye of SCOTT? Tis true those boys and youths and countrymen are led by the flower of the old army, who had disdainfully cast aside the trappings of a government which was calling upon them to subjugate their countrymen and overthrow the constitution of their country; tis true that they are inspired by a holy determination to die upon their ground or else march on to victory; tis true, as PERICLES said of the Athenians, "they place not so great a confidence in the preparatives and artifices of war as in the native warmth of their souls impelling theta to action", tis true, above all, that a nation's prayers are with them in the battle instead of a nation's boastings, but nevertheless the odds are fearful, and even the most confident tremble as the armies meet in deadly conflict.

The eyes of two nations are on them and the hearts of two people are throbbing responsive to every stroke. From morning until evening that dreadful battle raged, and all we yet know is, that our brave boys have made, upon the fatal field of Manassas., the name of Oglethorpe still more immortal, that our statesman hero has illustrated for all time his own beloved Georgia, that victory has perched upon our banners, and that defeat, shameful, overwhelming, almost inexplicable, has humbled to the dust the insolent myrmidons of a despotic democracy.

God was evidently there, strengthening the hearts of his struggling soldiers and bringing the haughty down to the dust. Could the eyes of our fainting, dying children, have been opened that day to see spiritual things, I feel sure that they would have seen horses and chariots of fire riding upon the storm of battle, and making those that were for them, more than those that were against them "Not unto us, O Lord, not unto us, but unto thy name give glory, for thy mercy and for thy truth sake."

It is but seldom, in the annals of war, that so signal a victory has been granted to the arm of valor and the prayer of faith. We should have been satisfied with even a doubtful field; more than satisfied with a decided repulse. How loud then should be our thanksgiving, how deep our gratitude, when God has granted us a triumph which must resound through the civilized world, and give us a name at once among the nations of the earth, when he has permitted us totally to demoralize that insolent army, to drive them back in shame and confusion of face upon their strongholds, to strip them of their batteries which they boasted to be invincible, to despoil them of all the stores which they had been so painfully gathering for so long a time snatch from them the prestige of power which their partisan writers had given them abroad.

And this victory has been given to us by God just at the moment when it was most important to us. There are circumstances in all conflicts which make certain battles decisive, decisive riot because they end the struggle, but decisive because of the effects produced upon the human mind. Man, with all his greatness, is very infirm in his judgments and is apt to measure a cause more by its success than by its principles. The one requires to be examined and decided about, the other is a thing of sight and sense, the one is modified by our feelings and prejudices, the other carries man by storm. Besides, it is hard to separate success from God's favor, and the superstitious mind — and by far the larger part of the world is superstitious instead of religious — almost invariably connects the finger of the Almighty with man's triumphs. Such effects it was most important should be produced at this crisis of our affairs.

Hitherto our successes had been ascribed to numbers, as at Sumter — to treachery, as in Texas — to the inexperience of officers, as at Bethel. In this fight we were acknowledged to be inferior, both in numbers and in arms. The enemy was led by officers of high reputation, under the experienced eye of the great Captain himself, and there was no room for any other fraud than such as stands connected with the legitimate stratagems of war.

The eye of the civilized world was upon this battle — of statesmen, to understand how to conduct their negotiations — of bankers, how to regulate their loans — of merchants, in what channels to float their commerce — of timid and doubting men, how to decide their politics. Much depended upon it for ourselves. For strange to say, imperceptibly to ourselves, our confidence in ourselves had been seriously impaired by the imbecile dependence upon the North for all the material comforts of life into which we had permitted ourselves to fall.

Even while we were guiding the Union by our statesmanship and illustrating it by our valor — even while we were giving it its Presidents, its Generals, its Admirals — even while we were furnishing it by our well-directed and well-managed labor with its great staple of exchange, we were permitting the North to take all the credit of advancement to itself, to absorb, into its great centers of commerce, wealth, literature, science, fashion, and to call it all its own, no matter whence it came or whose brain or pocket produced it, and to persuade even ourselves that we were a helpless race, who were dependent upon it for all we were and all we might hope to be.

They provided the historians, and so the battle-fields of the North were the only ones which were known to the world; they did all the criticism, and so the science and the literature of the South were buried under the mass of charlatans and poetasters and scribblers who claimed to be heard because of their birth-place, and who were willing to buy a fame which they could not otherwise produce, they furnished Europe with all her information of our affairs, and so we were as much unknown as if we had been mere dependencies, or if known, known only as uncivilized frontiersmen who were hewing down the forests and preparing the way for the educated North to come in and refine us.

All the sins of the nation were heaped upon us; we were the pirates, the slave-traders, the filibusters, the repudiators, the demagogues. All the vulgar bullying of the European powers which has been disgracing our country for the last thirty years, was laid — the bastard bantling — at our doors, and not only Europe and the North, but we ourselves, were getting fast to be persuaded that there was no wisdom, no learning, no virtue, no power in the South.

In this battle, then, we were upon trial; trial not only by the world, but trial by and for ourselves. A defeat would have riveted upon us all this false opinion and false character, and it would have required many fields of blood to break the chains of prejudice and calumny, and would have produced upon ourselves an effect which might have hung, for long, years, as a crushing weight upon all our efforts. Honor then to the noble spirits who have achieved this victory for us! Others may die upon the battle-field, but none can die so gloriously as they!

Others may rise up and be baptized for the dead, but none can ever supplant her first martyrs in the admiration of their countrymen. Whatever illustrious deeds may be done in the future — whatever glorious victories may inspire hereafter new songs of thanksgiving and of praise, none can ever eclipse the fame of these deeds and of this victory. They will ever be the first who cast themselves before the insulted form of their mother and received in their young hearts the wounds that were intended for her, they will ever be the first who gave their blood to wash out before the world the stains that had been slanderously cast upon her honor and her virtue, they will ever be the first who have offered up upon the altar of justice and of truth, a hecatomb of victims to soothe her insulted spirit.

Boys many of them were in years, but lions in heart! They have died young, but they have lived long enough to gain an enviable place in history, to entwine their names with the independence and glory of the South. But, above all, honor to the noble spirit who led them to the battle-field; who, having taught them by his virtue, his integrity, his unspotted character, how to live, was now about to teach them how to die! Before he left his home, he wrapped the Confederate flag around him and said that it should be his winding sheet, and all through that bloody day be courted the fulfillment of his prophecy. Wherever the storm of war was fiercest, there was he, wherever death was busiest in his bloody work, there raged he, the very impersonation of a hero.

Even that cruel tyrant seemed loth to take away so grand a soul, and it was not until victory was about to perch upon his crest and snatch him from his grasp, that he struck the fatal blow! And when his gallant boys surrounded him, even while his tongue was faltering in death, he uttered words that will be as memorable as the battle-field — "I am killed, but don't give up the fight."

Like Nelson, he died in the very arms of victory, and his blood, like the dragon's teeth which were sown by Cadmus, sprang up armed men who hurled back the cruel invaders! Mourn for such a life and such a death as his was! We cannot mourn, and even his widowed mother should say with the noble Ormond, "I would rather have my dead son, than any living son in Christendom."

The effects of this victory will be, for the present, more moral than material. For the moment, it will only exasperate the North and spur the leaders on from wounded vanity to redouble their exertions. But it will be as a leaven working among the people, and teaching them, slowly but surely, how hopeless is the task of subjugation which they have taken in hand.

When the first excitement is over, and the shrewd citizens of the North begin to look to the end of all this, and to see before them inevitable failure, they will take the matter into their own hands and call to a terrible account all who have deceived them and led them into their present distress. So long as they were made to believe that their armies could rapidly overrun the South and bring back to their allegiance their most profitable customers, they were ready and willing to hale on the war, but when they shall discover that all their efforts must be unavailing, that an enormous debt will have to be incurred that they themselves must pay, that there is no hope of succor from any of the sources whence they anticipated help, and that nothing is before them but a series of bloody fields to end in discomfiture and disgrace, then may we look for a change of counsels and the rainbow of peace.

This victory is the first step towards such a result, and through its blood and carnage may we see a glimmering of hope for returning reason among those who have suffered themselves to be deluded into the belief that the South would fall an easy prey into their hands. In Europe its effect will be more decided, and it will give a shock to Northern interests in that quarter from which they will find it hard to recover.

It may not lead to the immediate acknowledgment of our independence — European governments are not hasty in their action, because what they do they intend to adhere to and carry out — but it will give us a status abroad which will be of immeasurable advantage to THE CONFEDERATE STATES. Monarchies and Empires do not understand trifling, but when such a blow as this is struck, it at once commands attention and wins respect. However much our enemies may desire to conceal the severity of this blow, and however much we may fear that justice will not be done us abroad, both parties may rest assured that the Ministers and Consuls of foreign governments will keep their statesmen accurately informed of every movement in this important game.

The commercial interests at stake are too enormous to be trifled with, and every honorable effort will be used by both England and France to throw their weight into the scale of commercial freedom. And nothing will give such power to their movements or such strength to their reasoning as blows upon our enemy like that just dealt at Manassas.

Its effect upon ourselves is what I most fear. If we continue humble and give the glory to God, we shall go on from victory to victory, until our independence shall be acknowledged and our homes be left to us in peace. But if we suffer ourselves to be elated and to ascribe our success to ourselves — if our heart be lifted up and we forget the Lord our God and say in our heart, "My power and the might of mine hand bath gotten me this victory," then shall our peril be imminent, for the Lord hateth the proud and smiteth those who would rob him of his glory

This victory is, we firmly, believe, an answer to prayer, and while we would detract nothing from the skill of our leaders or the bravery of our troops, which are the secondary causes of success, we can yet see enough in its circumstances to satisfy us of the presence of God. Let us not lose this vast advantage, but crushing the pride of human nature, let us lay all the glory at the feet of Jesus and acknowledge him to be our Saviour and mighty deliverer.

The triumphant song of Moses was accompanied by a determination to show forth his gratitude to God by a thank-offering. The Lord had always been the strength and the song of the children of Israel, but now he had become their salvation. He had bared his mighty arm in the face of the nations and had delivered them from bondage and from destruction. This was a new relationship which had been established between them, and he determined to acknowledge it by preparing an habitation for God. "The Lord is my strength and my song and he is become my salvation: he is my God and I will prepare him an habitation, my Father's God and I will exalt him."

Moses and the children of Israel were not satisfied with an empty-handed thanksgiving. They were determined that God should perceive that they valued His protection and truly rejoiced in His presence and their earliest resolution was to keep him with them by building an habitation for him in midst of them. They courted His presence. They did every thing they could do to keep Him near to them in the national struggle which had been ushered in by the glorious victory over Pharaoh.

Theirs was not a day of thanksgiving and then a cold dismissal of their God until such time as they should need his services again, but they determined, in the exuberance of their joy, to make it a thanksgiving forever; to bring God into their camp and keep him there forever. What an ally! the Lord of Lord and King of Kings! He who holdeth in his hands the hearts of all men! He who can ride upon the whirlwind and direct the storm! He who can send forth hosts innumerable, horses and chariots of fire to do his bidding! He who can give courage to the fainting spirit and strike fear into the man of war! He who can distract the counsels of the wise and bring to naught the experience of the aged!

How would our hearts leap with joy should we hear that the banner of St. George or the blood-stained tri-color of France had been unfurled and was preparing to wave, in alliance with ours, above our battle-fields! What an assurance of success would it give us! What a triumphant march to victory would it seem to shape out before us! And shall we not endeavor to keep on our side an ally as much greater than these, as the Lord is greater than his servant?

Look all the way back through our young history — for although young, it has been full of marvelous incidents — and see how His power has shielded us, his wisdom directed us, His spirit harmonized us, His sword smitten our enemies. To preserve the favor of such an ally we should prepare, not one, but a thousand habitations, if necessary; we should exalt

Him, we should glorify Him, we should magnify His glorious name! Honor should be done to him daily; the song of praise and thanksgiving should be forever sounded before him.

Man should lead the chorus of rejoicing, "I will sing unto the Lord, for he hath triumphed gloriously, the horse and his rider hath he thrown into the sea," and woman should echo back the song of triumph with timbrels and with dances "Sing ye to the Lord, for he hath triumphed gloriously, the horse and his rider hath he thrown into the sea."

The Church of Christ, my beloved hearers, is his habitation upon earth, and we call upon you this day to prepare it for the presence of the Lord. It is always your duty and now it should be your delight. In this crisis of our national history, there is no element of society which is so important as the Church.

It wields the most powerful instruments for good or for evil at a moment like this. It carries the prayers of the people to the mercy seat of Christ, and brings back blessings upon its wings — it guides the sentiments of the people in the channels of duty and of devotion — it works upon conscience, upon heart, upon spirit — it sends the soldier to the battle inspired with more than animal courage, and it ministers comfort to those who remain behind to endure the terrible anxiety of suspense, and to bear the misery of the heart's desolation.

Prepare, then, habitations for the Lord that he may be induced to dwell among us; give him, for your own and for your country's sake, a glorious and exulting welcome. Exalt him, whose is "the earth and all that therein is, the compass of the world and they that dwell therein." Say unto your homes, unto your temples, unto your hearts. "Lift up your heads, O ye Gates; and be ye lift up, ye everlasting doors, and the King of Glory shall come in."

Since this Sermon was written, the body servant of Colonel BARTOW has returned and has delivered to his family the Prayer Book which had belonged to his Father, and which, although quite a large one, he had carried with him through the campaign. It was marked at the Collect for the Sunday after Ascension, which he was using when summoned to the battle-field. I subjoin the Collect, as indicative of the feeling with which he went into the conflict:

"O God, the King of Glory, who hast exalted thine only son Jesus Christ with great triumph unto thy kingdom in Heaven: We beseech thee, leave us not comfortless; but send to us thine Holy Ghost to comfort us and to exalt us unto the same place whither our Saviour Christ is gone before, who liveth and reigneth with thee and the Holy Ghost, one God world without end. *Amen.*"

# God In The War

A SERMON

DELIVERED BEFORE THE

LEGISLATURE OF GEORGIA,

IN THE CAPITOL AT MILLEDGEVILLE

ON

FRIDAY, NOVEMBER 15, 1861

BEING A DAY SET APART FOR

## Fasting, Humiliation and Prayer

BY

### His Excellency the President of the Confederate States

BY REV. HENRY H. TUCKER, D.D.

PROFESSOR OF BELLES LETTRES IN
MERCER UNIVERSITY

1861

## SERMON

"Come behold the works of the Lord, what desolations He hath made in the earth.

He maketh wars to cease unto the end of the earth; He breaketh to bow, and cutteth the spear in sunder; He burneth the chariot in the fire." Psalms 56:8:9.

Desolation! Desolation! Thousands of our young men have been murdered. Thousands of fathers and mothers among us have been bereaved of their sons. Thousands of widows are left disconsolate and heart-broken, to struggle through life alone. The wail of thousands of orphans is heard through the land, the aegis of a father's protection being removed from over their defenseless heads. Thousands of brave men are at this moment lying on beds of languishing, some prostrated by the diseases incident to the army and camp, and some by cruel wounds.

Every house within reach of the seat of war is a hospital, and every hospital is crowded. Huge warehouses emptied of their merchandize, and churches, and great barns, are filled with long rows of pallets beside each other, containing each a sufferer, pale, emaciated and ghastly. Some writhe with pain; some rage with delirium; some waste with fever; some speak of home, and drop bitter tears at the recollection of wives soon to be widows, and babes soon to be fatherless.

The nurse hurries with noiseless step, ministering from bedside to bedside. The pious chaplain whispers of Jesus to the dying. The surgeon is in frightful practice, bloody though beneficent; and as his knife glides through the quivering flesh and his saw grates through the bone and tears through the marrow, the suppressed groan bears witness to the anguish.

A father stands by perhaps, to see his son mutilated. Mother and wife and sisters at home witness the scene by a dreadful clairvoyance, and with them the operation lasts not for moments but for weeks. Every groan in the hospital or tent, or on the bloody field, wakes echoes at home. There is not a city, nor village, nor hamlet, nor neighborhood that has not its representatives in the army, and scarcely a heart in our whole Confederacy that is not either bruised by strokes already fallen, or pained by a solicitude scarcely less dreadful than the reality.

Desolation! Desolation! Hearts desolate, homes desolate, the whole land desolate! Our young men, our brave young men, our future statesmen, and scholars and divines, to whom we should bequeath this great though youthful empire with all its destinies; the flower of our society, — contributions from that genuine and proper aristocracy which consists of intelligence and virtue, — thousands, thousands of them laid upon the altar! And alas! the end is not yet.

Another six months may more than double the desolation. Relentless winter may aid the enemy in his work of death. The youth accustomed at home to shelter, and bed, and fire, and all the comforts of high civilization, standing guard on wintry night, exposed to freezing rain and pealing blasts, and having completed his doleful task, retiring to his tent, to lie upon the bare ground, in clothes encrusted with ice, may not falter in spirit in view of his hardships; the fires of patriotism may still keep up the warmth at his heart; when be remembers that he is fighting for the honor of his father, and for the purity of his mother and sisters, and for all that is worth having in the world, he may cheerfully brave the terrors of a winter campaign; but though his soul be undaunted, his body will fail.

Next spring when the daisies begin to blow, thousands of little hillocks dotted all over the country on mountain side and in valley, marked at each end with a rough memorial stone, and a brief and rude inscription made perhaps with the point of a bayonet, will silently but ah! how impressively, confirm the sad prophecy of this hour. Thus the work of desolation may go on winter after winter, until the malice of our foes is satiated, and until our young men are all gone. But let us not anticipate. The present alone presents subjects of contemplation, enough to fill the imagination and to break the heart.

These are the desolations of war. Do you ask why I present this sad, this melancholy picture? Why I make this heart-rending recital of woes enough to make heaven weep?

In so doing I am but following the example of the Psalmist when he says, "Come behold the works of the Lord, what desolations He hath made in the earth!"

If in the midst of victory when the God of Israel had given success to the arms of his people, their leader and king called upon them to forget their successes and meditate on the desolations of war, it must be right for the man of God now, to call upon his countrymen in the midst of a series of victories such as perhaps were never won in a war before, to forget their triumphs, and contemplate for a little the expense of life and of sorrow which those triumphs have cost.

Come then my countrymen, and behold the desolation. What emotion does it excite? What passion does it stimulate? To what action does it prompt? Indignation at the fanaticism, folly and sin of those who brought it all about. Rage at the authors of our ruin.

Retaliation! To arms! To arms! Let us kill! Let us destroy! Let us exterminate the miscreants from the earth! Up with the black flag! They deserve no quarter! They alone are to blame for this horror of horrors. We had no hand in bringing it on. We asked for nothing but our rights. Our desire was for peace. They tormented us without cause while we were with them.

What we cherish as a heaven-ordained institution they denounce as the "sum of all villainies." They regarded us as worse than heathen and pirates; they degraded us from all equality; they spurned us from all fellowship; they taught their children to hate us; their ministers of religion chased us like bloodhounds, actually putting weapons of death in the hands of their agents with instructions to murder us.

They made a hero and a martyr of him, who at Harper's Ferry openly avowed his design, to enact over in all our land the horrid scenes of St. Domingo, — thus by the popular voice dooming us to death and our wives and daughters to worse than death; and when after these outrages, we sought no retaliation but besought them to let us go in peace, they still clutched us with frantic grasp, in order to filch away our substance, and reduce us to a bondage more degrading than that which they affect to pity in the negro.

I will not continue to give expression to thoughts which alas! have already taken too deep hold on us all. But in the midst of all the rage, resentment, and fury, which a contemplation of these facts of history is calculated to engender, let me repeat to you the words of the text, with an emphasis which perhaps will lift your minds above the consideration of second causes. "Come behold the works of the Lord, what desolations He hath made in the earth!" If it be important to regard the desolations of war, it is still more so, to be mindful of the source whence they come. This perhaps was the chief object of the Psalmist. If he pointed to the rod, it was that all hearts should be turned towards Him who held it. And this my countrymen it is all important for us to remember, — that GOD is in the war. He brought it upon us.

The wickedness and folly of our enemies may have been the occasion of it, but these could not in any proper sense be the cause. That is but a shallow philosophy which sees a cause in anything outside of God. The idea of cause involves by necessity the idea of power, and what power is there independent of God? Aside from the will of God, what nexus can there be, between an effect and the antecedent which by a sad misnomer we denominate the cause?

Satisfied with a slovenly nomenclature, we apply the term cause to that in which there resides no power. That profounder wisdom which we learn from the inspired oracles demands a better vocabulary; it calls for a word to designate the cause of so-called causes. In want of this, it disallows to earthly antecedents even if invariable, a name which describes that which is to be found only in the Almighty.

The guilt of our enemies is what we term a second cause, that is to say, it is no cause at all, but only the occasion of a chastisement inflicted by an Almighty arm. God is in the war. God is in everything; in the doings of earth, for "He knoweth our sitting down and our rising up;" in the raptures of paradise, in the flames of perdition. Yea saith the

Psalmist, "If I ascend up into heaven Thou art there. If I make my bed in hell, behold Thou art there! Psalms 139:8.

In the economy of God the wicked are often used as instruments for the accomplishment of divine ends. Satan, when he introduced sin into the world, was the instrument of preparing the way for a brighter display of God's goodness than ever yet had amazed the universe, and was as really the herald of Jesus of Nazareth as was John the Baptist.

Those who cried out "Crucify him! crucify him! his blood be upon us and upon our children!" all guilty as they were; — in piercing the veins of a Savior opened the fountain of eternal life to the millions of them who shall be redeemed unto God by his blood, out of every kindred and tongue and people and nation.[4]

Thus does God cause the wrath of man to praise him. If there be any possible wrath, such as could not by divine almightiness, be so perverted from its wicked end as to promote the glory and exhibit the goodness of God, that remainder of wrath is restrained. In other words, sin is allowed only in so far as God brings good out of it. Thus every evil is the precursor of blessing. The greatest calamities that ever befell the Universe were but the harbingers of glory.

A Christian poet has said:

> We should suspect some danger nigh
> When we possess delight.

Thank God it is also true, that whenever evil comes, we may know there is good at hand. In national or in individual experience, when the godless soul sees only a dark cloud, fraught with terror and with wrath, to the Christian the cloud resolves itself into a blazing star that guides to the best of blessings. When God says to his children "All things work together for good to them that love God," the heart of the

---

[4] Many parallel cases might be referred to; for an interesting one see Gen. 45. 6.

believer makes no exceptions, and thus "rejoices in tribulations, also."

It is also a part of the divine economy to use the wicked as instruments for the chastisement of each other. — Two individuals indulge in mutual animosity. Each is wrong; and each by a series of unkindnesses, or acts that deserve a harsher name, inflicts upon the other a well deserved penalty. Neighborhoods give way to ill-will. — Nothing short of a miracle could prevent them from distressing each other; and Providence works no such miracle.

Nations burn with hate against nations, and as an appropriate punishment for their crimes God turns them loose upon each other, and their perpetual wars result in mutual ruin. History, profane as well as sacred, is full of examples where "Nation was destroyed of nation, and city of city; for God did vex them with all adversity." 2 Chron. 15:5.

Even in the control of his own children God makes use of the wicked as his instruments of discipline. When Israel did evil in the sight of the Lord, the inspired record declares that "The Lord delivered them into the hand of Midian; and the hand of Midian prevailed against Israel; and Israel was impoverished because of the Midianites." Judges 6:6. Individual experience too, may often make appropriate the prayer of David when he says "Deliver my soul from the wicked, which is thy sword; from men which are thy hand." Ps. 17:13.

The sin of the wicked is not diminished by the fact that it is over-ruled for good by a superior power. There can be no interference with the personal responsibility of moral creatures. Thus the guilt of those who wage this diabolical war on the unoffending people of these CONFEDERATE STATES, finds no apology in the providence of God. "It must needs be that offences come but woe unto him by whom they come." Luke 17:1.

Our aggressors must answer for their awful account before the bar of God. — There let us leave them. Our text which was written when the death-smell was fresh on the field of battle, makes no reference to the outrages of the enemy, but points only to God, as the author of the desolation.

The Psalmist does not confound the cause of trouble with the occasion of it. He is engrossed, not with the doings of earth, but with those of heaven. He has no eyes to see the wickedness of his foes. He forgets he ever had a foe, and sees only God in the war. Let his example be for our imitation.

Surely it is as contrary to religion as it is to a sound philosophy to banish God from the most striking act of his Providence that has occurred within the memory of living man. If it be true then that the hand of God is in this thing (and who can doubt it?) and if we lose sight of that fact, surely a worse evil will come upon us.

Among other evils, we may expect to receive in our own souls the consequences of our sin. Resentment, rage, and hate, will be so developed as to take entire possession of us. We shall become blood-thirsty as tigers, cruel as death, and malicious as fiends. All that we expect to accomplish by the war, if bought at such expense to our own character, would cost more than it is worth. If we cannot be free without transforming ourselves into devils, it were better not to be free; for any thralldom is to be preferred before slavery to sin.

But if we exclude God from our thoughts, and regard the desolations around us as coming only from the enemy, how is it possible to keep from violating the injunction "avenge not yourselves!" Whose blood would not be set on fire, whose soul would not be carried away with fiercest passions, by contemplation of the frightful evils we sustain, if they be traced to no cause outside the wicked hearts of our enemies! Alas, all of us are too prone to confine our attention to second causes.

Methinks I see the apparition of the spirit of David rising from the sleep of centuries, as that of Samuel did under the incantations of the witch of Endor. His form is venerable, his beard is flowing, and on his brow rests the crown of Israel. He touches the harp of solemn sound, and peals forth the notes of the sublime ode whence our text is taken. He waves his hand to the scenes of sorrow wrought by the war now upon us, and making no allusion to our foes, says "Come behold the works of the Lord, what desolations He hath made in the earth!"

When we regard the evils we suffer as the chastisement of the Almighty, there arises within us no spirit of resentment. The fiercer elements of our nature all subside. — We humbly submit to the judgments of the Almighty. Our eyes instead of flashing fire, are melted to tears; our tongues instead of curses and defiance, utter words of penitence and contrition.

Whatever comes from God we can bear. We acknowledge his authority. We know that at his hands we deserve nothing but indignation and wrath, tribulation and anguish. We know that he is a gracious Father as well as a righteous judge; and we recognize his benevolence even in his chastisements; for "whom the Lord loveth he chasteneth." We only say "It is the Lord, let him do as seemeth him good."

Surely this is a better spirit than results from a view of second causes. Surely this is more likely to secure the divine approbation and the divine aid; and if God be for us who can be against us? This is the very spirit which his chastisements are intended to excite; and when the end is accomplished the means will be laid aside. Thus shall war afflict us no more, and God will not allow "the wicked which is his sword" to harm us further.

But that other spirit which instead of forgetting the enemy and looking to God, reverses the order and forgetting God looks to the enemy, and which stimulates to frenzy the worst passions known to human nature, tends only to make us more wicked than we were before, and therefore to perpetuate the very causes which made these chastisements necessary. If instead of profiting by the afflictions which God sends upon us, we make them the occasions of additional guilt, what can we expect but that billow after billow of his wrath will overtake us until we shall be utterly destroyed.

The sweet singer of Israel having depicted the desolations which God sends by war, devotes the next strain of his inspired verse to the announcement of the truth that "He maketh wars to cease unto the end of the earth."

It is He who brings these evils upon us and it is He who takes them away. Nor is it needless for the Psalmist to remind us of what we might have known, that the blessings of peace are from the hand of the Almighty. Here too as in the former case, we are prone to be satisfied with second causes.

We are anxious for wise legislation and for skillful generalship. We congratulate ourselves on having such able statesmen as Davis and Stephens, such able generals as Johnston and Beauregard. We glory in the belief that our troops are as brave as the bravest in the world, and that our enemies though outnumbering us four to one as they did at Leesburg, cannot stand before Southern valor in the open field for one moment.

We exult (alas! our exultation is not unmixed with sin) when we see the terror-stricken fugitives leaping by hundreds over the steep embankment, and like devil-possessed swine plunging headlong into the Potomac. We are making abundant arrangements to supply ourselves with all the munitions of war. We are casting cannon, manufacturing arms, and fortifying our coasts. Hundreds of thousand of us are already under arms, and hundreds of thousands more are ready and anxious to step into the ranks.

We feel safe when we remember that we are so many and so strong, and so brave, and so well prepared to re-enact the scenes of Sumter, and Bethel, and Manassas, and Springfield, and Lexington, and Leesburg, and Columbus. We feel sure that if the enemy will only give us battle once more on the Potomac, our brave boys will again send them shrieking and screaming back to their Northern homes. We doubt not that we shall whip them whenever we come in conflict with them. We shall whip them, and whip them, and whip them again. We shall whip them again and again. We shall whip them until they are satisfied to their hearts' content, that the only safety for themselves is in letting us alone.

My countrymen! it is right for us to resort to all the means of defense which Providence has placed within our reach. It is proper to call into action our best civil and military talent, to strain every energy to the utmost in supplying the material of war. As for that sublime faith which we have in the unconquerable valor of our troops, I admire it, I partake in it. But we are here on dangerous ground.

We must not step over the line where God says "Thus far shalt thou go, and no farther." Let us not lean on an arm of flesh. Saith the prophet, "Cease ye from man whose breath is in his nostrils, for wherein is he to be accounted of." Isa. 2:22. Is our confidence in our success based on the wisdom of our statesmen and generals? That Providence which sustains the flight of the sparrow and numbers the hairs of our head might direct the death-bringing bullet to the vitals of our greatest chieftain. Instead of the horse, the rider might have been slain. "It is better to trust in the Lord than to put confidence in man. It is better to trust in the Lord than to put confidence in Princes." Ps. 118:8-9.

Is our trust in the valor of our troops? The same God who struck terror into the hearts of the Midianites when they heard the cry "The sword of the Lord and of Gideon!" the same God who sent confusion and dismay into the ranks of our enemies when the sword of the Lord and of the South prevailed at Manassas, might send a panic among us which would scatter us like chaff before the wind. He might send his angels in armies to descend upon us, and filling the air with their unseen presence, every heart might quiver with undefinable dread from unknown cause, and they might smite us with invisible weapons, the very touch of which would curdle our blood.

Oh! there is no bravery that can stand before the hosts of the living God. The outward appliances of war, the chieftains and captains, the arms and munitions, the shot and shell, the rifles, infantry, artillery, cavalry, all these are useful in their proper places. But let us not put our confidence in them. They are not to be trusted. — They all may fail. They never yet have made a war to cease.

This is the very sentiment of the scripture which says "There is no King saved by the multitude of an host; a mighty man is not delivered by much strength. An horse is a vain thing for safety, neither shall he deliver any by his great strength. Behold the eye of the Lord is upon them that fear him!" Ps. 33:16. "Battle is the Lord's." 2 Chron. 20:15. "He shall cut off the spirit of princes; he is terrible to the kings of the earth. At thy rebuke O God of Jacob both the chariot and the horse are cast into a dead sleep." Ps. 75:6-12. "He maketh wars to cease unto the end of the earth!"

So earnest is the Psalmists in declaring that the ending of the war as well as the beginning of it is from God, that he reiterates the sentiment four times in the text. First in literal terms, "he maketh wars to cease;" then in figure of speech "he breaketh the bow;" again in similar figure, "he cutteth the spear in sunder;" and for the fourth time he enunciates the same idea in another figure when he says, "he burneth the chariot in the fire."

The destruction of the bow, the spear, and the chariot, ancient instruments of war, was a symbolical way of describing peace. The figurative expressions then, mean the same as that which is literal; and if this portion of the ode were stripped of its poetic dress and expressed in plainest terms, it would be simply a fourfold declaration of a single truth.

"He maketh wars to cease! He maketh wars to cease! HE MAKETH WARS TO CEASE! HE MAKETH WARS TO CEASE unto the end of the earth!" Let this tremendous energy of quadruple emphasis, be for the rebuke, and discomfiture and silencing of those who look to earthly sources for the power to stop this awful war.

Ye worshippers of human Deities, who by supposing that the efforts of mortals can terminate the bloody strife, exalt the creature to a level with omnipotence, listen to the voice of the Almighty! "Be still and know that I am God! I will be exalted among the heathen, I will be exalted in the earth!"

While it is true that we need constant admonition to wean us from trust in human resources and lift our thoughts to a higher Power, yet it is also a fact, and one most gratifying to the Christian, that thus far in the war, there has been a wonderful turning of the hearts of the people to God. — When Col. Hill wrote to the Governor of North Carolina that the Lord of Hosts had given us the victory at Bethel, he spoke the sentiment of the whole army.

Our soldiers, from the highest officer to the humblest private in the ranks, habitually ascribe our victories to God. Even the irreligious seem to pause for a moment when they speak of Bethel or Manassas, and reverently acknowledge God in the battle. So universally does this feeling pervade our troops that it excites the wonder of all who have had an opportunity of observing it.

When Mr. Memminger introduced into THE CONFEDERATE CONGRESS the ever-memorable and sublime resolutions ascribing the victory of the 21st of July to the King of kings and Lord of lords, a thrill of acquiescence and hearty appreciation flashed over the whole Confederacy, and the hearts of all the people were melted together.

When the news reached this Legislative Hall only day before yesterday, that the Providence of God had brought across the ocean to our shores a ship laden with weapons of defense, and shoes for our feet, and other articles of necessity and comfort, the Representatives of the people here assembled, almost unanimously and simultaneously fell to their knees, and while tears of gratitude streamed from many a cheek, and amid a wide spread murmur of scarcely suppressed sobs, their presiding officer as the spokesman of the Assembly, offered up to God a tribute of prayer and thanksgiving! — Oh! that was a thrilling spectacle, and on which doubtless angels looked with beaming eyes and a new delight. Surely such a scene never occurred before.

The record has been entered on the Journal and is now a chronicle of the times. Posterity will read it centuries hence with moistening eyes. Heartstrings will quiver and bosoms will heave with emotion all over the world on perusing this sublimest page in history. It is cheering to believe that the record is copied in heaven, and that this outburst of gratitude which thrilled the breasts of men and angels with such sweet and strange emotion, was not unacceptable to Him, to whom the tribute was paid and whose goodness was the cause of it.

And now that His Excellency THE PRESIDENT OF THE CONFEDERATE STATES has set apart this 15th day of November as a day of fasting, humiliation and prayer, calling on all the people to flock to a throne of grace, as a father calls on his children to surround the family altar, the whole people respond; all business has ceased, and the nation is prostrate before God.

The scoffer and the infidel may question the sincerity of the Christian, or if not, they will perhaps be surprised to learn that to his mind the most cheering evidence of our success in this war is this acknowledgment of God so wide spread in the hearts of the people. This pious and reverent feeling is not the natural offspring of the human heart. If it comes to us from external sources it comes from none that are bad. Satan never turns the heart to God. None but God himself could have inspired this confidence in himself: and he never inspires confidence merely to betray it. —

This then is the chief reliance of the Christian patriot in this emergency. It is gratifying to see that this devout and proper spirit so generally prevails, and it should be the great aim of all who love God to cultivate and cherish it. The very best of us though we acknowledge God with one breath, are prone to forget him at the next; and while we ascribe the victories of the past to him, we are apt to trust for future victories to our own strong arms and stout hearts, and abundant preparations. No greater calamity could possibly overtake us than to yield to this disposition to forget God.

If I were to say that it would be the certain precursor of overwhelming defeat, I should be only repeating what the prophet Isaiah said three thousand years ago, but which like all other truth is not impaired by time: — Woe to them that stay on horses and trust in chariots because they are many, and in horsemen because they are very strong, but they look not unto the Holy One of Israel, neither seek the Lord." — Is. 21:1.

Woe to you then ye people of Georgia! Woe to you all ye people of THESE CONFEDERATE STATES! if you are engrossed with outward preparations for battle, and seek not the Lord nor put your trust in the Holy One of Israel, and in the King of glory! Who is this King of glory? "The Lord strong and mighty, the Lord mighty in battle!" — Ps. 25:8.

Many of the ways of God are past finding out, for "his thoughts are very deep," but in regard to the matter before us, it is not surprising that high and unfaltering faith in God should be the precursor of success. On the contrary it can be shown to be in keeping with all the dealings of his providence with us.

Of course when faith is spoken of, reference is had to real faith, not to counterfeits. Real faith either in God or in anything else is never an inert and unproductive principle. There is in its nature an element which prompts to action. Faith in God prompts to obedience, and if to obedience then to repentance, to reformation and to every virtue. The apostle not without reason places faith first, and hope and charity afterwards. For though charity be the greatest of the three, yet faith is the seed-virtue from which the others spring, certainly without which the others could not exist.

Now let us remember the point already made, that God is in the war. Let us further remember that he has not brought these calamities upon us without a purpose. Without presuming to know any of the secrets of Infinite wisdom, the Almighty has revealed himself to us sufficiently to warrant us in saying, that these afflictions must have been brought upon us either as a punishment for sins that are past, or as a means of making us better in future, or for both these ends.

Suppose the object be the first of these. Then such faith in him as prompts to repentance and reformation while it might not logically remove the chastisement, would at least prevent further occasion for it from accruing; and there is reason to hope, that the divine benevolence would not be bound by so strict a logic as not to remove the penalty when the sin that occasioned it is repented of and abandoned.

Suppose the object be to make us a better people. When the object is accomplished, there will be no further use for the instrumentality which brought it about. Suppose the object be both retrospective and prospective. The same reasoning that applied to the cases separately will apply to both together; except that the former case being coupled with the latter would receive strength by the connection, and we should have still better reason to hope that if we cease to sin our Heavenly Parent would cease to chastise.

It is not irreverent to suppose that the divine procedure would be governed by the same principles which control us in the discipline of our children. What father ever continues to use the rod when he is convinced that his child is so heartily sorry for his fault that he will never commit it again? What master would chastise his servant if he knew the servant's grief for his fault to be sincere and profound enough to prevent him from repeating the offence?

We are God's children. He is chastising us. Let us acknowledge him; and say "though he slay me yet will I trust in him." Let us confess the sins that brought these evils upon us. Let us repent of them, and so repent as to abandon. Let us do all this, and this war will come to an end. "He maketh wars to cease." He will make this war to cease.

When we become what we ought to be there can be no motive in the divine mind to continue the chastisement, and the war will cease. The skeptic may ridicule this conclusion. Let him ridicule. "A brutish man knoweth not neither doth a fool understand this." — Ps. 92:6. He who is enlightened from above, without stopping to ask the opinions of politicians, soldiers or philosophers, and preferring higher authority, goes straight to the oracles of God for a solution of the problem, and is satisfied when he reads: "He maketh wars to cease unto the end of the earth; he; breaketh the bow and cutteth the spear in sunder; he burneth the chariot in the fire."

The caviler may object, and talk about military and political necessities, and physical and moral impossibilities, and philosophic difficulties. But while he is prating, the providences of God will go right on, and will say to him in due time, "Be still and know that I am God."

How strange that we should ask men to predict what the end will be, without asking God who knows all things from the beginning. How strange that we should rely on our puny efforts to bring this dreadful strife to a close, when we know that God only can stop it. For is it not He who makes wars to cease? We have been trusting in horses and in chariots. Let us rather remember the name of the Lord our God.

Let us pay our vows unto him, and we shall have no further use for these dread instruments of war. — Here then is great good news for the people of THESE CONFEDERATE STATES! These desolations may be stopped! The red tide of life that flows from the veins of your sons may be staunched! Prosperity may again be established! — "What," exclaims one, "can we entice the enemy from their entrenchments into open field? Then indeed we shall soon destroy them and the remainder will sue for peace!"

No my friend, there is no certainty that that would close the war. "What then? shall we cross the Potomac, deliver Maryland, push on to Philadelphia and still farther North until we conquer a peace?" No, no. There can be no assurance of success in such an enterprise. "Shall we then court the friendship of foreign powers, and thus reinforce our army, and re-supply our wasting resources?" Yes! Let us court the friendship, not indeed of a foreign power, for the God of our fathers is not foreign to us, but let us court the favor of heaven, and verily an alliance with the Almighty will make us omnipotent!

My countrymen, before God! in my heart and from my soul, I do believe that if the people of this Confederacy were to turn with one heart and one mind to the Lord and walk in his ways, he would drive the invader from our territories and restore to us the blessings of peace.

I wish I could express myself with more plainness and with more force. Let me say again, I believe that the quickest and easiest way to terminate this war, and that favorably to ourselves, is for us all to be good. We imagine that the only way to get out of our difficulties is to fight out.

There is a more excellent way. Let us by faith, obedience and love, so engage the Lord of Hosts on our side that he will fight for us; and when he undertakes our case we are safe, for "he maketh wars to cease," and he will break the bow of the enemy, and cut his spear in sunder, and burn his chariot in the fire, and say unto him, "Be still and know that I am God!"

Call it superstition if you please ye men of the world. Say that we are deluded by a religious enthusiasm. But know ye that faith in Israel's God is not superstition, and that confidence in an over ruling providence is no delusion. Enthusiasm there may be, there is, there ought to be, we avow it, we glory in it. The heathen may rage and the people imagine a vain thing, but we rejoice when we can say, — God is our refuge and strength, a very present help in trouble.

Therefore will not we fear though the earth be removed, and though the mountains be carried into the midst of the sea, though the mountains shake with the swelling thereof, Selah! The Lord of Hosts is with us, the God of Jacob is our refuge, Selah!"

Lay what plans you will, and set what schemes you please in operation, and at the summing up of all things at the end of the world, it will be found that God ruled and overruled all things according to the working of his power; and that the great statesmen and great captains who figure so largely in history, were but the unwitting instruments of accomplishing his purposes.

We look back over the past and see God in history. We look forward and see him bringing generation after generation upon the earth to work out his designs and not theirs, for before they existed they could have had no designs. Why should the present be an exception? Let us then do justly, and love mercy and walk humbly before God, and by thus falling in with his plans, we shall be on his side and he will be on ours, and those who make war upon us will either see their folly and cease, or if they continue will do nothing more than work out their own ruin.

They have no power to harm us. We have no power to make ourselves safe. "Once hath God spoken, yea twice have I heard this, that power belongeth unto God." — Ps. 62:2. Let us fly to that Power and engage it in our behalf, and he who smote great nations and slew mighty kings, Sihon king of Amorites, and Og king of Bashan for his people's sake, will smite the hypocritical nation that wars against us, and will give to us and to our children the heritage of our fathers forever.

I have said that the way to enlist this almightiness on our side is to make the law of God the law of every man's life. Perhaps these terms are too general to convey the idea with power. What then more particularly is to be done. What specific duties must we discharge? What special evils must we forsake? All, all! The whole head is sick, the whole heart is faint, the whole body is corrupt.

How small a proportion of our population are disciples of Jesus! — Counting out avowed unbelievers and false professors, how few are left! Here is the place to begin. A pure Gospel is our only hope — I repeat it, a pure Gospel is our only hope. If the Kingdom of Christ be not set up in the hearts of the people no government can exist except by force. All you then who have no personal experience of the grace of the Gospel are so far, in the way of your country's prosperity.

The first step for you to take is to believe in the Lord Jesus Christ, confessing your sins and giving him your heart. But aside from this, let us look at our public morals. Passing by profanity, for we are a nation of swearers; passing by drunkenness, for we are a nation of drunkards; passing by Sabbath-breaking, for our cars thunder along the track on the Sabbath as on any other day, and our convivial gatherings are too often on the day of the Lord; passing by covetousness and lying, for two many of our citizens alas! will for the sake of defrauding the public out of a few dollars make false oath in giving in their tax returns; passing by neglect of our children, for too few of them receive that religious instruction and training which is their due; passing by injustice to servants, for while their physical wants are in some cases unsupplied their moral wants are too generally neglected; passing by all these things, and each of the sins of private life which ought to be exchanged for its opposite virtue; let me call especial attention to three things of more public nature, and which are fairer samples of the average of public morals.

In the first place, how is it that in the State of Georgia it is almost impossible to convict a culprit of crime? The most atrocious murders and other outrages are committed with impunity, in the very face of our so-called Courts of Justice. Is the Bench prostituted? Is the Bar prostituted? Or is it the Jury box? In either case it is clear that public virtue is at fault; otherwise these evils would not be tolerated.

So notoriously defective is the administration of justice, that in many cases fresh within the memory of us all, citizens have felt it necessary in self-defense to execute criminals without the forms of law. Is not this a step towards barbarism? The example of disregarding the law being set by reputable citizens, will be followed by others not so reputable. When this system is inaugurated where will it stop? Whose life will be safe? This reign of the mob, this lawless execution of men which is little short of murder, will become the rule and not the exception, unless a more healthy public opinion shall correct the evils in our Courts of Justice.

The second evil is kindred to the first. How is it that in all the history of this Legislative body pardon has been granted to every criminal, almost without exception who has ever applied for it? Can it be that all who have been pardoned were innocent? If so there must have been horrid injustice in the Courts which convicted them.

The bloodthirsty Jeffreys would scarcely have sent so many innocent men to the gallows. No; under the loose administration of justice already referred to, none but the most glaring cases (with possibly a rare exception) could ever be convicted. — How comes it then that our Legislators turn loose these culprits upon society?

It is because they are more anxious to secure a re-election than to promote the good of the State. How comes it that a vote adverse to pardon would endanger their re-election? It is because public opinion is rotten. The fault lies in the low standard of public morals.

But for the third item. Without meaning to indulge in wholesale denunciation of any class of my fellow citizens, it may yet be pertinent to inquire, how is it that so few of our public men are good men? Is it to be supposed that all the talent, and all the learning, and all the wisdom, have been vouchsafed to the bad rather than to the good?

Does Satan claim a monopoly of all the intellectual power and administrative ability in the world? Perhaps it is not surprising that he should; for he once offered to give to their rightful owner "all the Kingdoms of this world and the glory of them" on condition of receiving his homage in return.

But it is preposterous to suppose that there are no good men to be found capable of discharging the highest public trusts. — Why then are they not oftener found in eminent position? It is because the public in estimating a man's fitness for office, throw his morals out of the account; and because popularity can be obtained by means which bad men freely resort to, but which good men eschew. How sad a comment on public virtue!

Every voter who allows personal interests, or preferences, or prejudices, or party zeal or anything to influence his suffrage in favor of a bad man in preference to a good one, if the latter be capable, is doing what he can to banish virtue from our councils and God from our support. It might be a fair subject of inquiry, whether he or the outbreaking felon whose place is in the Penitentiary inflicts the greatest injury upon society.

It is time that the preachers of the Gospel, who ought to be if they are not, the great conservators of public morals, had made way upon these monster evils; and I rejoice that I have the opportunity on this public day, before this Legislative body, and before the people of the whole State, to bear my testimony against them.

The three evils just specified are only outward manifestations of an internal distemper, the mere efflorescence of evil deep seated in the public heart. The disappearance of these would indicate a radical change. Suppose public justice to be rightly administered, suppose the influence of virtue in our councils to be predominant; and this is to suppose that thousands upon thousands of individual men have grown wiser and better, that myriads of private faults have been exchanged for corresponding virtues, that the whole complexion of society is changed, and its whole nature improved.

Suppose that the Gospel of Christ which alone can work these changes, should continue thus to elevate, refine, ennoble and sanctify, until every heart were brought under its sacred influence. How much like heaven our earth would be! Can any one suppose that in such a state of society as this, the heavenly tranquility would ever be disturbed by the clangor of war!

Let our whole people at once renounce their evil works and ways with grief, and follow hard after God, and I confidently declare that he would with a mighty hand and an outstretched arm deliver us from our enemies and restore peace and prosperity. — Think you that I ought to modify this positive declaration into a mere expression of opinion? I reiterate the same sentiment in words which no man will dare to question: — "When a man's ways please the Lord he maketh even his enemies to be at peace with him." — Prov. 16:7. And again. "Let the wicked forsake his way and the unrighteous man his thoughts, and let him turn unto the Lord, and he will have mercy upon him, and unto our God for he will abundantly pardon." — Is. 55:7.

Is it said that these words refer to individuals and are not applicable to States? The same conditions of mercy that would suffice for one man would suffice for two, and if for two then for any number, for nations and for all.

From these teachings of Holy Writ, it appears my countrymen, that in carrying on this war which the providence of God has brought upon us, we ought to use a new set of instrumentalities; instrumentalities the object of which shall be not to injure our enemies but to benefit ourselves; to benefit us not in things visible and tangible but in the inner man. Thus shall those faults in our character which made these chastisements necessary be removed, and as matter of moral certainty the sad consequences which we suffer would cease.

Here then is joyful news to thousands of Christian patriots who burn with desire to aid their country's cause, but who know not what to do. All you have to do is to be good, and in being good you are doing good; and in doing good you are securing the favor of God and contributing your share towards enlisting Him on the side of our armies.

Joy to our venerable fathers, who bowing beneath the weight of years, are unable to gratify their intense desire to fly to arms! Fathers, learn from the word of God; the sins peculiar to old age. Struggle against them. Fixed as your habits may be, try to improve your hearts and lives; and be sure that every success you meet with in the improvement of your graces will tell upon our enemies with more power than the missile from the musket.

Joy to our mothers and wives and sisters and daughters! While with busy fingers you ply the needle and the loom for the benefit of our brave defenders, remember that you can render aid far more efficient. Cultivate the graces and practice the virtues enjoined in the Gospel; and though no famous report will be made to the world, God will observe it; though no influence be seen going out from it, yet its influence will be felt in heaven and will descend to earth again. God yearns towards them who seek Him; and when His affections are drawn out towards us, He will be more ready to defend and deliver us.

Joy to the invalid, to the blind, and deaf and dumb, and maimed, and poor, and all who by afflictive dispensations are seemingly helpless and apparently a burden to their country in these times of peril. You too can help us in the war. Bear your sorrows with patience, receive the attentions of your friends with gratitude, copy the spirit of Jesus, and as little as the world may think of it, you too will help to drive the invaders from our soil.

Scoff skeptic if you please, but we rejoice in the assurance that whatever brings God nigh to us will drive our enemies far away; and what brings God so nigh as the exercise of the spirit and the practice of the duties which His word enjoins?

Joy, Joy to you ye preachers of the Gospel! Know ye that whatever makes the people better makes them stronger; that in spreading truth and virtue you are supplying the true sinews of war. Your mission is one of love and peace, and yet in more senses than one you are warriors. Your profession may be thought valueless in these times of bloody strife, but in truth yours is the most efficient branch of the service.

The influence of the Gospel is a wall of defense against enemies carnal no less than spiritual. Every pulpit is a battlement whence great moral Columbiads hurl huge thunders against all who would harm us. Joy, joy! ye ministers of the Gospel of peace, for you can fight for your country and yet keep your hands unstained with blood.

See what an accession there is here to our forces in the field. We thought we had an army of some two hundred thousand. Here we have added the whole army of the saints, male and female, of every age, and color, and condition; — a motley band whose uneven ranks excite the sneers of men and devils. But on their banner is inscribed, "Not by might nor by power but by my Spirit saith the Lord." Zech. iv. 6. By that sign they will conquer.

Each in his sphere moves quietly along, and men of the world think they are doing nothing, but they are the best soldiers in the war. Their spiritual weapons make no loud report; no blood is seen to follow their stroke; the stroke itself is not seen. The still closet is remote from the scene of battle. But when our enemies rush on a praying people, they rush on their own destruction.

Every closet is a masked battery, from whose mysterious depths there goes forth an influence unseen and unheard, but carrying swift disaster to the ranks of our foes. Terror seizes upon them; they feel the dread influence but know not whence it comes, and bewildered and confounded by these assaults on their spiritual nature while yet their bodies are unhurt, they fly, they fly, supposing that they fly not from men but from devils. They know not that they are flying from before the saints of God, from before the armies of the Most High.

My countrymen, we are certain of success in this war if we but use the right means. But those means which are the last that men think of, and the last that they adopt, are the first in order and the first in importance in the Divine estimation. The first and last and only thing that men are apt to do, is to gather together the implements of war and prepare for battle. God forbids not the use of these things; nay, to lay them aside would be but to tempt His Providence. But paramount to this is the purifying of the heart.

Let us "seek first the kingdom of God and his righteousness," and trust that all other things will be added. Mat. vi. 33. Let our people forsake their sins and practice goodness, so that it call be said of our land, "thy people shall all be righteous," and the sweet prophecy will be fulfilled in us, which declares, "Violence shall no more be heard in thy land, wasting nor destruction within thy borders; but thou shall call thy walls Salvation and thy gates Praise. A little one shall become a thousand and a small one a strong nation. I the Lord will hasten it in his time." Is. xvi. 18.

Yes! when this happy day comes it will be of God, for "He maketh wars to cease unto the end of the earth; He breaketh the bow, and cutteth the spear in sunder; He burneth the chariot in the fire." Suppose every nation were thus to turn to the Lord. Then every nation would secure his blessing. Nation would rise up against nation no more, nor would men longer learn the arts of war. The spears would be beaten into pruning hooks and the swords into ploughshares; the days of Millennial glory would come, and the whole world would be subject to the gentle reign of the Prince of Peace!

# Christian Duty in the Present Time of Trouble

A SERMON
PREACHED AT

ST. JAMES' CHURCH,
WILMINGTON, N. C.

ON THE

## Fifth Sunday after Easter, 1861

BY THE

RIGHT REV. THOMAS ATKINSON, D. D.,
BISHOP OF NORTH CAROLINA

WILMINGTON, N. C.

1861

## A SERMON

"Blessed is the man that endureth temptation; for when he is tried, he shall receive the crown of life which the Lord hath promised to them that love Him." — St. James 1:12.

We stand today, dear brethren, in the midst of circumstances of great doubt and anxiety, with provocations tending to kindle the bitterest and most vehement passions, and with the line of duty in many instances difficult to trace, and difficult to follow, even when traced. Never did we stand more in need of right counsels, deliberate and conscientious reflection, earnest purpose to do our duty, and heartfelt dependence on God our Saviour, for guidance and strength to enable us for its performance.

We stand today, face to face with civil war, a calamity, which, unless the experience and universal testimony of mankind deceive us, is direr and more to be deprecated than foreign war, than famine, than pestilence, than any other form of public evil. The cloud we have all been so long watching, which we have seen, day by day, and month by month, enlarging its skirts, and gathering blackness, is now beginning to burst upon us.

It seems to me that no one but an Atheist, or an Epicurean, can doubt that it is God who rides in this storm, and will direct the whirlwind, and that He now calls upon us to look to Him, to consider our ways and our doings, to remember the offences by which we have heretofore provoked Him, and to determine on the conduct we will hereafter pursue towards Him, toward our fellowmen, and towards ourselves.

I feel that we have some solid grounds of encouragement to hope for His favor. This Commonwealth, with whose fortunes our own are linked, cannot be said to have had any hand in causing, or precipitating the issue before us.

She has sought, till the last moment, to avert it, and she his incurred censure by these efforts. But when compelled to elect between furnishing troops to subdue her nearest neighbors and kindred, and to open her Territory for the passage of armies marshaled to accomplish that odious, unauthorized and unhallowed object, or to refuse to aid, and to seek to hinder such attempts, she chose the part which affection, and interest and duty seems manifestly, and beyond all reasonable question, to require.

What she has done, and is about to do, she does, as an old writer finely says in such a case, "willingly, but with an unwilling mind," as an imperative, but painful duty. Such is the temper, we may be well assured, in which it best pleases God, that strife of any sort, especially strife of this sort, should be entered on.

There is another consideration from which I derive great comfort, and which is certain to give comfort to all who receive it. It is that whatever we may think of some of the earlier steps in these disputes, yet as to the present questions between the North and the South, we can calmly, conscientiously, and, I think, conclusively, to all impartial men, maintain before God and man that *now* at least we of the South are in the right. For we are on the defensive, we ask only to be let alone.

That old Union to which we were all at one time so deeply attached, is now dissolved. It cannot be, at this time, amicably reconstructed. No one proposes it shall be done — no one supposes it can be done. Shall there then be a voluntary and friendly separation, or an attempt at subjugation. This is really the question before the people, lately known as the people of the United States. How strange that there should be any doubt as to the answer!

That men should hesitate which to prefer, a peaceful separation of those who cannot agree, or civil war, with all its horrors, and all its uncertain issues! We ask the former — those so lately our brethren demand the latter. Should they insist on this, and should they succeed in this detestable strife to the very height of their hopes, it would be worse than a barren victory. It would be a victory that would cost the conquerors not only material prosperity, but the very principles of government on which society with them, as with us, rests.

I cannot then doubt, and it seems a singular hallucination that any man should mistake, the righteous cause in this present most lamentable controversy, and I hope and I believe that God will bless with temporal success the righteous cause. He may not, however, for He does not always see fit to make right visibly triumphant. — But succeed or not, it is the cause on the side of which one would desire to be found.

Yet, however this thought may cheer us, we cannot disguise from ourselves that success, should we obtain it, will not probably be reached until after an arduous and painful struggle, involving severe trials of the feelings, and of the character of the community, and of ourselves individually. And no man yet knows how he shall meet these trials. The most self-confident are usually the first to fail. "Let not him that girdeth on his armor boast himself as he that taketh it off."

Since, then, a searching trial seems to await us, let us, in God's strength, endeavor to prepare for it, and in order thereto, listen with obedient faith to the instructions of that holy man, whose righteousness was so exemplary that Jews, as well as Christians, knew him by the name of James the Just. "Blessed, says he, is the man that endureth temptation, for when he is tried, he shall receive the crown of life, which the Lord hath promised to them that love Him."

Temptation or Trial (for they mean the same thing) comes to man in two forms, Prosperity or Adversity, of which the former is the more generally dangerous. Prosperity tempts us by inclining us to forget God, and to love the world which so smiles upon us, by slackening the reins on the necks of our appetites and passions, by opening the door to vices which our very circumstances might otherwise shut out from us, by nourishing selfishness, by deadening sympathy, and by weakening faith.

Great prosperity has been the ruin of many countries, and of many men in every country. It has surely been the occasion of a large part of our present miseries. Never in the history of the world was there such a rapid advance made by any people in all the elements of power, abundance and splendor, as was made by this nation in the last forty years.

We passed, as in a day, from national childhood to a most robust and formidable manhood. We were the admiration, the envy, the wonder, and I may say, the fear of all other people. — England and France bore that from us which they never would have endured from each other. It was not of our Army and Navy that they stood in awe, but they were reluctant to give umbrage to a people who fed their commerce, and upheld their manufactures.

With this influence abroad, when we looked at home we saw villages growing up in a few years into great cities, a soil which today was a quaking morass, tomorrow sustaining immense blocks of buildings, warehouses bursting with their stores, dwellings not merely provided with comfort, but decorated with splendor, and this not in one or two favored spots, as sometimes in Europe, but on the contrary, we saw vast territories where the Buffalo roamed, and the Deer bounded, and the form of man had not appeared, except as the Indian was observed marching along his war-path, or the solitary trapper gathering his furs; we saw these wild regions changed almost as in the shifting scenes at a Theatre, into great, rich and populous States.

Astonished Europe heard year by year, that another million had been added to the numbers of the mighty Republic, and that its agriculture and commerce, and manufactures were increasing even more rapidly than its population. Then came the Mexican war, like another volume of steam, and made the rush and roar of our rapid progress still more astounding. Then came more and more of gold and glory, and expanding territory.

We have been tried by prosperity as no nation ever was tried before, and we have yielded to temptation as completely and unresistingly as any people ever did. Those old stories we have all read were outdone. Rome corrupted by the conquest of Greece and of Asia, Spain demoralized by the subjugation of the Indies, were prophetic of our destiny.

Our material prosperity, swift as was its advance, did not keep pace with our moral deterioration. Within the memory of any middle-aged man we were regarded in Europe as rigidly, perhaps ridiculously precise and scrupulous in morals and manners. No one dreams of this being our character at present. In one single state, and that a small one, the number of suicides average annually nearly a hundred. What the number of homicides is, no statist, I presume, would undertake to tell.

This we know, that if the blood of man, shed by his fellow-man calls to God for vengeance, the cry that pierces the ear of the Lord of Hosts from our land ceases not day or night. Need I say any thing of other forms of vice — drunkenness, lewdness, gaming, fraud, bribery, peculation, public and private? And with this such lawlessness, such haughtiness, such self-glorification!

Who that looks abroad on our country, can read without a shudder, the prophetic language of St. Paul in that last Epistle written from Nero's Dungeon with the axe and block at hand, when with purged eye he reads the signs of the last times, and thus describes them: "This know also, that in the last days, perilous times shall come, for men shall be lovers of their own selves, covetous, boasters, proud, blasphemers, *disobedient to parents*, unthankful, unholy, without natural affection, truce-breakers, false accusers, incontinent, fierce, despisers of those that are good, traitors, heady, high-minded, lovers of pleasure more than lovers of God."

Is there a trait in this dark picture, to which our country does not furnish a living likeness! We have been tried by prosperity then, and we have not stood *that trial*. It seems clear that God is now about to withdraw, at least for a time, the favors we have so abused, to try us with calamity. There is no man this day in that wide land which was called the United States, who does not know trouble and affliction. It has come to us all, in some form or other, and to many in many forms.

See how our national wealth, which was so dear to the national heart, is disappearing! Whose property has not, within a few months, been reduced in value, a fourth, or a half, whatever his personal care or diligence may be. The idolaters of money are crying out like Micah of old, "Ye have taken away my God, and what have I left!" Indeed who knows now how much property any man has!

This time of trouble, like the grave, levels all distinctions, and rich and poor meet together. Factories and shops are closed, schools are deserted, churches are thinned, in every family the husband, or the father, or the son, or the brother has marched, or is preparing to march to the uncertain issues of the siege, or the battle-field.

Thus we stand today. — How or where we shall stand three or six months hence no human wisdom can inform us. And how shall we bear what may await us? As yet but a few drops have fallen on us from the cloud, how will it be when its full fury is upon us? "If thou hast run with the footmen, says the man of God, and they have wearied thee, then how canst thou contend with horses? and if in the land of peace wherein thou trustedst they wearied thee, then how wilt thou do in the swelling of Jordan?"

Let us then remember that we are now entering into a time of temptation, and of very severe temptation, and that temptation does not necessarily do any man good, but may do him great harm, while, however, the *endurance* of temptation will do him the greatest good, "for when thus tried, he shall receive the crown of life." Everything which comes to us from God, is in some sense a temptation; that is, tries us, reveals our character, and brings us a benefit, or an injury, according to the use we make of it.

The sunshine which ripens the sound fruit, rots the unsound. The storm which prostrates the decayed oak, sends deeper into the soil the roots of the living and healthy. So with ourselves. Health, wealth, wisdom, power, life itself is a blessing or a curse, according to the use we make of it. So it is with trouble and calamity. They are medicines in the hands of the Great Physician, but we may so receive them, as that to us, they shall become poison.

Affliction, alas, often hardens men's hearts, makes them unthankful and rebellious against God, envious and malignant towards their fellow-man. The worst men on earth are those who have passed through the extremes of the two conditions, who have known nothing but unbroken prosperity, or unmitigated misery. On the other hand, the best men the world has ever seen, are those who have borne great affliction, and by God's grace have endured the trial.

Such were Noah, Daniel and Job, the Prophets and Apostles, the great Saints, and the blessed Martyrs, while on the other hand, vice has never been so shameless, and so pitiless as in times of great public and private calamity, such as the destruction of Jerusalem, the plague at Athens, and the great pestilences in Florence and London. Out of the furnace of affliction men come either purified or hardened.

I repeat it then, it is not necessarily good for us to meet trouble, but that it is of all things the best and most Christ-like, victoriously to endure it.

Permit me, as one whose duty it is to watch for your souls, in view of the great account, to offer you in all humility and affection, some counsels on this momentous subject. In the first place then, believe and lay to heart, and keep constantly before your minds this most certain truth, that whosoever may be the *instruments* of our present troubles, God is the efficient author of them.

Hear the word of the Lord which He spoke to His ancient people by His Prophet Amos. "You only have I known among all the families of the earth, therefore will I punish you for all your iniquities." Mark the cause and effect. Because he so peculiarly loved them, He would punish them. And He adds: "Shall the trumpet be blown in the city, and the people not be afraid? Shall there be evil in the city, and the Lord hath not done it?"

And so the blessed Jesus said to Pontius Pilot, "Thou couldst have no power at all against me, except it were given thee from above." And to the same effect is the message of God to Sennacherib, King of Assyria, by Isaiah the Prophet, saying with regard to that proud King's boasted victories: "Hast thou not heard long ago that I have done it, and of ancient times that I have formed it?" And then he adds: "I will put my hook in thy nose, and my bridle in thy lips, and I will turn thee back by the way by which thou camest."

The first requisite to success against our enemies is reverent obedience towards God, for again as holy scripture sayeth: "When a man's ways please the Lord, He maketh even his enemies to be at peace with him." Let us then earnestly and perseveringly seek the favor of Him without whom our enemies can do us no hurt — without whom not a hair of our heads can fall to the ground.

Let us seek His favor by that which He so loudly calls for at this time, by repentance, national and individual, by prayer public and private, by fervent, faithful, constant, prevailing efforts to keep God's holy will and commandments, and to walk in his holy ways.

Secondly, we must be careful to cherish unity and mutual affection among ourselves. A censorious, suspicious, denunciatory spirit, always evil, always pernicious, is especially to be deprecated by us at present. Let us avoid as the last, greatest, and most shameful of calamities, a fall into that abyss of misery which engulfed the wretched Jews at Jerusalem, when assailed by enemies from without, and deserted in spirit and counsel by God, they gave themselves over to hating and slaughtering one another.

Again let us, as far as may be, seek to check in ourselves and others the growth of rancorous, vindictive, malignant feeling and the use of bitter, scornful opprobrious language concerning those once our brethren, now, alas, it would seem our enemies. For after all we are Christians, or we have been deceiving ourselves, and the world, and all but God, for a long time.

We are the servants of Christ, and our master's eye is upon us in this hour of trial. We are the servants of Christ, and in our master's visible presence we shall soon be. We are the servants of Him who spoke the sermon on the mount. What injunctions does he there give us? What feelings does He there bid us to cherish; what language to use concerning our enemies?

We are the servants of Christ — what language did he use to Judas Iscariot when he came to betray Him? What prayer did He offer for those who nailed him to the cross? And how shocking does the language of some of our adversaries, and of some of the professed followers, and even ministers of Christ, among our adversaries, appear to us? Shall we imitate them in their faults and sins?

Again, let us take care not to have our minds possessed by this one subject of our national troubles. A man whose thoughts are engrossed by one idea, especially if that be an agitating and exciting idea, is on the verge of insanity. And, already, men heretofore of firm and well-ordered character, have committed suicide from the pressure of this one distracting thought, the troubles of the country. And I have heard already from a certain Lunatic Asylum, (and what is true of it is probably true of all,) that its inmates have recently become much more numerous from the same cause.

The best remedy is the calm, soothing, elevating influence of religion. Remember the testimony of the Psalmist, as it is expressed in our prayer-book version: "The Lord is King, be the people never so impatient. He sitteth between the cherubim, be the earth never so unquiet." Acquaint thyself with him, and be at peace. You will be tempted to intermit, or at least diminish the performance of your religious duties. Never yield to that temptation — dread it, abhor it. Never had you such occasion to be fervent in spirit, serving the Lord as now.

Be more assiduous than ever heretofore in reading the Scriptures and the works of devout men, in public prayer, and the use of the sacraments, and above all, in your closets, in calling earnestly upon God, yea, importunately beseeching Him to send peace, to advance righteousness, to purify and bless the land, and to prepare us, even by these troubles, to expect, and to be ready for His coming. Make prayer more than ever a real communion with God.

Temporal deliverance you may well and properly supplicate; indeed it is your duty to ask this, but have still nearer to your souls the deliverance of those souls from sin and obduracy, and worldliness, and bad passions, and His wrath, and eternal death. Cry to Him in the all-prevailing name of Jesus, not for yourself only, but for your country, wretched and imperiled, for the Church weakened in its efforts, uncertain as to the future before it; and cry to Him likewise for those near and dear to you, for husband, brother, father, son, that He would guard and preserve them, body and soul, amid the exceeding fury of this storm which now shakes our land.

And lastly, remember that you yourselves are now under trial; that the issues of that trial are for eternity, that though sharp it will be short; and that if you endure to the end you will be saved, and that the sharper the trial endured the more glorious will be the salvation.

And now, dear brethren. what will be the result? Scripture prophesies it, and history prophesies it. Some of you will fail in this time of temptation, and will not endure it. Some of you, I fear, will sacrifice to the passions of the hour the Christian character, and the Christian hope. Some of you will come out of the trial purified and refined, and assured of a brighter crown.

Resolve, oh Christian hearer, this day, in God's strength, to which class you will belong; whether to those who will cast away the crown to which perhaps for years they have aspired, or those who hold on to their hope with greater resolution than before.

# A Tract for the Times

# SLAVERY & ABOLITIONISM

BEING THE

## SUBSTANCE OF A SERMON

Preached in the Church of St. Augustine, Florida

ON THE 4th DAY OF JANUARY, 1861

Day of Public Humiliation, Fasting and Prayer

By the

## Right Rev. A. VEROT, D.D.

VICAR APOSTOLIC OF FLORIDA AND

NOW BISHOP OF SAVANNAH.

1861

## TO THE PUBLIC

Although this Sermon be of a remote date, having been preached on the 4th of January last, before the Secession, war consummated, still it is so well adapted to our Institutions, that we thought we would render service to the community at large, by reprinting it and spreading it all over the country.

Tho' written in a plain and unpretending style, it is quite forcible, and presents the most instructive and most practical tract we ever read, on the rights and duties of Slaveholders.

*New Orleans, December 8th 1861.*

THE EDITOR

# SERMON

Justice exalteth a nation: but sin maketh nations miserable. Prov. 14:34.

BELOVED BRETHREN:

This is a great, a most important truth, involving the most momentous, interests, which I deem expedient and necessary, on this melancholy occasion, to present to your earnest Consideration. Justice exalteth a nation: but sin maketh nations miserable."

We learn this important lesson from the Wise Man who has written the Book of Proverbs; but it is not the result of his individual and personal Wisdom which I present to you: it is the unerring dictate of the Holy Ghost, who inspired and directed the sacred penman to record, in that portion of Scripture, a maxim which is an imperishable truth, because it is the word of Him who is truth itself, who can neither deceive nor be deceived; and indeed, heaven and earth shall pass away; but His words shall not pass away.

But, independently of the unexceptionable authority of Him who has promulgated this sublime maxim of true and genuine statesmanship, and of sacred and divine politic we have history to bear witness to the truth of the sentence of the Wise Man — "Justice exalteth a nation: but sin maketh nations miserable." The rise and fall of nations, consigned in the pages of history, is but a continual application and confirmation of this principle of unerring truth.

The great Doctor of the Church — the patron of this city and congregation — St. Augustine, in his admirable work, "Of the City of God," undertook to show the true reason of the unexampled prosperity of the Roman Empire.

That Empire was the most extensive and the most prosperous that ever existed: it extended itself to the remotest corners of the known universe. Even the wild nations that could not be reached by its authority, respected and dreaded the very name of the Romans.

That illustrious Doctor does not hesitate to say, that this temporal prosperity of the Empire was the reward of the moral virtues which illustrated the Roman nation in the first centuries of her existence, and which were never more conspicuous than in the men whom she placed at the head of her armies, and to whom she gave the direction of her civil and political affairs. They have left us admirable examples of justice, integrity and fortitude, on, most trying occasions.

Such was their love of justice, that one of their enemies, who had even fought against them with success dearly bought, knowing that gold, which is so powerful on men, could have no effect on the chief officer of Rome to bribe him and corrupt him, remarked that it would be easier to turn the sun from his course, than the Roman Consul from the path of justice. As long as this love of justice lasted, the Supreme Ruler of events gave success to their arms, and extended their conquests far and wide, until the whole earth was under their sway.

But, at a later period; injustice, iniquity, ambition, covetousness, and bribery crept into the Empire, and were found disgracing even the leaders of the nation. It was then that Almighty God permitted that hordes of Barbarians should invade that Empire, now fallen from its pristine justice and integrity; and those Barbarians devastated and overturned the colossal Empire, and swept its authority, its grandeur, and its very name from the earth.

Such is then the plan of Divine Providence in the government of this world. If iniquity, injustice, rapine, and bloodshed seem sometimes to meet with success, it is only temporary and ephemeral, similar to the devastation produced by a swollen torrent, but such causes cannot establish, settle, and place on a permanent basis; any civil and political institution: any government that rests upon injustice, must necessarily crumble with its tottering foundation.

"Justice exalteth a nation: but sin maketh nations miserable."

Our beloved country is now undoubtedly under the operation of that stern and inflexible rule of justice, at the hands of the Author of justice. We have hitherto been a nation prosperous beyond even the most exaggerated conceptions of a wild imagination; productions of every kind lavished by our soil; an abundance, not to say an overflowing, of the circulating medium; extensive factories, an active commerce, and the rich and exuberant fruits of industry, by sea and by land, have; made the United States a paragon of riches, a sort of elysian fields in which the overflowing population of Europe came to enjoy abundance, riches, peace, and freedom.

The aspect is suddenly changed: the political horizon has become gloomy; a day of humiliation, fasting, and prayer is kept over the land, to avert impending evils; discord and disunion are rapidly spreading over the length and breadth of the land; the horrors of war, and of the worst kind — of civil war — are staring us in the face, and the prosperity, hitherto unparalleled, of the country, has given, way to mutual distrust, uneasiness, suspension of commerce, stagnation of industry, suffering, and the anticipation of evils yet worse to come.

The cause must no doubt be, that we "have forgotten justice," and that sin has crept frightfully among us to make us miserable; for Almighty God hates in us only sin, and the disorderly bend of our wills; by which we transgress His law.

Slavery is the origin of the present disturbances, and is the fatal sand bank upon which the Ship of State has already made a total or partial shipwreck. Injustice has then been committed on this point, and I deem the present occasion to be a very favorable one, to place before your eyes some truths which are of great importance to the nation at large, — to the North, and to the South, to the people collectively, and to individuals, to masters, and to servants.

I wish to show on the, one side, how unjust, iniquitous, unscriptural, and unreasonable is the assertion of Abolitionists, who brand Slavery as a moral evil: and a crime against God, religion, humanity, and society; whereas; it is found to have received the sanction of God, of the Church and of Society at all times, and in all governments. On the other side, I wish to show the conditions under which servitude is legitimate, lawful, approved by all laws, and consistent with practical religion and true holiness of life in masters who fulfill those conditions.

Servitude is the state of a person dependent on a master, so as to be obliged to work all his life for that master, with the privilege, in the latter, to transfer that right to another person by sale.

Divines and civilians who examine the foundations of social life, inquire what things can come under the domain or ownership of men, and they agree that we have not a perfect domain or property over our own life and limbs, but only the *usufruct* of them, — that is, a life-interest in them; and hence a master, not being the true owner of his own life and limbs cannot be the owner or proprietor of the life and limbs of a slave; this high domain belongs exclusively to our Maker: a master can claim no other right than the *usufruct* of his slave, — that is, a right on his labor and industry, and the labor and industry of his children.

This being premised, we can show, to the satisfaction of every one who is not determined to shut his eyes against the truth, that the state of servitude is reprobated neither by natural, law, nor by the Divine positive law, nor by the ecclesiastical law, nor by the civil laws. Those four kinds of laws are the sources of all justice, of all right, and from them emanate all the directions and prescriptions which govern the actions of men.

Natural or moral law is that which arises from the nature or essence of moral and reasonable beings, and is engraved in our hearts by our Maker, the Author of Nature. Such are the Commandments *Thou shalt not kill,* — *Thou shalt not* &c. Divine *positive* law is that command of God which requires something in addition to natural law. Such was the circumcision prescribed to the Jews, or baptism prescribed now to Christians. Ecclesiastical law comes from the Church, which God has established, with an express command to us to hear her: — "He that heareth you, heareth me: he that despiseth you, despiseth me. — Luke 10:16."

Civil law comes from the governments under which we live, and which it is our duty to obey; — "Let every soul be subject to higher powers." — Rom. 13:1. Now Slavery is condemned by none of these laws, as it is easy to show.

As to natural law: — it must be said, indeed, that natural law does not establish or institute Slavery: no one is, by nature, the slave of another; but natural law approves of reasons and causes by which a man may become the slave of another man. The case stands here precisely as with regard to the division of property. No land belongs to anybody by the right of nature, but legitimate titles constitute it the property of individuals.

Any one, ever so little conversant with history, finds Slavery, established among all nations of antiquity, and it is not improbable that it is coeval with the division of property. Writers on this branch of science assign the various titles which legitimate a state of Slavery, and which, no doubt, must have been originally the source and beginning of its introduction among men.

The first title they assign, is the sale that a man makes of himself to a master. A man may sell his labor, and work for a day, a week, a month or a year: why may he not sell it for all his life?

If it be said that a sale requires a consideration, and an equivalent between the contracting parties, this is very true. But the master gives an equivalent, namely — food and clothing to the slave, with; the assurance and security to him to find them at all times, and especially the promise of support and maintenance in sickness and in old age; when ho will be unable to work. The equivalent given by the master may be sufficient inducement for some individuals to offer their work and liberty for ever.

The slave receives indeed an equivalent, in this certainty: of being always provided for — a certainty, which many distressed and starving families in Europe, and in the large cities of America, would indeed appreciate highly, as they know what a source of interminable care, anxiety, and solicitude this matter is for them.

It is truly remarkable, how: gay, cheerful, and sprightly are the slaves of the South. I do not hesitate to say, that they seem to be better contented than their masters; assuredly more so than the sullen and gloomy population found in the work shops and factories of large cities. The master therefore gives an equivalent.

This is so true, that, for me personally, I would not accept persons who would offer, their services for life; on condition. of maintaining them for ever, precisely on account of the danger of, having services that might prove unacceptable, and, on account of the heavy charge such persons occasion in sickness and old age.

I know of masters who were poor when they had slaves; and had to become rich by setting them free; and I have no doubt it is one of the reasons, for which Slavery has become gradually extinct in Europe.

Another title of servitude mentioned by our canonists and jurists, is capture in a just war, as history tells us how the captives in war used to be sold as slaves. The conqueror could put them to death; it is assuredly a better for them that they be sold as slaves.

Christianity has introduced a more humane legislation in reference to prisoners of war; for which we must thank our Redeemer; but nature alone and strict justice declare that in a just war, the vanquished forfeits his life to the victor, who does him kindness by granting life at the expense of liberty.

Another title I must mention, is condemnation to Slavery for crimes committed, or even for non-payment of debts. This is likewise a point on which Christianity has introduced milder forms; but we must not forget that they are a boon, and not a strict right: he who is condemned to hard labor in a penitentiary, would find his lot much improved in the condition of a slave.

Again if a man cannot pay his debts, he maybe compelled, in justice to work in order to pay them and this, no doubt, must have been a frequent title of servitude. Our Lord mentions it in one of His parables, without a word, to censure what was then a general practice.

"One was brought; who owed his lord ten thousand talents, and as he had not wherewith to pay it, his lord commanded that he should be sold, and his wife and children, and all that he had; and payment be made. — Matt. 18:25.

A spirit of philanthropy (Whether judicious or not I do not examine) has induced modern legislators to suppress imprisonment, much more Slavery, for debt, and dishonest debtors are very partial to such a legislation, but the ancients entertained, different ideas of stern and strict justice, for which we are not at liberty to blame them.

Nativity, or birth from a mother in a State of Slavery, is also admitted by writers to be a just cause of servitude; *partis sequitur ventrem* is an axiom in law. A child follows the condition and state of his parent's, and the child must perish, unless it be maintained and supported by the master.

If the child could speak, he would prefer being a slave to being exposed to the necessity of dying for want of sustenance, and hence, this title has been readily admitted wherever Slavery has at all existed and the Scripture, as we shall soon see, confirms it.

Finally, We mention long possession in good faith, with an apparent title, to be a legitimate cause for holding slaves. This title was called prescription by the Latins, and has retained that name in almost all modern European languages. This is a title introduced by the general consent of nations, for the, security of property.

If we have possessed something for a long time in good faith; thinking it is ours, it is really ours, although there might arise, after a long lapse of years; some contestations about the validity of the original title.

We see, therefore, that there are many ways in which Slavery may lawfully exist, and that such a State is not reprobated by reason, or by the natural and innate, notions of justice, when some of those titles exist. Civil laws may condemn some of these titles, in the present refined state of society: in that case, such titles will be invalid, not because they are adverse to the natural law but because they are made void by the law of the land.

Let us now examine whether the Divine positive law condemn Slavery. If Slavery is immoral in itself, no Divine law can commend it or approve of it, because God cannot commend or authorize something immoral. If it be not immoral in itself, still God could forbid it, as He forbade, in old times, the eating of blood and of other things.

In this respect, however, we find that God, in the Old Testament, under the law of nature, and under the law of Moses, not only did not prohibit Slavery, but sanctioned it, regulated it, and specified rights of masters, and the duties of slaves.

It would certainly be tedious to adduce all the proofs of my assertion which could be extracted from the Old Testament; — a few of the most striking will be amply sufficient.

Abraham assuredly was a good man; now Abraham was a Slaveholder, and a very large one indeed. When his nephew, Lot, was taken prisoner (Gen. 14:14) "he numbered the servants born in his house three hundred and eighteen well appointed." pursued and defeated the invaders, and delivered Lot and all the people.

The Scripture here approves of the title of nativity, by mentioning that these Slaves were born in his house. In the same page of Genesis, chap. 16, we find a more striking, and pointed approbation of Slavery. For reasons stated in that chapter, Sara the wife of Abram; was obliged to treat with severity her handmaid — or female servant — Agar; the latter ran away, and "an angel of the Lord having found her by a fountain, of water in the wilderness, he said to her: Agar, handmaid of Sarai, whence comest thou? and wither goest thou? And She answered: I flee from the face of Sarai, My mistress. And the Angel of the Lord said to her: Return to thy mistress, and humble thyself under her hand," — v. 7.

How strange must all this be for Abolitionists who retain their belief in the Bible! God sends an Angel purposely to tell a runaway slave to return to her mistress, and humble herself to her; and Abolitionists have set aside all laws; and torn the fundamental articles of the Constitution to enable runaway slaves to escape the pursuit and just demands of their masters; the angel proclaims obedience and submission to slaves, and they excite them to revolt, and are ready to aid them in shaking off the authority of their masters.

Nothing more is wanted to show that the spirit of Abolitionists is not the spirit of the Angels of God, the spirit of the Bible, the spirit of truth and justice, but the demon of anarchy, discord, stubbornness, and pride. Again, the following chapter of Genesis mentions that Abraham circumcised all the males of his house, not only those who were born in his house; but also "the bought servants," — v. 23 and 27, — which shows that the sale of slaves is not condemned by Scripture.

Indeed, it seems that every, page of Holy Writ contains some statement to demolish the false and unjust principles of Abolitionism. Those men must be ignorant even of the Ten Commandments of God; for the Tenth Commandment also forbids coveting our neighbor's property: "new his servant, nor his handmaid, nor his ox," &c. — Exod. 20:17.

The Lord here forbids desiring and designing to take servants from their master's, and the modern fanatics not only desire, but actually take iniquitous means to release servants from their masters, in defiance of the plainest laws of God.

Finally, the twenty-first chapter of Exodus contains laws emanating from God himself, to regulate Slavery among the Jews. The Jewish Servant or slave who had sold himself could be retained only until the year of the general jubilee, by a special law of the Jews. The same chapter contains several provisions relating to the same subject. they all suppose servitude to be lawful.

The twenty-fifth chapter of Leviticus allows Jews to have bond men, and bondwomen of the nations that are round about them: "These you shall have for servants, and, by right of inheritance, shall leave them to your posterity, and shall possess them forever" — v. 44-46.

Here is Slavery again sanctioned and approved by the law of God himself, consigned in a Book which, all revere as the Word of God. Can there be anything, then, more unscriptural than Abolitionism: and; if this country be the country of the Bible, as some have asserted Abolitionism must be then of exotic growth.

I am aware of an objection — which is indeed a serious one but which I meet at once, because it will wonderfully strengthen my argument. The Jews were a rude and carnal people: their religion was but rudimental and figurative, and very imperfect. These defects have been amended in the New Law, which has brought all things to perfection. Hence some might think that Our Lord Jesus Christ, the Founder of the New Law, has abolished Slavery, although it was allowed, in times past.

Indeed, this is what has taken place with, regard, to some points relative to marriage. Divorce, and polygamy were allowed to them of old. Still no one, could sanction the practice of them by the example of the good men of the Old. Testament, or by the Law of Moses. But the case is as clear and obvious as possible. Our Lord has expressly, formally, and pointedly abolished divorce and polygamy: "They shall be two in one"; What God has joined, no man can put asunder"; but He has not proscribed or forbidden Slavery.

There is not a word in the New Testament to prohibit it, but there are on the contrary, plain and evident approbations of it. In the eighth, chapter of St Matthew, a Centurion Slaveholder comes to Our Lord to ask for the cure of his servant, and, in the course of the conversation, the Centurion says: "I have soldiers under me; and I say to this man go, and he goeth; and to another come, and he cometh; and to my servant, do this, and he doeth it; and Jesus' hearing this wondered, and said: "Amen, I say to you, I have not found so great faith in Israel."

How different was this way of acting from that of an Abolitionist. The latter would have reproached the Centurion for the crime of injustice, barbarity, and inhumanity in keeping slaves. Jesus, on the contrary, not only has no rebuke to Administer on the score of Slavery, but admires and praises the faith of that man, and grants a cure to his servant, a manifest and incontestable proof that Our Lord did not hold the Centurion guilty for having a slave.

Let it be remarked that the word servant, here in the passages already quoted, means a slave, in Latin, *servus*, — and when the Scripture speaks of servants in a limited sense, as are the white servants among us, they are called hirelings or laborers.

The Apostles, who were taught by our Lord, and, who preached His Gospel, and established His Church in every part of the world, had also to speak of slaves, and they have done so in their inspired writings, so as to leave no doubt on the right which a master has to keep his slave, and on the obligation of the slave to honor and obey his master.

St. Paul, in the seventh chapter of the first Epistle to the Corinthians, says positively, that each one ought to remain in the state of life in which he was when called to Christianity, — slave, if he was a slave; free, if he, was free — for this is of little consequence, Viewed in reference to the next life: "Let every man abide in the same calling in which he was called. Art thou called being a bondsman? care not for it; but if thou mayest be made free, use it rather. For he that is called to the Lord being a bondman, is the freeman of the Lord. Likewise he that is called being free, is the bondman of Christ."

From which we see how far the Apostles were from the doctrine and practice of modern fanatics, who exhort slaves to make themselves free by any means they can, per fas et nefas.

St. Paul, in several of his Epistles, speaks of the manual duties of slaves and masters; he never dreams of the new duty invented by the Abolitionists — the pretended duty for the master to liberate and manumit his slave, and the duty of the slave to run away from his master, even by using violence, and causing bloodshed. The inspired Apostle tells the slave to obey, as a point of conscience, as a necessary means of salvation; and he tells the master to treat his servant with justice and kindness.

Thus Col. 3:22: "Servants, obey in all things your masters according to the flesh, not serving to the eye, as pleasing men, but in simplicity of heart, fearing God . . . . . Masters, do to your servants that which is just and equal; knowing that you also have a Master in Heaven. Similar admonitions occur in, several other Epistles: it would be superfluous to quote them.

There is a passage yet more pointed. I Tim. 6: Whosoever are servants under the yoke, let them count their masters worthy of all honor, lest the name and doctrine of the Lord be blasphemed. . . . . These things teach and exhort. If any man teach otherwise, and consent not to the sound words of Our Lord Jesus Christ, and to that doctrine which is according to piety, he is proud, knowing nothing;" and truly Abolitionism is but a compound of insufferable pride and unpardonable ignorance.

St. Peter, First Epistle, 2:18, points out the duty of obedience to servants in all cases whatever: "Servants, be subject to your masters with all fear; not only to the good and gentle, but also to the froward."

But facts instruct us better than words: and we have to see the conduct of St. Paul with regard to a fugitive slave, to judge better of the glaring opposition of Abolitionism to the Apostles, and to the Sacred Scripture.

The Epistle to Philemon is a short, page of the Sacred Volume, which they should indeed desire to expunge. Philemon had a slave called Onesimus; who ran away from his master, a citizen of Colossae, and whom St. Paul found in Rome, and converted to Christianity.

Now St. Paul found in Onesimus qualities which made him desirous of his services in his ministry. What did the great

Apostle do? Did he tell Onesimus that he had been right to ran away, and procure his liberty at any price?

No, he sent back Onesimus to his master with an Epistle, which is a perfect model of sweet, persuasive eloquence, begging Philemon to forgive his slave, and send him back to, him, as he needed his services in the bonds of the Gospel.

Paul had just claims on the gratitude of Philemon, still he would not detain his fugitive slave without his consent, but sent him back, that his master might be perfectly free to grant or to, refuse the favor asked of him. How different are these views of St. Paul and of the Word of God, from those which are entertained by Abolitionists!

We have now seen how both the New and Old Testaments admit, sanction, and authorize Slavery, from which we conclude that this state of life is not against the Divine and positive law.

We add now that the Church has made no general law against Slavery, but has kept up the teaching and the examples of the Apostles on this point, leaving masters at liberty to keep or to manumit their slaves, as they thought. proper.

The book I have in my hands, beloved brethren, is the Canon Law, or Law, of the Church. Now the book is full of passages relating to slaves; and to attempt to prove that the Canon Law recognizes Slavery, and countenances masters in retaining possession of their slaves, would almost be ludicrous, and would be tantamount to an attempt to prove that the sun shines in the heavens, at mid-day, as there are whole chapters, indeed, and sections on that matter.

Not to detain you too long, beloved brethren, I will content myself with one or two quotations that will, indeed, cover the whole ground of the discussion. The Canon Law contains several provisions in relation to the ordination of slaves, as the example of St. Paul ordaining Onesimus, seems to have been a precedent for such appointments.

The Eighty-first Apostolic Canon says that slaves may be ordained, if manumitted by their masters; but if they be admitted to the clergy without the will of their masters, they must be returned to their masters.

Now we see this to have been done from the same Canon Law, Distinct. 54, cap. 10, where the Pope orders one Leontius, who had been promoted to the lower ranks of the clergy; to be under subjection and obedience to his master in the condition of a slave.

Assuredly the Church could not have recognized the rights of masters in a more forcible and pointed manner; no one, then, has a right to take slaves from their masters against the will of those masters.

The Canon Law, can. xvii., ques. 4, c. 37, contains a decree of the Council of Langres, held in the beginning of the fourth century, which condemns heretics who maintained the principles of modern Abolitionists; whence, we see that the fanatics of our day have not the merit of having invented their hypocritical schemes of false philanthropy; they had predecessors in the early ages of the Church, who wished to liberate slaves; and who denounced masters as guilty of injustice and inhumanity.

Here is now the decree of the Council against those heretics:

"If any one teaches the servant of another, under the plea of religion, to contemn his master, and to quit his service, instead of teaching him to serve his master in good faith and with all respect, let him he anathema."

No law could be framed more expressive and more pointed against. Abolitionism. The highest penalty inflicted by the Church, that of anathema or excommunication, is pronounced against those who teach the doctrine of Abolitionists, and it is only an aggravation of their guilt to allege pretexts of religion; and wrest Holy Writ, in support of their attempts. This is indeed more than sufficient to show that Slaveholders have the sanction of the-Church and of Religion in retaining the possession of their servants.

Ecclesiastical History tells us, as we gather from authentic documents, that the Church and Monasteries owned slaves;

and St. Gregory the Great — the learned and pious Pope, to whom England is indebted for her conversion to Christianity — with the money of the Roman Church bought English slaves, and also Barbary slaves — to use the former in evangelizing England, and the latter in the service of the sick in a Roman hospital. We learn this from the letters of the Pontiff himself. Assuredly no slave owner need scruple to what so holy, so zealous a Pope has done.

We come now to the civil law in relation to Slavery. The civil law can modify, introduce, or suppress things or practices whenever such enactments are not in direct opposition to moral and natural law. Hence the civil law may prohibit Slavery, and it does prohibit it in several countries, and perhaps in the greater part of Christian nations. But such a prohibition takes its force and efficacy solely from the civil law.

As for the United States, it is as plain, that the Constitution, framed after the War of Independence, recognizes the relations of master and slave, and that the law of the United States gives a right to the master to reclaim and seize his fugitive slave, wherever he may be found within the United States. These statements are undeniable, and there is no occasion for me to dwell on a point known to everybody.

Those States which have enacted laws against the Constitution and the Legislation of the United States, have sapped the very foundation of social order, and are the true and responsible causes and agents of the misfortunes which have already befallen the nation, and of the greater calamities with which it is threatened. The words of my text receive here their application: "Justice exalteth a nation but sin maketh nations miserable."

Before concluding this first part of my address, I must take a cursory notice of the reasons and objections raised by Abolitionists against the doctrine delivered in the preceding remarks.

I will not notice the allegation of agrarians and anarchists that "all men, are born free and this assertion, although liberal and popular with a certain class of persons, is however, false and a glaring falsehood. Some are born poor, and others rich. Some are born weak, puny, and unhealthy; others strong, and healthy. Some are born dull and stupid, others of quick and penetrating intellect, etc., etc.; for the enumeration would be too long.

The true ground of *equality* in men is that we will be condemned by our Maker only for guilt voluntarily and freely incurred, or rewarded in the next life only for the supernatural good we will have accomplished in this life. In all these respects a slave is absolutely on the same footing with his master.

But the Bible is brought forward against Slavery, and, Abolitionists of course quote the Bible in support of their theories, although it must be apparent to every one from the quotations already-adduced, that if the battle of abolitionism is to be fought on Scripture ground, they are already discomfited.

Indeed it is enough to remark that some of the modern fanatics have gone to that length of impiety and blasphemy to assert unblushingly that if the Bible upholds slavery, the Bible must be amended. No better confutation on abolitionism need be adduced than the necessity to which it drives its defenders of uttering execrable and blasphemies.

Those who would not set aide the authority of the inspired volume, allege from it these general maxims, that Christ has liberated us; that there is no slave in the Christian religion. But it is evident, they speak of spiritual liberty, of the true liberty the only one which deserves the name, liberty from sin, from corrupt inclinations, from Satan, and not liberty from civil powers, and masters, to whom they teach positively and expressly that obedience is due, so that to resist them, is to resist the appointment of God.

Hence, the passage which says there is no slave, runs thus, Galat. 3:28. "There is neither Jew, nor Greek; there is neither bond nor free; there is neither male nor female. For you are all one in Christ Jesus." Words which it would be ludicrous to allege as intimating the extinction of domestic Slavery: The passages of Scripture, however, which the abolitionists urge with greater confidence, are these which command men to pay the wages of their laborers and hirelings.

The following are those they quote: Lev. 19:13. The wages of him that hath been hired by thee, shall not abide with thee until the morning. — Deut. 24:14, 15, has a text of the same import; and St. James, in the New Testament, rebukes thus the rich. — Ch. 5 v. 4. "Behold, the hire of the laborers, who have reaped your fields, of which you have defrauded them, crieth; and the cry of them hath entered into the ears of the Lord of Sabaoth."

But it is perfectly obvious that these quotations have no bearing whatever on the question. When our slaveholders hire laborers, they pay them according to the agreement made, and this is all that the Scripture speaks of. The texts, here quoted, speak of laborers and hired servants, and not of slaves belonging to the masters, for whom they work.

The very fact that the Scripture makes the distinction between hired men, or laborers and slaves, shows that the slaves are not entitled to any wages, because they are not hired by the day. Slaves, however, receive their hire or a compensation for their Services in the food, clothing and dwelling, which, they receive, in the care that is taken of them during their infancy, and in the assurance they have to be provided for in time of sickness, and in old age.

The preceding remarks must convince every candid mind, that the pretentions of Abolitionists have no foundation whatever. in nature, or morality, or the word of God, either in the Old or New Testament, or in the enactments of law-givers of the religious or the political order.

The fact is that there has been, in the northern part of the country, an actual conspiracy against justice and truth; and I am sorry I have to state, (but a just regard for truth and justice compels me to do it,) this conspiracy against justice and. truth, is headed by fanatical preachers, whose only object is to inflame the wicked passions of their hearers.

Yes, beloved brethren the chief cause, the true source of the misfortunes which weigh already upon the land, and bid fair to increase a hundred fold, lies in the misrepresentations of ignorant and fanatical zealots, who desecrate and pollute the Divine word, speaking in the name of God, although they gainsay all the teachings of God. They are the false prophets of whom Scripture says, Jer. 23:21: "I did not send prophets, but yet they ran; I have not spoken to them, yet they prophesied."

Now, beloved brethren, they are the same who have heretofore assailed, calumniated, vilified our church, and have resorted to the vilest and most iniquitous devices which infernal malice can suggest, in order to destroy our holy religion, or that church which is founded on the chair of Peter, and recognizes the Pope as the visible head of the church on earth.

It is to their nefarious machinations that we are to ascribe the burning of the Charlestown Convent, which in the middle of the night drove innocent and defenseless females out of their home into the fields, and the Philadelphia riots, where arson and murder against unoffending Catholics, became the order of the day; and so many other acts of crying injustice, cruelty and barbarity, during that religious excitement from which we are just now emerging, I mean the movement of Know Nothingism.

During that period, the press, which is more or less under the sway of those fanatical leaders, has teemed with the most absurd, unjust, obscene, and, revolting slanders and lies against Catholic Institutions, chiefly Convents, (as in the case of Maria Monk,) and against Priests, Bishops, and the Pope. That party, although a thousand times unmasked and convinced of perjury, lies, and palpable injustice, has kept on its course of violence, deception, misrepresentation.

It seemed quite impossible for it to learn any lesson from truth, moderation and justice, because it was urged on by blind fanaticism, and by the demon of religiosity rather anti-religious bigotry. Those blind leaders, quitting the sphere which they seem to claim when they style themselves reverend, have sent remonstrances to Congress on points evidently out-of the pale of political and civil legislation; they have also invaded State legislatures, and those places have disgraced their proceedings by iniquity and injustice.

It is that same party, which, baffled in its attempts against the Catholic Church, which has opposed only patience, silence and prayer to its unholy attacks, and exasperated by the rebuke it received from the ration, (for, it could not destroy the sense of justice so deeply engraved in the American breast,) has now turned its weapons against the South, advocating; in the name of the Bible, the liberation of slaves.

But the South has not been, and will not, as a Nation, be as patient as the Catholic Church. As an additional proof-that this Abolitionism is the same party which has lately waged war against the Catholic Church, I have only to state a fact asserted by the late illustrious and eloquent Bishop of Charleston, Dr. England, in his treatise on Slavery, which his death left imperfect, a fact of which he had been an eye witness, namely, that the Abolitionists of England. presented regularly every year two petitions to Parliament, one to ask that the slaves of America be set free, the other to ask that the vexations and bloody penalties enacted against Irish Catholics be executed and strictly enforced.

I must likewise make another remark, the truth of which struck every thinking mind at the outbreak of the present disturbances. Protestant writers have been extolling the Republic of the United States, as endowed with wonderful strength, stability and order, when compared with the 'Republics' of South America, in which the majority of the people profess the Catholic religion.

The invidious comparison has often been made; as if free and liberal institutions could not prosper under our Church, and as if Protestantism alone could found, establish and foster Republican Institutions. The present state of affairs show show how ill grounded these views have been. The fact is, that religion has nothing to do with the disturbances and agitations of the Governments of Spanish origin which have sprung up South of the United States.

The true cause of those agitations lies in the ambition, and other wicked passions of men who are unwilling to be controlled by religion, and who deem it right to attack religion in order to become rich from its spoils. But in the United States, it will be properly and clearly religion or rather bigotry that will have destroyed the beautiful fabric of Washington and the other great men who wished so much to keep the Government and religion separate from each other.

The Catholics of America have scrupulously adhered to those constitutional provisions, and have interfered only by praying for the republic, the general peace and welfare of their fellow citizens.

As for the Protestant Clergy, with, of course, honorable exceptions, they have brought about this deplorable state of things, in which the South is arrayed against the North, and in which war, bloodshed, and all the atrocities of civil discord may yet have their sad exhibition. Protestant intolerance and bigotry have demolished this beautiful edifice, which wisdom, moderation and prudence had reared to political liberty.

I must now, brethren, pass to the second part of my discourse, and having shown the lawfulness of Slavery in general, I must show the conditions upon which this state of things receives the sanction of justice, of God himself, and of the church — the visible guide given us by Our Lord Jesus Christ.

It is in this part that I may have to mention wrongs which the South ought to acknowledge and confess; and if these wrongs be persevered in this may be the reason why the Almighty; in his justice and wise severity, may sweep Slavery out of the land, not because Slavery is bad in itself but because men will abuse it through wanton malice.

The necessity of some conditions for the legitimacy of Slavery must appear evident to everybody. A man, by being a slave, does not cease to be a man, retaining all the properties, qualities, attributes, duties, rights and responsibilities attached to human nature, or to a being endowed with reason and understanding, and made to the image and likeness of God.

A master: has not over a slave the same rights which he has over an animal, and whoever would view his slaves merely as beasts, would have virtually abjured human nature, and would deserve to be expelled from human society. I will then state the various conditions which must accompany a legitimate possession of slaves.

In the first place it is domestic Slavery which we advocate to be lawful, and to have the sanction of God himself, but it is not the "slave trade", or the African trade. The slave-trade is absolutely immoral and unjust, and is against all laws natural, divine, ecclesiastical, and civil. The slave-trade consists in kidnapping negroes by fraud and violence on the coasts of Africa, and bringing them to America for sale.

This trade is evidently condemned by justice and humanity. What right has any man to steal another man and, enslave him? This, next to murder, seems to be the grossest violation of justice that can be conceived. It is no palliation of this trade to assert that the condition of those poor creatures will be bettered by selling them to Christian masters in America: for evil is not to be done, in order to obtain a good result.

It is absolutely evil to deprive them of liberty without. any just cause; no good effect can render it lawful. Besides, that good effect is doubtful, as the religion and civilization of the whites who commit such horrible theft, must be hateful to those poor negroes.

It is not an excuse for the trade, but an additional monstrosity to say that those negroes are sold to the captains of vessels by other tribes who have captured them in war; for the war is for no other reason than to, make prisoners; it is not a war, but an abominable plunder of human beings.

Hence the slave-trade has been most severely prohibited by nearly all European Governments; it is, as all know, expressly forbidden by the United States, and we hear frequently of vessels engaged in that abominable traffic, having been seized and captured by the men-of-war of the Nation.

As to the ecclesiastical law, his Holiness, Gregory XVI; in the year 1839, issued apostolic letters forbidding most expressly this shameful commerce, forbidding any one to teach that it is lawful. In that document, his Holiness quotes decrees of his predecessors who had condemned the slave-trade. The letter of Pope Gregory XVI, was solemnly read in the council of American Prelates, held in Baltimore in the year 1840. All laws stigmatize, and reprove the slave-trade, and it must be a subject of regret and mortification for the true friends of the Southern cause and Southern rights, that some people have expressed, or hinted, a desire, that the trade should be revived, and that the prohibition of it by the Government should be repealed.

Fortunately the number of the advocates of this infamous trade is so small, that it may well be considered as nothing. Indeed if a Southern Confederacy was to authorize this worst of piracies, we could predict with certainty its speedy downfall, because it would not be founded on justice, but on iniquity. "Justice exalteth a Nation, but sin maketh Nations miserable." But there is not the slightest fear of this.

The second condition of legitimate Slavery is that the rights of free colored persons be respected. The moment some colored people have acquired, or possess lawful exemption from Slavery it is as unjust to enslave them again, as it would be to enslave a white man, because the ground of Slavery is not in the color of the skin, but the titles which make one the legitimate servant of another.

It would be then a palpable and unreasonable violation of all justice to sell them, or to expel them from the State, or to vex and molest them merely because they are colored. There is as much injustice vexing the free colored population, as there would be in vexing white men, either on account of their origin, because for instance, they are Irish or German, or on account of their religion.

It has been a subject of bitter mortification for the lovers of justice and .humanity to learn that some State legislatures have had before them laws for banishing or selling such persons. I trust the escutcheon of Florida will not be sullied by such unjust statute, and that the love of justice in which all are equally interested will for ever prevent the attempt of such unwise legislation. Some Slaveholders may imagine that the expulsion of free negroes would strengthen their tenure of slaves, but they are mistaken; injustice will not uphold anything: injustice is a rotten prop, which will only accelerate the fall of whatever rests on it.

Hence the friends of justice and order have been highly gratified at the late proceedings of the South Carolina Legislature, on the occasion of a bill which was introduced to sell all free persons of color. The gentleman who had to report on the bill, following the dictates of justice, which is never more imperious and more sacred than in the case of a contest between the strong and the weak, pointed, out both the injustice and the impolicy of such a measure, and concluded energetically against it in the following strain, which I can quote only in substance:

"Forbid it justice, forbid it humanity, forbid it conscience. Let us not by such a "glaring act" of injustice disgrace our cause, and render ourselves unworthy of the smiles and countenance of the Supreme Arbiter of all events, in this the hour of our need."

This conclusion of the report does great honor to the head and heart of those who lead politics in Charleston, and indeed there is not a more crying, cowardly, infamous tyranny than that of a strong Government on colored people, precisely because the latter are weak, defenseless, and incapable of protecting themselves.

Here is another condition I must mention in the name of morality, in the name of public decency, in the name of religion, in the name of Christianity it is that the whites do not take advantage of the weakness, ignorance, dependence, and lowly position of colored females, whether slaves or not — availing themselves of the impunity which, hitherto, laws in the South have extended to this sort of iniquity.

It is indeed right that the two races should be kept distinct, and public sentiment repudiates amalgamation, and hence such connubial alliances are not to be encouraged and formed. But, things being on that footing, every outrage against morals should be repressed. It is the duty of the clergy to protest against every violation of the moral law, and by making the present remark, I discharge but too weakly and imperfectly a sacred obligation. attached to the responsible and dangerous office of Bishop, which I hold in the Church of God.

I am a sincere and devoted friend of the South, to which Divine Providence has sent me, and I am ready to undergo any hardship — to make any sacrifice — for the true welfare of the people among whom I live; still I must say it for conscience sake who knows whether the Almighty does not design to use the present disturbances for the destruction of frequent occasions of immorality, which the subservient and degraded position of the slave offers to the lewd.

I hope I am a false prophet: but, at the same time, I must admonish my countrymen that obscure, secret, and hidden crimes, often call for an open, public, and solemn, chastisement at the hands of the Supreme Moderator of events; and I must remind them that the waters of the flood, in which the whole race of mankind was swept off, save a small remnant; were sent by the Almighty to punish an impure and lewd generation; I must remind them that Sodom and Gomorrah were consumed in a shower of: burning pitch and brimstone, because of the unnatural lusts of its profligate inhabitants.

It is but right that means should be taken to check libertinism and licentiousness, and that the female slave be surrounded with sufficient protection to save her from dishonor and crime. The Southern Confederacy, if it should exist, must rest on morality and justice, and it could never be entitled to a special protection from above, unless it professes to surround Slavery with the guarantees that will secure its morality and virtue.

This leads me to another condition on a subject kindred to the preceding. It is that matrimonial relations be observed among slaves, and that the laws of marriage be enforced among them.

All know that there, have: been, and there are frightful abuses about this point, and I leave it to the conscience, reason, and good sense of any upright and virtuous man, whether God can bless a country and a state of things in which there is a woeful disregard of the holy laws of marriage. It is my duty to proclaim to masters that they have indeed a right on the labor of their slaves; they can justly require of them obedience, respect, and service. But they are not the masters of their slaves in such a way that they can forbid them marriage, or prescribe it at pleasure.

Although they can give directions and advice to their servants on this point, still those servants are their own masters as to that. The titles to Slavery include only labor and service, but they cannot change the nature of men. It would be unnatural and foolish to suppose that the whole race is deprived of the faculty of marrying by their servile dependence; and it would be a shocking, hideous, and abominable conclusion, to admit that they live in concubinage and adultery.

Hence religion and morality point out to masters a strict and rigorous duty, not only not to oppose marriage of their servants, but to promote it, and to procure for them all the necessary means of avoiding immorality and crime. Slaves must be encouraged to marry, and the laws of marriage must be observed among them exactly as among the whites. The law of God admits of no distinction in this respect: the laws of morality are not different with the different races of Men, and a state of things which is criminal with the whites, cannot be excusable with the colored people.

Their is one Christian code of morality and of domestic order. Our Lord Jesus Christ has appointed laws and sacred prescriptions for marriage, which He has, indeed, raised to the dignity and excellence: of a sacrament. He has not excepted anybody from the operation of these Divine laws. Divorce and polygamy must be excluded from Christians, or else the anger of God will necessarily be provoked by the violation of His laws.

Slavery, to become a permanent institution of the South, must be made to conform to the laws of God; a Southern Confederacy will never thrive, unless it rests upon morality and order; the Supreme Arbiter of Nations will not bless with stability and prosperity a state of things which would be a flagrant violation of His holy commandments. Hence marriage must be established and enforced among Slaves, and all the laws of Christian marriage must be held up to their faithful observance, as they are among the whites in every decent form of society; and the law of the Apostle must apply to servants: "Marriage honorable in all, and the bed undefiled." — Heb. 13:4.

Another condition arises from the nature of connubial society — it is that the husband and wife are joined together until death parts them. Our Saviour's word on this cannot pass away: "What God has joined together; let no man put asunder." Hence families ought never to be separated, when once established. It is unreasonable, un-Christian, and immoral to separate a husband from his wife and children, and to sell, the husband North, and the Wife South, and the children East and West.

A master ought not to be allowed to do this merely for the sake of greater profit. Covetousness and cupidity would not render that conduct excusable, but would only heighten its black hue. Legitimate gain from slaves cannot be censured; but gain at the expense of morality, religion, and humanity is a horror which can but bring to a speedy ruin a fabric that would rest on it and admit of it.

The separation of families is fraught with evils and inconveniences which shock the moral sense of everybody at once; but in the eyes of Religion it presents yet a greater inconvenience. This married man, this married woman, now separated from each other, cannot live in continency; it would be requiring a miracle of fortitude and virtue, which cannot be expected from the generality of men, much less from a race more inclined to pleasures than any other.

Indeed, the strength and violence of animal propensities is in the inverse ratio of intellectual and moral faculties, which are decidedly weaker in the African race, as all persons of experience will testify. Hence these people will be necessarily exposed to adultery; for the laws of God cannot be set aside or ignored; the former marriage still subsists, and hence the separated parties will live in adultery and crime, and be in the impossibility of serving God and of working out their salvation.

What a dreadful responsibility for any master who has not yet extinguished altogether in himself the fear of his Supreme Judge! There ought to be, therefore, a provision made and sanctioned by the civil law, to be a bar against cupidity, that families shall never be separated and especially, that husband and wife will be looked upon as one person, inseparable and indivisible.

The only exception to this law would be the commission of great crimes by one of the parties, which would render them subject, to legal punishments, as imprisonment in the penitentiary, for in such cases even among the whites the husband is separated from his wife.

Abating the conditions necessary, to render Slavery lawful an reasonable, it is scarcely necessary to mention that the master must really and in good faith provide food, clothing, and dwelling for his servant. This is a duty of the master which requires no proof, and is admitted by all, and practiced by all generally speaking; and it is indeed a, striking feature of the South, that the slave is better fed and clothed than the free negro.

There is, we know, much misrepresentation and calumny resorted to on this point by Abolitionists; their appalling stories about the hardships of slaves are no more than a malicious fiction. If there have been cruel, tyrannical, tiger hearted masters, it is only a proof that there may be monsters in the human race — but such monsters are found as well in free as in slave regions.

As for the generality of masters in the South, they are humane and kind, and more inclined to be too mild than too severe to their servants. This kind treatment is the necessary effect of religious feeling and practical religion among masters. and hence it ought to be the great study of ministers of religion to spread the spirit of Christianity among the people; it will do incomparably more for the relief and the happiness of the slave than all the fanatical efforts of Abolitionists.

This spirit of Christianity will teach the master to treat his slave with humanity and kindness, as a fellow being, and as a partaker of the same nature, the same promises, the same hope of eternal happiness, which exalt so much the human race when received in the light of faith and Christian revelation, and hence I can do nothing better than to write down here the teaching and recommendation of the inspired Apostles concerning the relative duties of masters and servants:

"Servants, obey in all things your masters according to the flesh, not serving to the eye, as pleasing men, but in simplicity of heart, fearing God. Whatsoever you do, do it from the heart, as to the Lord and-not to men, knowing that you shall receive of the Lord the reward of inheritance. Serve ye the Lord Christ. For he that doeth an injury shall receive for that which he hath done unjustly, as there is no respect of persons with God. Masters, do to your servants that which is just and equal, knowing that you also have a Master in heaven." — Colos. 3:22.

"Servants, obey your carnal masters with fear and trembling, in the simplicity of your heart, as Christ, not serving to the eye as it were pleasing men, but as servants of Christ, doing the will of God, from the heart, with a good will doing service, as to the Lord and not to men, knowing that whatsoever good every one shall do, the same shall he receive from the Lord, whether he be bond or free. And you, masters, do the same things to them, forbearing threatenings knowing that the Lord both of them and you is in Heaven, and there is no respect of persons with him." — Eph. 6:5.

"Exhort servants to be obedient to their masters, in all things pleasing, not contradicting, not defrauding, but in all things showing good fidelity, that they may adorn the doctrine of God our Saviour in all things. — Tit. 2:9.

What a useful and extensive subject of meditation for servants and masters. If both come up to the requirements and exhortations of Christian morality laid down by the Apostles themselves, then servants will truly be happy, and will love and serve their masters from their hearts, and masters will also find in their servants protectors, devoted friends, loving subjects,-who will take their interests to heart, and be more like children than slaves.

Such, indeed, were the servants of Abram, whose virtue, faith, and religion, are a theme of praise in the Sacred Scripture, who numbered three hundred and eighteen born in his house, who exposed their lives for the interests of their master, and obtained for him a glorious victory.

These are the dispositions which true religion would instill in the breasts of servants, and which we would witness generally among servants, if religion presided over our families and plantations. In the absence of this element of order and peace, alas! masters have often no greater fear than from their servants, and what blessing then would it not be for masters themselves, if their servants would imbibe the true and genuine spirit of Christianity?

This leads me to the last condition which I wish to mention for the lawfulness of Slavery. It is that servants must be provided with the means of knowing and practicing religion. This is a sacred, indispensable, bounden duty of masters, the neglect of which alone, if they had committed no other fault, would expose them to eternal damnation.

Servants are moral, responsible and rational beings, accountable to the Supreme Arbiter of all things, as the masters themselves. They must save their own souls, and have, as well as their masters, no other affair worthy of the name in this world.

They have an immortal soul, made to the image and likeness of God, and redeemed by the blood of Christ. The loss of such a soul is a greater misfortune than the destruction of the whole world. Man is on earth, only to save that soul by the love and service of God, and the slave has the same rights and duties as the white man:

"There is neither Jew, nor Greek, there is neither bond nor free, there is neither male, nor female; for you are all one in Christ Jesus." Gal. 3:28.

It is, therefore, evident that the slave must be made acquainted with everything necessary that he may save his soul. The master who has the time, and the services of his slave, is bound by natural law, as also by the divine and ecclesiastical law, to instruct his servants in their religious duties, or to have them instructed by proper persons.

He has, with regard to that, the same obligations which parents contract with regard to their children. Hence it would be a great crime, and a great folly at the same time, in masters to keep their servants in ignorance of every religious doctrine; those lost souls would cry out to heaven against them for vengeance; and this flagrant. injustice against the souls of slaves would be the sure way to render Slavery an untenable and ruinous institution, deserving the contempt of men; and the malediction of God.

It would be treating slaves like beasts, and as this is supremely unnatural; such a state of things would be a forced and violent one, and could not stand, and God would owe it to his mercy wisdom and justice, to bring about the speedy ruin or such an unjust and iniquitous institution.

On the contrary, if the slave be taught his religion, dire nature and destination of his soul, his duties to God, and the rewards as well as the chastisements a the next life, he will then act reasonably: many will follow the admonitions of the apostles, and thus the mutual happiness and satisfaction of servants and masters will be surely and efficaciously promoted.

A Christian and religious master may easily become a most effectual missionary, enforcing among his servants; by his words and examples, the love of morality and virtue, gaining them to God, and by his kindness winning their affection and love. He will thus be served far better in this world, and will be the instrument of the eternal happiness of many in the next world, which is indeed the highest aim of human ambition.

Happy are the masters who own those slaves, and happier the servants who belong to them. The number of such masters is not very large but we have known some who had truly upon this, the Christian Spirit, and did not hesitate to sacrifice one afternoon every week, calling in a Clergyman to give their servants once a week, a homily and familiar instruction adapted to their wants, besides the Sunday, which they had free for the performance of their religious duties.

The subject which I have presented today to your consideration, beloved brethren, is one of great importance, and is to have a powerful influence over the stability of the Southern Confederacy.

---

Such a Confederacy will, to all appearance, be formed, and such is the rapid march of events, that the dismemberment of the Union is already consummated, and the faint hopes of a permanency of the Union, which existed yet when the first pages of this paper were written, have altogether vanished, and the new flag of the Southern Confederacy is now given to the breeze, and waves under my eyes.

Now if that Confederacy is meant to be solid, durable, stable and permanent, it must rest upon justice and morality. "Justice exalteth a Nation: but sin maketh Nations miserable."

It is undoubtedly true that the law of God does not reprove Slavery; it is undoubtedly true that now the sudden and abrupt manumission of slaves would be a misfortune of appalling magnitude, more so yet for the slave than for the master. Let then the wise and the virtuous unite and combine their prudence, their patriotism, their humanity, and their religious integrity to divest Slavery of the features which would make it odious to God and man.

Now is the time to make a salutary reform, and to enact judicious regulations: I propose as the means of setting the new Confederacy upon a solid basis, that a servile code be drawn up and adopted by the Confederacy, defining clearly the rights and duties of masters, and the rights and duties .of slaves. This will be the means of proving to the world that the South is on the side of justice, morality, reason and religion.

This will be a just vindication of Southern views sanctioned by the Great Arbiter of Nations; this will be a most triumphant confutation of the charges which bigotry, ignorance, fanaticism and malice, cloaked under a reverend garb, have for years heaped against Southern Institutions.

We have assembled to humble ourselves under the remembrance of our manifold transgressions: the subject which has been presented to you on this occasion affords to the North and to the South just subjects of humiliation, sorrow, confusion and humble accusation before the Supreme Ruler.

Let us, beloved brethren, accompany these sentiments of humiliation and grief with great confidence in the mercy of God, who often permits transitory sufferings in order to derive from them substantial and lasting good. Let us remember how the Jews, under Esther, having recourse to penance and prayer were saved miraculously from their enemies, who themselves fell into the pit they had dug for their unoffending brethren.

Let us remember how the threats against Nineve were averted by the humiliation and penance of the people, and let us hope, in the midst of the said forebodings which reach us every day, and in the midst of the rumors and cries of civil war which seem to become every day nearer and nearer, that Divine Providence, who has in his hands the heart of kings, rulers, and statesmen, will avert calamities from our heads, or at least grant us the grace of so profiting by the temporal evils to which we may be subjected, that by patience, resignation, submission to the will of heaven, we may expiate our past faults, cancel at least a part of the debt which we owe to the Divine Justice, and render ourselves worthy of the eternal happiness which is promised to the true Servants of God in the next world.

# The Silver Trumpets of the Sanctuary

## A SERMON

### PREACHED TO

## The Pulaski Guards

### IN

### CHRIST CHURCH, SAVANNAH,

### ON THE SECOND SUNDAY AFTER TRINITY

### BEING THE SUNDAY BEFORE THEIR DEPARTURE TO JOIN THE ARMY IN VIRGINIA,

### BY THE

### RT. REV. STEPHEN ELLIOTT, D. D.,
#### RECTOR OF CHRIST CHURCH.

SAVANNAH
1861

## Sermon

NUMBERS 10:9. — "And if ye go to warn your land against the enemy that oppresseth you, then ye shall blow an alarm with the trumpets: and ye shall be remembered before the Lord your God, and ye shall be saved from your enemies."

The children of Israel were led out of their captivity by the outstretched arm of Jehovah himself He was their pillar of cloud by day, and their pillar of fire by night. He was not only their God, but their King. He made their laws: He guided their armies: He arranged every matter, not only of religious worship but of civil and military discipline, and, among other things, he instituted the usage to which our text refers.

He ordered Moses to make two silver trumpets, which were to be blown upon certain occasions, by no less persons than the sons of Aaron, the Priests of the Sanctuary. One of these occasions was when their armies went out to battle, that they might be animated and encouraged in the fight, and brought to the remembrance of the Lord for salvation from their enemies.

In this way was war consecrated by religion, and the heart of courage was lighted anew from the altar of God, and the arm of valor was strengthened by the knowledge that they were daily borne upon the wings of prayer before Him whose power no creature is able to resist.

But it was only one species of war which was thus surrounded with the holiness of religious blessing. These trumpets were not to be blown when their armies were mustered for a war of conquest, nor when they gathered themselves together for an alliance with the nations which surrounded them, but only when they went to war in their own land against the enemy that oppressed them.

The war which this usage hallowed and sanctified, was a strictly defensive war, one waged for a nation's rights against invasion and oppression. "And if ye go to war in your land against the enemy that oppresseth you, then ye shall blow an alarm with the trumpets."

Under these circumstances, children of Israel, is the paraphrase of the promise, ye may go to battle without any fear, and strike boldly for your homes and your altars without any guilt. The right, in such case of self-defense, will be on your side, and God sitteth in the throne judging right.

The church will sound the trumpets that shall summon you to the battle, and God dwelleth in the sanctuary between the Cherubim. The congregation will remember you at the morning and the evening sacrifice, and the High Priest will remember you when he sprinkles the blood of atonement before the Mercy seat, and God will remember you because of his everlasting covenant with you, and will save you from your enemies.

This close connection between God and his people has ceased with the incoming of Christ, and the Gospel is, in many respects, a very different system from the Law. But while different, it is yet the same. It is the perfect development of a Divine scheme, and therein it differs as a full-blown flower differs from its bud.

It is the full exhibition to man of a plan of mercy which the Law shrouded under types and shadows, and therein it differs as a landscape, flooded with light, differs from one seen obscurely through the morning's dawn. It is the spiritualizing of a Divine intercourse with man, which, under the Law, was carried on by sensible symbols, and therein it differs, as the ethereal flash of thought from the slow communication by signs.

But its moral principles remain the same, for the Law, comprised in the Ten Commandments, delivered from Mount Sinai, is still our rule of right and wrong. Christ spiritualized it, and thus made it more comprehensive, but he did not alter it. What was morally wrong under the Law, is morally wrong now — what was morally right then, is morally right now. The principles of God's immutable morality nothing can change — no lapse of time — no alteration of dispensations — no mutation of name or nation.

Christian morals stand upon no stronger basis than Israelitish morals, for those rested upon the word of the unchangeable I AM. If defensive war was right then, it is right now: and surely it must have been right when God himself commanded the battle shout to be sounded from his own sanctuary, and promised that he himself would take part in it, and save his people from their enemies.

It is a great error to suppose that our Lord taught the world to believe that his Gospel would make wars to cease over the earth. He knew too well that the wrong must ever battle against the right, and so he said: "I come not to bring peace, but a sword."

The principles of his doctrine must necessarily modify the horrors of war, and leaven that fearful scourge with humanity and mercy, but it was never the teaching of Him, who foretold that wars and rumors of wars should be among the most notable signs of the coming of the Day of Judgment, that they would ever blot it out. In the Apocalypse, that prophetic roll of the world's history, whose leaves we are perpetually deciphering under the march of events, conflict succeeds conflict, up to the very moment when the heavens shall be rolled together as a scroll, and warriors, with garments rolled in blood, usher in its terrors.

Great as is the glory of the Gospel — unspeakable as are its mercies and its blessings — they will never rid us of the curse which God has stamped upon the world. War will ever, while the world endures, mingle its miseries with that full tide of sorrow which sin has brought upon mankind. When sickness shall cease, when sorrow shall cease, when affliction shall cease, when poverty shall cease, then will war cease, for they are all only branches of the same root of evil which nothing can eradicate from the earth.

Christ has limited their duration, but that limit is coeval with the world's existence. When the heavens and the earth, that now are, shall pass away, there shall arise new heavens and a new earth, wherein dwelleth righteousness, and therein shall be no more curse. All evil will cease, because all sin will cease, and together shall all man's enemies be cast into outer darkness.

But, while this is so, another question may press itself upon the tender conscience and give it embarrassment. While, as is evident, wars will continue unto the end, is there anything in the Gospel which forbids a Christian man from bearing arms and fighting in his country's service?

We unhesitatingly answer, that there is nothing; no shadow of a prohibition where the war is defensive. In the Gospel, as in the Law, when Christian men "go to war in their land against the enemy that oppresseth them," they may go with the certain assurance that they are doing no wrong, that they are acting according to the purest reason, and that nothing can be found in the word of God which shall condemn them.

"Whatsoever is absolutely necessary, says Jeremy Taylor, is certainly lawful: and since Christ hath nowhere forbidden kings to defend themselves and their people against violence, in this case there is no law at all to be considered: since there is a right of nature, which no law of God hath restrained: and, by that right, all men are on an equal footing, and, therefore, if they be not safe from injury, it is their own fault, or their own unhappiness; they may if they will, and if they can: and they have no measures in this, but that they take care they be defended and quit from the danger, and no more." — vol. xii 448-449, (Heber's edition.)

This is the abstract argument derived from the silence of our Lord, but there are indications in the New Testament that the profession of a soldier was not contrary to the doctrine of Christ. When John the Baptist came rebuking sin in the spirit and power of Elijah — the sternest of all the ancient prophets — and preparing the way of the Lord, the soldiers demanded of him, "And what shall we do?" And he said unto them, "Do violence to no man, neither accuse any falsely: and be content with your wages."

Not a word against the lawfulness of their occupation: not a word indicating that He was near at hand who would strike by his Gospel at the root of their profession, but simply an injunction to observe in their conduct the principles of mercy, of justice, and of obedience.

And if it be said, that this answer was given by John ere yet the Holy Spirit had been sent by our ascended Lord to guide his people into all truth, we have the yet stronger case of Cornelius, an officer of the Roman army, in active service, whose history is contained, singularly enough, in the second lesson of the morning service.

As a soldier and an officer he had served God earnestly, so that the writer of the Acts of the Apostles calls him "a devout man, and one that feared God with all his house, and gave much alms to the people, and prayed to God always." His position did not interfere with his religion, nor did it hinder the grace of God, for that found him in the daily performance of a soldier's duty, and an angel of God was commissioned to say unto him, "Thy prayers and thine arms are come up for a memorial before God:" and he was chosen to be the first Gentile convert, and to illustrate the divine truth that on the Gentiles, also was poured out the gift of the Holy Ghost.

The baptism of God came upon him, although a soldier, and then followed the baptism of man, and we are nowhere instructed that because he became a Christian, therefore he ceased to be a soldier. And in one of the early apologies for Christianity, we hear Tertullian saying to the Roman Emperor: "We, Christians, fill your cities, your islands, your towns, your boroughs, your camp, your senate, and your forum." And this could not have been true, had the early Church forbidden her communicants to enter into service as soldiers.

The military life seems to have been treated by Christ as was every other department of domestic and social arrangement. It was placed by him upon its proper principles, and his spirit was left in the world to work, silently yet surely, its conformity to those principles. He never denounced it, although his Gospel was come to preach peace on earth, good will towards men.

Upon these principles, soldiers, I feel that the trumpets may sound in your behalf from the sanctuary of God, and that you may go where duty calls you, believing that you will be remembered before the Lord your God, and your country saved from its enemies. The conflict in which you are about to mingle is one waged upon the holiest grounds of self-preservation and self-defense. Everything most dear and sacred to every one of us is involved in it.

We are contending for SECURITY, the object of all government and law and the basis of all domestic and social happiness. In ancient times, nations contended for conquest, for dominion, for spoils: in modern times, they contend for security. That phrase, which for some centuries, has molded the politics of Europe — the balance of power — is no idle figment: it rests upon this very necessity for security among the nations which insist upon its preservation.

Nearly all the later wars of England have turned upon this very point, that she might be secure in her interests from the ambition of powerful or jealous neighbors, and might prevent any one of the great powers from accumulating too much territory or too much influence. Hence the pertinaciousness with which she hung upon the skirts of the first Napoleon, and the jealousy with which she watches all the movements of his successor. For, without security, there can be no growth in any of the elements of a people's greatness — no accumulation of capital — no advancement in arts or elegance — no independence of thought or feeling — nay, no comfort abroad or at home.

No people can be happy or contented, can feel any self-respect, or deserve any respect from others, who are not secure in their rights or property. The consciousness that they are consenting to live in a state of sufferance humiliates them and unfits them for self-government. They lose the spirit of independence; they forfeit their place in the rank of nations, and as inevitably as the brave man holds dominion over the coward, will the usurper and the tyrant hold dominion over them.

The feeling of INSECURITY, soldiers, was that which lay at the basis of all our sectional movements. The Anglo-Saxon race has never waited until the stroke of tyranny actually descended. It has ever snuffed tyranny at a distance and armed itself against its advent.

The barons who wrested Magna Carta from John, at Runnymede: the bold commoners who brought the Stuarts to the proper knowledge of a people's rights: the colonies which struck the blow against taxation without representation, all acted upon this principle. They demanded security for their rights, and when it was not granted them, they cast their swords into the scale.

None of these were suffering from any overt act of tyranny, but they perceived that principles had been advanced and sanctioned which must end in utter servitude. And this was precisely our position. We foresaw that there could be no security for us under the constitutional interpretation which had been adopted by an irresponsible and ever swelling majority: that there could be no national life for us when we were no longer reckoned as equals, but were pointed at as barbarians and lepers, carrying about with us our manifest taint of infamy. We should have been leaving to our children an inheritance of shame and a life of unceasing conflict.

The time had come when it was essential that we should enter upon this struggle for life and death, that our State governments should cast over us the shield of their protection and give us, under a new government, that security which was essential to our peace and prosperity. This legitimate action has brought upon us the barbarous invasion which you are marching to hurl back upon its unprincipled projectors. The Mother of States — the nursery of heroes, of orators and of statesmen — the shrine which contains the ashes of Washington — summons you to her defense, and points you to the ruthless hordes who have dared to pollute her soil with their unhallowed tread, and to violate all the charities of civilized life.

Against such a warfare you may advance, soldiers, with the assurance that you will be remembered before the Lord your God, and will be saved from your enemies. As you mingle in the strife, you will rejoice that from every sanctuary in the land the silver trumpets will be sounding and bearing your cause into the presence of Him who giveth not always the battle to the strong, but can save by many or by few.

Soldiers, this is no holiday work in which you are about to engage. For the first time will you witness the stern realities of war, and you must prepare yourselves to encounter them. Before you are labor, fatigue, hardship, privation, danger, the battle field. So far in life you have known these things only by name. Count them not as trifles, lest when they come upon you they may find you amazed at their severe and cruel visage.

They must be borne, and they can be borne with courage and with cheerfulness, but not unless you put your trust in Him "who giveth strength and power unto his people." If you call upon him, he will be with you in the day of trouble if you acknowledge him, he will acknowledge you. And the soldier, of all men, is he who should keep nearest to his God and Saviour.

No man carries, so emphatically, his life in his hand, and none, therefore, should be more ready, at any moment, to return it to his God. What men need in war, is not mere physical courage — most men have that in common with the brutes — they require moral courage to withstand temptation, to practice temperance, to endure hardships like good soldiers, to be watchful, obedient, patient, merciful.

Many more soldiers perish in war from careless habits than from the stroke of the enemy — from sickness and disease engendered by recklessness, than by the sword. Military discipline, to which you are now subjecting yourselves, will force upon you this attention to temperance and moderation, but it will require moral cultivation to make you what true soldiers should aim to be.

The Duke of Marlborough, the profoundest military genius England has ever produced, perceived the importance of the moral element among soldiers, and he enforced, throughout his army, the strictest attention to prayer. He never went into battle, he never sat down before a fortress to besiege it, without first calling his army to prayer: and wonderful to say, through all his long career of war — battling as he did against the most powerful monarch of Europe, and the most consummate generals of the time — he never lost a battle, nor ever raised a siege.

And if, from this moment of your departure for your field of action, you would adopt this practice in your corps, of daily morning and evening prayer, of prayer upon the eve of every conflict, of thanksgiving for victory and deliverance, you might be known in the army as the "praying company," but you would certainly be known as the moral, the brave, the efficient company of your regiment. To carry with you into battle, besides your own strength, the strength of the Lord of Hosts, is to be irresistible. May you be thus doubly armed — knowing no fear, save the fear of God.

And in this contest will you be called upon, most especially, to cultivate mercy and humanity. All war has a tendency to excite the passions, to infuriate the temper, harden the heart, but especially a war such as this, which aims at our destruction and strikes its blow at the very heart.

It will be very difficult to observe the limits of Christian warfare in a conflict which is begun by summoning thieves and burglars and cut-throats to the contest. If the gentlemen of the North had come forth to meet the gentlemen of the South, all the rules of chivalry might have been observed, and this war, cruel as it is likely to be under any circumstances, might have worn the aspect of civilization and Christianity.

But when it has been committed to the hands of such men as haunt the purlieus of all large cities, when our homes and our firesides are threatened with pollution by the savages who have been swept together from the prisons and penitentiaries of the North, it will require an almost divine moderation to stay the arm of vengeance. But the Christian must never forget that his God has said, "Vengeance belongeth to me — I will repay, saith the Lord."

Even with such enemies, let mercy and humanity predominate. Strike no more blows than are necessary for victory, and wherever and whenever the cry for mercy shall reach your ear, listen to it and grant its prayer. Let the flag under which you fight be stained with no unnecessary blood. Let no mother's heart be wrung, no sister's bosom lacerated, by your ferocity. The attribute of him, from the door of whose sanctuary the silver trumpets shall animate you to battle, is "The Lord, the Lord God, merciful and gracious." And he will bless you, if you honor his attribute of mercy.

And now, soldiers, I send you forth with the Church's benediction and blessing. Your cause is just — your leaders are skilful — your comrades are brave and earnest. Before you, is a ruthless enemy — behind you, are your homes and your firesides. Who can doubt the issue if you will but keep the Lord on your side?

Remember him always, for to him belong the issues of life and death. And we, Priests of the Sanctuary, who are not permitted to put on the armor of the warrior, will yet be with you blowing the silver trumpets in the ears of the God of battles, praying him ever to remember you, and to be your defense, now and evermore.

# A Sermon

## DELIVERED IN THE MARKET STREET M. E. CHURCH PETERSBURG, VA.

BEFORE THE

## CONFEDERATE CADETS

ON THE OCCASION OF
**THEIR DEPARTURE FOR THE SEAT OF WAR**

Sunday, Sept. 22d, 1861,

BY

## REV. R. N. SLEDD.

1861

# SERMON

Be of good courage, and let us behave ourselves valiantly for our people, and for the cities of our God, and let the Lord do that which is good in his sight. — 1 CHRON. 19:13.

Our blessed Redeemer is called by the prophet Isaiah, "the Prince of Peace." His advent into the world was celebrated by "a multitude of the heavenly host praising God, and saying, Glory to God in the highest, and on earth peace, good will toward men."

Said he, in his first sermon, "Blessed are the peacemakers: for they shall be called the children of God." His kingdom is said to be a kingdom of "righteousness, and peace, and joy in the Holy Ghost." And we are exhorted to "follow peace with all men": in other words, "If it be possible, as much as lieth in you, live peaceably with all men."

We conclude, therefore, that the spirit of Christianity is eminently pacific, and that nothing can be more in harmony with the genius of the gospel, and with the purposes and plans of God as unfolded in His Word, than the reconciliation of all contending parties, the adjustment of all differences, and the establishment everywhere of relations of amity and good will among men and nations.

But though such be its spirit — though its object be the diffusion of the blessings of peace — though it be the revealed purpose of its Author that the sword shall ultimately be beaten into the plough-share, and the spear into the pruning-hook, and nation no more lift up sword against nation — we are not to suppose that it requires of us passive submission to all the insults and encroachments of others.

As individuals, it is true we are to cherish no personal revenge. We are rather to love our enemies, to bless them that curse us, and pray for them which despitefully use us, and persecute us. But "the powers that be are ordained of God"; ordained "for the punishment of evil-doers"; ordained for the settlement of the conflicting claims and the protection of the rights of men. And hence, whenever our individual rights are assailed, it is in perfect accordance with the object of government, and with the purest morality for us to resist the invasion by seeking the defense and protection of law.

But nations have no such tribunals to which they can appeal for the adjudication of their differences. And when compromise and concession are unavailing, there is no alternative but a resort to arms, and a resentment of injuries by force, or the loss of all position and influence as a government, and a failure to secure any of those benefits or accomplish any of those objects for which governments are divinely established.

Moreover, the design of our being is that we may be happy. And it is God's will that we should occupy the position most favorable to the realization of that end. If our capacity be such that a condition of subjection and dependence will best promote our welfare, then does it accord with the purpose of our being and with the will of God that we should occupy that position.

If on the contrary we be qualified for self-government, and for the appreciation and enjoyment of the blessings of freedom — if a state of independence be most conducive to our happiness and to our accomplishment of the objects of life, then have we an inalienable moral right to that state, and to the unmolested fruition of its advantages. And when any foe would degrade us from that position, and deprive us of its privileges, neither the principles of morals nor the laws of God enjoin non-resistance.

Both justify the individual in calling to his aid the strong arm of the law, and the government in appealing, as a last resort, to the great arbiter of national difficulties — the sword.

While, therefore, the gospel requires the individual to restrain hand from violence — forbids his assuming the place and authority of law and in the blood of a fellow-man seeking satisfaction for his injuries, it cannot, without coming in conflict with God's will concerning us, demand that a government, founded in justice and mercy, shall keep back its sword from blood when the destruction of its enemies is essential to the security and happiness of its subjects.

So far from it, when the interests of humanity are imperiled — when the cause of equity and religion is at stake — when all that men hold dearest, all that makes existence desirable is in jeopardy, then does God, by His providence, if not by His word, bid us buckle on our armor, and "behave ourselves valiantly for our people, and for the cities of our God."

Numerous illustrations of the correctness of this position are to be found in the history of the Jews. Their government was a theocracy, strictly so until the days of Saul. But though under the immediate direction and control of God, but few nations of antiquity were more frequently engaged in war.

Their territory was acquired by the conquest and expulsion of its original inhabitants, and its possession maintained by force of arms. God required of them no compromise of their honor, no surrender of their freedom for the sake of peace. But when their rights were assailed and their security threatened, Himself summoned them to arms, and led them to victory. And while His hand was less prominent in their government in the days of the kings, He no less distinctly manifested His approbation of their efforts to defend themselves against the encroachments of their neighbors.

David, in many respects their greatest king, was preeminently "a man of war." His reign was characterized by almost incessant conflicts with the surrounding nations. In no instance did he hesitate to take up the sword when the honor, the liberty, or the life of his subjects was in danger. And yet he was a man after God's own heart, a man whose "heart was perfect with the Lord" — a man inspired by God's Spirit, guided by God's counsel, and honored with the highest evidences of His favor and love.

If therefore examples from the Word of God are of sufficient authority as testimony, then have we in the history of God's ancient people ample confirmation of the righteousness of a war of defense, or the consistency of such a war with sound morality and pure religion.

Such do we regard the contest in which you are soon to become active participants. You go to avenge no merely private injuries. Your country's freedom, her dearest privileges and richest blessings, her God-given rights are in danger. And voluntarily denying yourselves the comforts and fond endearments of home and friends, you have placed your all on her altar, counting not your life itself a price too great to be paid for the discomfiture and overthrow of her enemies, and the achievement of her independence.

And it is but appropriate before entering into such a struggle — a struggle which may result disastrously to you, and bring many sorrows to hearts that love you well — that in God's house, and from God's Word, you should seek those instructions that will best prepare you for the eventful scenes before you.

There is no condition in life, there are no circumstances in which men may be placed which God has not anticipated and for which He has not provided. His "Word is a lamp unto our feet and a light unto our pathway," whether that pathway lie amid the flowers and fruits of a prosperous peace, or the desolation and ruins of "grim-visaged war."

I. The first lesson which it inculcates on this occasion has reference to the temper of mind with which you should engage in this contest. "Be of good courage." Nothing is more essential to success in any avocation than genuine courage. The path of life is thronged with obstacles: beset with difficulties at every step. And if we achieve any triumph, or obtain any eminence in our respective callings, it can only be the result of firm resolve, steadiness of aim, and unyielding perseverance.

"He that wavereth is like the wave of the sea driven with the wind and tossed." "Unstable as water thou shalt not excel." Indecision and instability, vacillation of will and that cowardly spirit that prefers obscure ease to an encounter with difficulty but seldom transcend the limits of a miserable mediocrity. Genius may sometimes enable even the irresolute and fickle to achieve distinction. But if unsustained by a strong will and a stout heart its most brilliant successes are but transient and unsatisfactory.

On the other hand, not more certainly does the morning star foretell the splendor of coming day, than do stability and decision, resolution and fortitude, founded in a strong conviction of right, and warmed into life by a love of the right, guarantee permanent prosperity, and lead ultimately to the realization of the desired end.

Courage, however, in the popular sense of the term, is a temper of very doubtful character, and often of unquestionable immorality. It is usually ascribed to all who are fearless of danger, or reckless of life. But such fearlessness may be the result simply of incompetency to comprehend and appreciate the reality and extent of the danger.

It may be the fruit of an unjustifiable sensitiveness to public opinion. It may spring from sympathy, from love of plunder, or from any passion which is of sufficient strength to overpower the passion of fear and banish all thought of peril. In its popular sense, therefore, it may not only be associated with the worst of vices, but may have its origin in the basest of motives.

Indeed its best illustrations are to be found in the history of duelists, who hazard their lives and the happiness of their families, and with vindictive barbarity seek the life of a fellow man on false principles of honor, or merely to escape the suspicion of cowardice; or, in the history of pirates, who willingly brave every peril and commit every enormity merely to gratify an unhallowed lust for gain.

And as the effect partakes of the moral quality of the cause, a courage originating in such motives, though lauded by a corrupt public sentiment, cannot be otherwise than grossly immoral in its character and tendency, and unbecoming the true man.

Such courage we cannot recommend to you. We would not have you exhibit a spirit of brutal ferocity. We would not have you actuated by an insane disregard of consequences, or a savage prodigality of life. Be the soldier of enlightened principle — not of wild enthusiasm or malignant passion. Enter the conflict with an intelligent, deliberate fixedness of purpose: with an invincible resolution to do and suffer whatever the success of your cause may demand: with the spirit of a Christian, not of a demon.

Take as your model "the father of his country," our Washington — him to whose memory poetry and eloquence delight to pay the tribute of their homage, and to perpetuate whose fame the canvas glows and the marble speaks. In him you find an inflexibility of will which seven years of doubtful experiment could not swerve from its purpose: an iron nerve which the prospect of danger but strung to a higher tension: a fortitude which disaster and defeat, which the unspeakable sufferings even of a Valley Forge could not overcome: and above all an integrity and a devotion to right which no lure of ambition, no prospect of personal aggrandizement and glory could tempt to a violation of justice and mercy.

Be this your courage. Be his virtues the fire that shall warm your heart, the power that shall invigorate your arm, and the light that shall guide your steps. Be his renown your highest ambition, and his laurels your coveted reward.

To have this good courage it is essential that you have "the peace of God which passeth all understanding" in your hearts. You have within an immortal spirit — a spirit that shall outlive time, and be happy or miserable forever. And if your "heart is not right in the sight of God," already has the prospect of coming peril awakened within you a strange misgiving. You cannot be indifferent to the future. You cannot forget the terrible retributions of eternity. And while conscious that you are guilty before God, and convinced that death will be followed by banishment from His presence and from the glory of His power, whatever the strength of your nerve and the stoutness of your heart, the one will relax, the other will quail when the dreadful issue is confronted.

"A guilty conscience makes cowards of us all" — often palsies the arm when most its strength is needed, and overwhelms with disaster even in the moment of victory.

Often, indeed, is its victim panic-stricken and flying before dangers which exist only in his own imagination. But while "a sinful heart makes a feeble hand," conscious innocence is an impregnable bulwark of defense against all those ghostly fears and suspicions that "haunt the guilty mind" — a safeguard against mad passion, and the surest spring of that well-advised, yet vigorous action so essential to success in great emergencies.

And while it is incumbent upon us always "to have a conscience void of offence toward God, and toward men," now that you are about to hazard your life in the cause of your country, it is peculiarly important that you should at once secure forgiveness of sin and the favor of God.

Reared as most of you have been by godly parents, you cannot escape the remembrance of their pious admonitions. Persuaded as all of you are of the truth of the gospel, you cannot blot out the vision of its plagues. And with these clinging about your spirit you can but shudder and shrink back at the prospect of death. Oh, then, let the guilt of your past misdoing be cancelled by faith in the Son of God. Hasten without delay to the blessed Jesus!

Give Him no rest until He bids thee "Go in peace." Then mayest thou be strong, and quit thyself like a man. For if thou fallest, thou hast a higher life — a life which is "hid with Christ in God" — a life, whose joy and blessedness "no rude alarms of raging foes" can interrupt or destroy. Death in its most revolting form will but bring thee into possession of an eternal home of peace and rest.

It is true that some have imagined that religion is inconsistent with that contempt of danger and death so requisite to the good soldier. But let the life of a Washington, who was never greater than when on his knees, refute the objection. Let the history of a Havelock, at once the ornament of Christianity and the pride of the British army, noted no less for his piety than for his soldierly qualities, silence the infidel insinuation.

Or go to the bloody field of Manassas: behold the dauntless courage of the heroic Harrison: and hear him, after receiving the death-wound while nobly pouring out his heart's blood on the altar of liberty, faintly whispering of the love of Jesus and the hope of heaven! Yes, and ere the victors' shout rang o'er those plains, his spirit on the wings of the battle-cloud, sprang upward to God, shouting in its flight, "Victory! victory! over death and hell!"

And, oh, say not in view of that scene, a scene that might well thrill the heart of an angel, that the humble Christian, the child of God, cannot fight the battles of his country! Nay, "godliness is profitable unto all things": not only adorns and elevates the character of the votary of peace, not only lights up and beautifies the death-scenes of a quiet home, but showers her benefits and blessings amid the sterner realities of war, inspires the soldier of freedom with the loftiest patriotism, breathes into his heart the sublimest courage, and when he falls throws about him her grandest charms and scatters around his grave her richest perfumes.

Oh, be the soldier of Christ! Let this be the element of good in your courage. While on your banner may be inscribed Liberty's device, let there be another banner, all unseen yet even unfurled before the eye of your faith, on which is inscribed the reeking cross with its bleeding Victim encircled with the promises of the Gospel, and bright with the dawning glories of heaven. Then may you afford to be brave — to encounter embattled hosts — to encounter death itself! For that banner's magic inscription

> Lights life in death,
> Turns earth to heaven;
>
> to heavenly thrones transforms
> The ghastly ruins of the mouldering tomb!
> And falling beneath its folds,
> thou fallest but to rise again in triumph,
> incorruptible, glorious, immortal!

II. We may likewise learn a lesson with respect to the conduct that should characterize us in the field. "Let us behave ourselves valiantly." Courage has respect chiefly to our temper of mind, and is subjective in character. Valor has respect to our mode of action, and is objective. It is courage in exercise. The one is usually the concomitant of the other. He who is truly courageous in heart is seldom otherwise than valorous in action.

He who has that strength of will and firmness of purpose, that invincible fortitude and resolution, originating in an intelligent perception of right and duty, which are the essential elements of true courage, will seldom be wanting in vigorous action when the good of his cause demands exertion, or shrink from danger when it demands exposure.

But however necessary and commendable individual valor may be, in a great contest in which tens of thousands are engaged, it can be of but little real benefit unless it be subject to control and exhibited in the execution of some established plan.

An army without a commander is usually worthless. And an incompetent commander, one who has not sufficient merit to inspire confidence, and sufficient nerve to exact obedience is oftener an injury than an advantage to the cause which he espouses. There must of necessity be in every army a ruling mind: one planning, directing, controlling all.

Otherwise, in the conflict of opinions and plans naturally arising from the absence of all control, and in that disorder and confusion of action which such conflict will occasion, there will exist the elements of certain disaster. A body of men, all governed by one mind, may effect in a few hours that which the same number, each acting independently of the other, could not accomplish in a lifetime.

It is, therefore, not only wise, but necessary to your efficiency, that for the time you surrender your will to that of your officers, and they in turn to their superiors, and all yielding an implicit obedience to the incumbent of the highest office, be intent simply on the execution of his orders.

This lesson of submission to control is a difficult one for many to learn; but until you have completely mastered it, though you may be individually brave, yet as an integral part of a great army, you are not prepared to behave yourself the most valiantly and the most efficiently in the field of conflict.

It is necessary, too, that you keep a perpetual curb on those passions which, in a contest like this, are so apt to be awakened and cherished. You may perceive the effects of ungoverned passion around you on almost every day. You see it in the child who inflicts a severer punishment on himself in his effort to punish the stone which he imagines has done him injury.

You see it in the conduct of the man whose heart is fired with jealousy or burning with revenge. You see it everywhere blinding the understanding, overpowering the reason, stilling the voice of conscience, disqualifying its victim for all deliberate action, and leading to the perpetration of deeds at which even fallen humanity shudders.

You feel that your country is insulted and outraged. You behold her pleasant places made desolate by an infidel and fanatical foe. Her honor is your honor. Her insults, her injuries, her destiny, all are yours. And it is but natural that there should spring up in your heart, not simply a feeling of indignation, but a burning desire to be revenged on her enemies and despoilers. But curb that vindictive spirit.

Tis the spirit of the savage, not of the Christian hero: a spirit condemned alike by reason and religion, and which, unless checked, when the hour of conflict comes will precipitate you into dangers which reason would have escaped, and perhaps sacrifice a life which reason would have saved.

Your enemies may need the spur of the basest passions of their nature to give them a heart for their wicked work. You need it not. And he, indeed, must be a miserable craven, who, in a contest like this, has need of the excitement of passion or any artificial stimulus to nerve him for the onset. No. "Bid tumultuous passions all be still." Let reason have her sway. Recollect,

> Tis reason your great Captain holds so dear;
> Tis reason's injured rights his wrath resents;
> Tis reason's voice obey'd his glories crown;
> To give lost reason life, He poured his own.

Remember that you are Christians, and are struggling for the most precious boon, save the Son of God, ever bestowed on the children of men; and even in the midst of carnage and blood, let the Word and grace of Christ dwell richly in your heart, and the good pleasure of your God absorb every other motive and govern every impulse and effort.

And thus armed against confusion and panic by a wholesome discipline, and against the excesses and dangers of unbridled passions by reason and religious principle, with the determination of men who act from an unshaken conviction of the righteousness of their cause — with that determination which takes no step backward, relying upon God's arm for your support and His shield for your protection, move forward with the song of David as your battle-shout:

"God is our refuge and strength, a very present help in trouble. Therefore will we not fear, though the earth be removed, and though the mountains be carried into the midst of the sea"!

Your comrades on the right and left may bite the dust. You too may fall. But animated by this spirit, and falling in this spirit, all around you are the bright-winged messengers of God, ready to catch away your spirit and bear it in triumph above the tumult and storm of battle to the mansions of the redeemed.

III. We learn from the text a lesson of dependence upon God, and of submissiveness to the dispensations of His providence. "Let the Lord do that which is good in his sight." He is not an idle and uninterested spectator of the events that are transpiring in our land. He is not indifferent to the fate of the nations of the earth, nor to the wants and destiny even of the most insignificant of His creatures.

By Him "kings rule and princes decree judgment." "He doeth according to his will in the armies of heaven and among the inhabitants of earth." The universe, in all its measureless extent, is filled with the light, the power, and glory of His presence; and from the flaming archangel to the minutest insect, from the blazing sun to the imperceptible atom, all are upheld continually "by the word of His power." And let Him withdraw himself but for a moment, and creation, animate and inanimate, becomes at once a chaotic wreck.

What then more befitting His creatures, whose every blessing is from His infinite bounty and whose every breath is from His hand, than that they should carry about them continually a conviction of His presence, and a spirit of dependence on the decisions of His righteous will? "Go to now, ye that say, Today, or tomorrow we will go into such a city, and continue there a year, and buy, and sell, and get gain: whereas ye know not what shall be on the morrow — For that ye ought to say, If the Lord will, we shall live, and do this or that."

And "go to now," ye that build your hopes of triumph on the strength of your own arms, or the courage of your hearts, without regard to the will and providence of God: whereas ye know not that the next hour your eye may have lost its fire, your arm be palsied, and your heart still in death. For that ye ought to say, ALL our sufficiency is of God; the fortunes and events of war are all at His disposal; and if He will, victory shall perch upon our banners.

Saith the wise man: "Pride goeth before destruction and a haughty spirit before a fall." Said a greater than he: "Whosoever exalteth himself shall be abased." If as a people we have any thing to fear, it is the spirit that possessed the Assyrian monarch when he ascribed the splendor of his capital and the glory of his kingdom to the power of his own might — a spirit which God signally punished by driving him from men and compelling him to dwell with the beasts and eat grass like an ox.

If we look simply to the chivalry of the South, if we rely simply on the fiery valor of her sons for success, and ascribe all the glory of our victories, as we are prone to do, to our military chieftains, we may expect God to humble our pride and punish our impudent vainglory, by withdrawing His support and covering us with defeat.

He is God and there is none other beside Him, and on nothing is he more resolved than that men shall every where acknowledge his sovereignty. "I will be exalted among the heathen, I will be exalted in the earth." It is therefore our highest wisdom, yea, the noblest patriotism to cultivate a spirit of dependence upon Him, and while exerting ourselves to the utmost, look simply to Him for the success of our efforts and the prosperity of our cause.

And not simply dependence, but an attitude of perfect submission to the disposal of God is not only most becoming our condition, but the surest way to secure the accomplishment of the end we seek. It is thus that we are brought into union with Him — have access to his sympathy and exhaustless resources.

It is thus that we become parties to that covenant in which He declares, "I am the Lord thy God, the Holy One of Israel, thy Saviour. When thou passest through the waters, I will be with thee; and through the rivers, they shall not overflow thee: when thou walkest through the fire, thou shalt not be burned, neither shall the flame kindle upon thee."

And since in His hands are the issues of life and death, of victory and overthrow, since, whatever we may do, He will control our affairs according to the good pleasure of His own will, and since by submission we secure the benedictions of His grace, the guidance of His Spirit, and an interest in His special providential care, what so wise as a hearty surrender of our cause, and our all, to Him! True, He "resisteth the proud" and self-sufficient, and is resolved to crush out all rebellion and opposition to His will. But He "giveth grace to the humble," and honors their humility with His peculiar favor and blessing.

Then let life or death, let success or disappointment be the issue of this dreadful conflict, still let us say, "Let the Lord do that which is good in his sight." Though our homes may be invaded and dishonored, though our loved ones may be afflicted, and weep, and mourn, though throughout our land is heard the clanking of the despot's chains, and seen the blight of the despot's touch, still let the language of our hearts be, "Not my will but thine, oh God, be done"!

And surely if any one has need of the constant protecting care and power of an almighty hand, that one is the soldier. The admonition, "Boast not thyself of tomorrow; for thou knowest not what a day may bring forth," may be addressed to him with a peculiar propriety and force. For of him is it pre-eminently true that

> Dangers stand thick through all the ground
> To push him to the tomb.

And although he may escape the missiles of the foe, the air which he breathes is loaded with disease; and often when he thinks himself the most secure, the enemy is fixing its deadly fangs in his vitals. Oh, then, humbly submit yourselves to God! Seek shelter "in the secret place of the Most High," that you may find protection from "the arrow that flieth by day," and "the pestilence that walketh in darkness."

Let the God of Jacob be your God, His will your will, and his glory your end. Then may you claim that promise which saith, "A thousand shall fall at thy side, and ten thousand at thy right hand; but it shall not come nigh thee. Only with thine eyes shalt thou behold and see the reward of the wicked."

IV. The objects for which you contend are of sufficient importance to inspire you with a good courage, and stimulate you to behave yourselves valiantly: of sufficient importance to induce you to cultivate that spirit, and make whatever self-sacrifices may be necessary to your success.

You are actuated by no thirst for power, no desire for the gain and glory of conquest, no disposition to encroach on the rights and disturb the peace of the innocent and unoffending. No sacking of cities, no rapine and plunder enter into your program. Your mission is to repel lawless invasion, to avenge national injuries and vindicate the national honor.

We fight "for our people." The avowed purpose of our enemies is our subjugation, the extinction of liberty in our land: an end which they profess to be resolved to accomplish though it bring desolation to every home and "baptize every foot of Southern soil in fire and blood": a purpose which savors more of the heartlessness of an Alexander, or the barbarity of an Attila than of the civilization of the nineteenth century.

And hitherto their conduct has been characterized by a vandalism, a rapacity, and a contempt for virtue and religion perfectly accordant with their savage purpose.

To save those we love from their indignities — to shield our gray-haired sires and honored mothers, our noble wives and lovely daughters, our tender children and faithful servants, from the wanton violence of a despotism whose deeds would disgrace the annals of the Middle Ages; to drive from our soil the propagandists of principles subversive of all social order and domestic happiness; to secure to ourselves and transmit to our posterity the blessings bought by the blood of our fathers — these are the objects for which we contend — this the work to which God and every interest of humanity calls us.

Yea, our all has been staked on the issue of the struggle; and before us now is naught but the palm of the victor, or the chains of the slave and the doom of the traitor; naught but the liberty to think, and speak, and act for ourselves — the enjoyment of the inherent rights of every virtuous and intelligent people, or the holding of our property, our opinions, our lives, at the will of an unscrupulous and unprincipled tyranny.

To protect our people from the one, and establish them in the enjoyment of the other, is our simple desire and aim. This is the cause for which you are to battle — the cause to which our patriot sires pledged their lives, their fortunes, and their sacred honor: the cause, too, to which our fathers' God has hitherto given the encouragement of His smiles and the help of His hand.

Nor is this all. We fight "for the cities of our God." Ah, that allusion of the Jewish general must have thrilled his hearer, and given an intenser glow to the patriotic fire of his heart. Our God! the God of our fathers, who brought them out of Egypt with a high hand and a stretched out arm, who gave them bread from heaven forty years, guided them in their wanderings by a "fiery, cloudy pillar," and led them at last into this goodly land — the God who has chosen us as His peculiar people, made us the repository of His will and the light of the world — the God who has ever been about us as a wall of fire, a strong tower of defense, and who has lavished upon us the richest gifts of His love — His honor is assailed, and His majesty despised by these idolatrous Ammonites!

And the cities of our God! Their pleasant places, their peaceful homes and stately palaces, their vine-clad bowers and dancing fountains, where innocence sports and happiness lives — Jerusalem which he hath chosen, and Mt. Zion where his glory dwelleth — all are threatened with desecration and ruin! Then let us be valiant for Israel and for Israel's God!

You have the same motive to inspire your hearts and quicken your ardor. The cause of Christ, the interests of religion are involved in this direful conflict. The men in high places, the manufacturers of public opinion among our adversaries are avowedly the advocates of a higher law than the Bible. As a natural consequence, the leaven of infidelity is at work through all the ramifications of Northern society. Among the intelligent and among the ignorant, in the pulpit and in the parlor, in the bar-room and in the counting-house it is found, preying with an insidious but deadly virulence on morality and religion.

We would not do them injustice: but we believe that no people equally enlightened have ever originated and fostered so many infidel delusions; that nowhere has there been such a general degradation of the sacred office of the ministry to the purposes of fanaticism; that no people of equal religious privileges combine in their character and exhibit in their conduct so much that is inconsistent with that law which is "holy, just, and good."

And the great principle which seems now to animate every heart, and on the supremacy of which they seem determined, may be shown to lead, and in a multitude of instances has already led to an open rejection of the Word of God.

President Mahan, a man of learning, a Doctor of Divinity, uses these ominous words: "We are constrained to admit either that slavery is right or the Bible not of God. If I felt myself forced to take one or the other of these positions, I freely confess that for one I should take the latter."

When ministers of the gospel of high position and influence can thus proclaim to the world their readiness to sacrifice the Word of God rather than the principle of abolitionism, we need not wonder that among the masses that Word should fall into disrepute and contempt.

We refuse to admit that principle. And in resisting its forcible intrusion upon us, we are but refusing to surrender the principles of revelation for the falsehoods and deceit of a vain philosophy.

Only to yield to the idea of the fallibility of the Bible by admitting its error, or surrendering its teachings on this one subject, and the way is open for the rejection of whatever it enjoins that comes in conflict with human opinions and passions. Its authority is gone, its wholesome laws are of none effect, and its precious promises and inspiring hopes more baseless than the "fabric of a vision." We are afloat upon the ocean of existence without an anchor, without a pilot, without chart or compass, at the mercy of every storm, and the sport of every demon.

No, no! In God's name, give me the Bible, whatever it may cost and whatever it may enjoin! Say it is unworthy of credit if you please. Say its religion is but a dream. Ah, then, tis the sweetest delusion that ever entered the brain, or enchained the heart of a mortal! Tis a delusion that makes me strangely happy in life and gloriously triumphant in death! Tis all that makes life a blessing — tis my only support amid earth's sorrows — my only guide to eternity!

Yes, give me such a delusion rather than life itself. And, oh, let me hand it down to my children, the charm unbroken, that they too may enjoy some of its sweetness and reap some of its blessed fruits!

Nay, but the Ammonites are upon us with their strange gods. They would dispel the delusion. They would dissolve the charm. They would undermine the authority of my Bible. They would desecrate the temples of our God, and infuse into a pure Christianity the poison of their own infidelity.

You go to contribute to the salvation of your country from such a curse. You go to aid in the glorious enterprise of rearing in our sunny South a temple to constitutional liberty and Bible Christianity. You go to fight for your people and for the cities of your God. And though it may cost us many a tear of sorrow, we bid you Godspeed in your noble work.

Our prayers shall follow you wherever you go. But not more earnestly will we pray for your protection and safe return, than that you may "be of good courage, and behave yourselves valiantly for your people and for the cities of your God." May God's providence preserve you. May His grace dwell richly in your hearts by faith. May his glory be the aim and object of your life. May His love and smiles be your reward here, and a happy immortality your inheritance forever.

Be just, and fear not;
Let all the ends thou aim'st at, be thy country's,
Thy God's and truth's; then, if thou fall'st,
Thou fall'st a blessed martyr.

1862

# New Wine Not To Be Put Into Old Bottles

*A SERMON*

PREACHED IN CHRIST CHURCH, SAVANNAH,

On Friday, February 28th, 1862,

BEING THE DAY OF

HUMILIATION, FASTING, AND PRAYER

Appointed by

the President of the Confederate States

BY THE

Rt. Rev. STEPHEN ELLIOTT, D. D.

RECTOR OF CHRIST CHURCH, AND BISHOP OF THE DIOCESE OF GEORGIA.

"And no man putteth new wine into old bottles." — St. Luke 5:27.

1862

## To the Clergy of the Diocese of Georgia.

THE PRESIDENT OF THE CONFEDERATE STATES having issued his Proclamation appointing Friday, the 28th of February, instant, as a day of solemn humiliation before God, in view of His manifold mercies towards us as a nation and of our great unworthiness of them —

Now therefore, I, STEPHEN ELLIOTT, Bishop of the Protestant Episcopal Church in the Diocese of Georgia, do direct the Clergy of the said Diocese to invite their congregations to assemble together in their respective places of worship, and to keep the Fast before the Lord in all humility of mind and spirit, and while deprecating the wrath of God for our past sins, to invoke His blessing upon the new Government which has been so successfully inaugurated.

Upon the occasion of this Fast, the Clergy will use the subjoined service:

- Morning Prayer as usual to the Psalter.

- Psalms for the day — the 13th, 56th and 94th.

- 1st Lesson — II Kings ch. 18, from v. 17, and ch. 19 to v. 8.

- 2d Lesson — I Peter, ch. 2 vv. 11–18.

Use the whole Litany, and immediately before the General Thanksgiving, introduced the Prayers following:

### PRAYER

O most mighty Lord God, who reignest over all the kingdoms of men; who hast power in Thy hand to cast down and to raise up, to save Thy servants and to rebuke their enemies, let Thine ears be now open unto our prayers and Thy merciful eyes upon our trouble and our danger.

O Lord, do Thou judge our cause in righteousness and mercy, and wherein soever we have offended against Thee, or injured our neighbor, make us truly sensible of it and deeply penitent for it. We humbly confess that we are unworthy of the manifold goodness vouchsafed us in this struggle for our rights, yet we are bold, because of Thy long suffering, to pray for the continuance of it and to supplicate Thy blessing upon us and our arms.

Cover the heads of our soldiers in the day of battle, and send Thy fear before them, that our enemies may flee at their presence. Establish us in the rights Thou has given us, in our Government and in our Laws, in our Religion, and in all our holy Ministries.

The race is not to the swift, nor the battle to the strong, but our trust is in the name of the Lord our God. Hear us, O Lord, for the glory of Thy name and for Thy truth's sake, through Jesus Christ our Lord. Amen.

### PRAYER.

Almighty God, who rulest over all the nations of the earth and disposest of them according to Thy good pleasure, we yield Thee unfeigned thanks that Thou hast been pleased to bring these CONFEDERATE STATES in safety to the close of the first year of their political existence, and that Thou hast preserved Thy servant, THE PRESIDENT OF THIS CONFEDERACY, in health of body and vigor of mind to the commencement of his administration as the Chief Magistrate of our now settled government.

Let Thy wisdom be his guide, and let Thine arm strengthen him; let justice, truth and holiness, and all those virtues that adorn the Christian profession flourish in his days; direct all his counsels and endeavors to Thy glory and the welfare of these States; and give us grace to obey his government cheerfully and willingly for conscience sake, that neither our sinful passions nor our private interests may disappoint his cares for the public good; let his administration be prosperous and honorable, and crown him with immortality in the world to come through Jesus Christ our Lord. Amen.

# A Sermon

ST. LUKE 5:37-39.

"And no man putteth new wine into old bottles, else the new wine will burst the bottles and be spilled, and the bottles shall perish.

"But new wine must be put into new bottles, and both are preserved.

"No man also having drunk old wine straightway desireth new: for he saith, the old is better."

The meeting of Congress and the inauguration of a President under our permanent Constitution, have ushered us upon a new era in our national history, and in the wise judgment of our Chief Magistrate, afford a fitting opportunity for once more humbling ourselves before the mercy-seat, and invoking the blessing of the Christian's God upon our new Government and upon the conduct of our civil and military affairs.

We are learning the sublime truth of our daily dependence upon God, and we are learning it, where only it can be learned, in the school of adversity and affliction. Happy nation! which frequently and hopefully bows itself in prayer and supplication at the throne of Grace, for it is at least an outward and visible sign that we hear the rod and who has appointed it!

At such a moment it is well for us to pause in the wild career of action and consider profoundly the great principles which must lie at the foundation of our national structure, ere we may feel assured that it is builded upon a rock.

It is indeed, as Jeremy Taylor expresses it, meditating upon the outskirts of a camp, but that is better than not to meditate at all. Our whole future will depend upon the first years of our political existence, and we must weigh our position now, even amid the tumult and confusion of war, or let it depend upon chance or fortune.

All nations which come into existence at this late period of the world must be born amid the storm of revolution, and must win their way to a place in history through the baptism of blood. And this, because no people would ever throw off a beneficent government, and an oppressive one will always strive to perpetuate its tyranny by arms and violence.

If we wait, therefore, for peace, ere we ask counsel of God and wisdom from His throne, we shall permit the molding process of our future to have been finished ere we examine the form and shape which it is likely to put on. Our new wine will have found its way into old bottles ere we shall have duly considered the folly of such a course, and our labor and suffering may have been in vain and for nought.

We look very superficially at the revolution through which we are passing, when we consider merely the immediate causes which have produced it, and go no further back in our analysis. To say that the movement which has brought into existence the new Government, whose inauguration we have just commemorated, was made necessary by the avarice and fanaticism of an ever increasing sectional majority, is to speak the truth; but that measure of it only which lies upon the surface. Sterner questions lie behind that.

How happened it that among a Christian people, of Anglo-Saxon lineage, trained in all the great principles of English liberty, with every appliance of knowledge and experience — experience, moreover, worked out by their own ancestors — such vices should so early have gained such supremacy?

How did it come to pass that constitutional law should so completely have lost its power, that the moral sense of the nation should have been so drugged, that its Christianity should have exerted no vital influence over its actions?

Seventy years to terminate a nation's existence! Why Rome existed eight hundred years before she reached the culminating point of her greatness. It is now a thousand years since England commenced her career of power and of fame. Russia is only "mewing her mighty youth," although she has already outlived our age by centuries.

By what fatality is it that we have become effete at so early a period; that we were corrupt to the core ere we were well out of the bud; that, like a young spendthrift, we have wasted health, vigor, virtue, in our earliest manhood, and are already decrepit and breaking up under the diseases which belong only to old age?

Alas! that we should have to answer such appalling questions; to answer them, too, in the midst of the tumultuous and terrible results which they have naturally brought about. But they must be answered, or else we shall gain nothing from the revolution through which we are passing; shall reap no fruits from the seed which we are fructifying with the rich blood of our children.

It will not do to say that we were only the offshoot of a long existing nation, and that we came into being with its infirmities cleaving to us, and not with the vigor of a fresh and buoyant life. Tis true, husbandmen say that a graft from a tree, however young and living it may be, will droop and wither when its parent stem shall perish; but alas for us, our Fatherland is still mighty in its power, is still overshadowing the world with its wings of protection and of glory.

We have not decayed because England has decayed. We have not fallen to pieces like a house builded upon the sand, because the winds and the waves have swept her into oblivion. She is stronger today in her law, in her religion, in her arms, in her arts, than when we tore ourselves away from her motherhood. She yet rejoices in all the freedom which has been her birthright for centuries, and evinces no token that her eye is dim or her natural force abated.

If we would excuse our early decrepitude, we must find some other reason than one drawn from our having sprung from a people which had reached the spring tide of its glory. If the graft has withered, we must rather look for its blight from the stock upon which it has been grafted, for the parent stem, the oak of old England, still spreads its arms in ever increasing grandeur, defiant of the storms which rage incessant around its incorrupt heart.

Nor can we truly affirm that our early decay has sprung from the rapid influx upon our shores of foreign elements, which have overborne the native influence and subjected it to its control. The tides of avarice and of fanaticism which have swept over our fair heritage and changed it into a desolation, have flowed in upon us from the most ancient and best civilized of our States, and have ever found their increasing momentum from those peculiarly native fountains.

The Europeans who have settled the western States, and who have filled our cities, have been finally made their tools, but only after they had been deceived and made to believe that their own liberties were in danger from the slavery of the South.

They have given power to the destructive flood which has borne away all the barriers of constitutional law, but only as a lake whose waters have been turned by human art into the channels of the natural stream. What knew they, the simple-minded peasants of Germany and Scandinavia, of our political questions, until they were indoctrinated by the pestilent demagogues who undertook to introduce them to the tree of knowledge?

What cared they, the laughing, careless emigrants from the green fields of the Emerald Isle, about such points as have wrecked our Union, until wily politicians sat, like the toad at the ear of Eve, and whispered sin and mischief to their untutored souls? The disgrace of this early and incomparable corruption is our own, born of the soil, springing rank from the principles which were laid at the basis of our political nationality. We cannot get rid of it.

We cannot shuffle it off upon those who are as innocent of it as a deceived and cheated accessory is innocent of a crime into which he has been unwittingly drawn. We must bear it ourselves in the face of the world and evince our shame by clearing our skirts of it, and our penitence, by putting our new wine into new bottles.

Nor can we shield ourselves from the scorn of the world by affirming that this revolution has arisen out of political causes alone, and not out of moral causes; for they have eyes and can see, ears and can hear, minds and can understand.

I affirm that this revolution was as much a moral as a political necessity; that corruption had become deep-seated in philosophy, in letters, in ethics, in religion as well as in politics; that it had found its way into commerce and trade, and finance and social life; that cunning and trickery were becoming the normal conditions of intercourse, and that morals were fast losing their hold upon the public mind.

There is no instance upon record of such a rapid moral deterioration of a nation as has taken place in ours in the last forty years. Growing in all the elements of political and economical greatness at a pace unexampled among nations, their increase was not faster than the corruption which they engendered. So soon as the stern, honest, uncompromising men of the Revolution — men who had been trained under other principles — passed away, the new order of things began to manifest itself in political circles, and from them extended to the press, to the legislative chambers, to the primary assemblies of the people, and, finally, to the last bulwarks of every nation, the judiciary and the pulpit.

It became almost impossible to resist the torrent of evil, and men at last began to call good evil and evil good, sweet bitter, and bitter sweet, against their own better sense and wiser consciences. What was expedient was right; what was popular was just; what was low and cunning was smiled upon, if only it chanced to be successful. No government could endure under such a condition of things. No people could work out any destiny, but discord and anarchy, with such principles festering at its heart.

What has happened was inevitable. The irrepressible conflict between the slave and the hireling brought it to a point, but if that had never existed, some other discord would have arisen, which would have rent asunder a people, that, even in its yet early manhood, had exhibited and gloried in the vices of a nation tottering to its fall.

The question then recurs: "In what are we to find the causes of this rapid corruption and this early moral obliquity? What has made it necessary, ere a century has elapsed, to remold our institutions, and to look with dismay upon our late fellow-citizens, as they yield up to passion all their constitutional guarantees and bow, without a struggle, before the decrees of a maddened people?"

And my answer is: "We can find them in the principles upon which we planted our Government; principles which have reacted upon our whole social life; upon our politics, upon our literature, upon our morals, upon our religion, upon our homes. They were false and unscriptural, and have worked out very soon the inevitable law, 'That whatsoever a man soweth, that shall he also reap.'"

The principle upon which we rested our Revolution, that "taxation without representation is tyranny," was clearly true, and our forefathers were right in resisting its exercise and in meeting its encroachments at the very earliest moment.

The time had come, likewise, when it was well for us to manage our own affairs, and to be independent of other nations. But there was no necessity to cast to the winds all conservatism and to lay down principles, as the foundation of our Government, which were contrary to Revelation, and, therefore, to Truth.

Carried away by our opposition to monarchy and an established Church, we declared war against all authority and against all form. The reason of man was exalted to an impious degree, and in the face not only of experience, but of the revealed word of God, all men were declared to be created equal, and man was pronounced capable of self-government.\*

Two greater falsehoods could not have been announced — falsehoods, because the one struck at the whole constitution of civil society as it had ever existed, and because the other virtually denied the fall and corruption of man.

If man is capable of[5] self-government, what need of any government at all? If man is wise enough and virtuous enough to manage not only his own affairs, but to conduct with brotherly love — loving his neighbor as himself — all his relations with his fellow man, why such an apparatus of machinery as is every where required for the administration of justice?

Man is not capable of self-government because be is a fallen creature, and interest, passion, ambition, lust, sway him far more than reason or honor. As for equality among men, whether by creation or birth, or in any other way, it is a miserable *ignis fatuus*, not worthy to be followed, even for the purpose of exposure.

Upon principles as false and as foolish as these was our late Government founded, and although wise men attempted to place conservative barriers around their exercise, and did preserve them, during their life time, against the working of the principles which were perpetually undermining them, when they passed away, the process of demolition fairly commenced, and it required but a man's life time — and that not a long one — to place every thing that was valuable in home and in society at the mercy of the demagogues, who sounded these false doctrines in the ears of an irresponsible multitude.

Like the spawn of error in Spenser's allegory, the moment they were born, they began to gnaw upon the vitals of their mother. If all men are created equal, (thus consequentially did they carry out the principle), then should there be no classification of society, no master and no slave, no capitalist

---

[5] As this expression may be susceptible of misconception, inasmuch as any Government which may be framed by a people, however well checked and balanced, is to a certain extent self-government, I would state that my argument is directed against that doctrine which blasphemously affirms the "*vox populi*" to be the "*vox Dei*," and which would maintain that the will of a majority must always be right and should always rule — a doctrine from which we have been just forced to escape.

and no workman, no rich and no poor, no learned and no ignorant.

If all men are created equal, then is the Governor no better, no wiser, no more to be honored than the governed; then is the Judge to be no more learned, no more experienced, no more reverenced, than the parties at the bar; then is the Priest to be no more holy, no more educated in sacred things, no more consecrated to his divine office, than the people; then is the father to be as the child, and the grey hair and the reverend form to be upon a level with the presumptuous youth.

If man is capable of self-government, then is the whole framework of civil society to be arranged by the will of a majority; then are no guarantees necessary for life or for property; then are rulers from the highest to the lowest to be placed or displaced by caprice or faction; then is the sacred ermine of justice to be dragged through the mire of party, and to be soiled by all the miserable influences of selfishness.

Such are the legitimate fruits of these principles, and they have been produced to the destruction of our country. Like the apples of Sodom, they were fair to the eye and looked bright and healthful, but they have turned to ashes in the mouth. To our cost have we found that they would be utterly destructive not only to our interests, but to the peace of our whole social life, and we have withdrawn from those, who were prepared to carry them out to their full desolation, and to make us the first victims of their triumphant exercise.

This picture has not been overdrawn. It is the stern truth, and is witnessed to by the condition of society wherever they have had full sway. Among us they have been partially checked in their operation by our adherence to the doctrine of State Sovereignty and by the institution of slavery, which has forced upon us a certain measure of conservatism.

The falseness of these principles was too glaring to us to permit us to be entirely carried away by them. But even we have felt their influence in those arrangements of society which were not immediately connected with our local interests or local institutions. Where is there, even among us, guarded and protected as we have been, any reverence for age, or authority, or experience? What boy is there who does not think himself capable of self-government, fit for any position; who is not quite ready to sneer at the past and to consider the wisdom of the old as the dotage of infirmity?

What man is there who does not deem himself qualified to fill any office, or to discuss and criticize any matter, even though he may never have applied an hour's study or a moment's thought upon it? What politician will dare to stand up and tell the people that they are wrong, or fill the breach when they rush to the assault upon any of the institutions of the land?

What power has philosophy or morals, or even religion, against the popular will? Have not all the conservative influences of our General and State Governments been progressively overturned, and new doctrines, all based upon these principles, been worked into the public opinion of the people?

It is fearful to perceive what a low tone of ethics pervades our literature and our press; how morality has been dissevered from religion; how all form, which at last is the embodiment of spirit, is ridiculed and scorned. And when we read our Bibles, and note the catalogue of vices which St. Paul said should characterize the perilous times of the last days, we shudder at the number of them which have been the legitimate fruits of our national principles.

"This know also," writes he," that in the last days perilous times shall come, for men shall be lovers of their own selves, covetous, boasters, proud, blasphemers, disobedient to parents, unthankful, unholy, false accusers, incontinent, fierce, despisers of those that are good, heady, high-minded, lovers of pleasure more than lovers of God; having the form of godliness, but denying the power thereof."

Of his whole catalogue I have omitted but three classes, which may yet be developed, ere our struggle is at an end: "Without natural affection, truce breakers and traitors." Is not this enough to make us tremble? Does it not bear out every thing which I have written and spoken this day? Well for us that we have burst the bonds which bound us to such principles! Better for us, if we shall be able, by the grace of God and the virtue which is left in us, to put our "new wine into new bottles."

It is useless, upon these days of humiliation, in which we come before God to repent of our national sins, to spend our confession and our penitence upon the mere excrescences which show themselves upon the surface. It is a mockery of God, who looks far beneath that surface, and who sees and knows that a corrupt tree can never bring forth good fruit.

He expects us to pierce to the core, to dig down and stir up to the very roots whence spring these wretched consequences. Unless we do this, He will not help us. "Be not deceived; God is not mocked." He sees where the difficulty is, at what door the sin lies, and He sees, moreover, that we know it, and have not the courage to avow it. But unless we do confess it and humble ourselves before Him, and ask Him to remove away from us these idols of "human reason," and "man's natural virtue," all our present struggles shall be in vain; our valor, our sacrifices, our own blood and the blood of our children, shall all have been spent for naught.

The new wine will burst the old bottles and be spilled, and the old bottles shall perish, the example and scorn of the world. Let those whom we have left go on, if they please — but God forbid, for their sakes, that they should — upon such infidel principles; but let us, now that we have the opportunity, retrace our steps, and take once more to our arms the word of God and the wisdom of God.

But you may ask: "To what does all this tend? Shall we go back to monarchy, to aristocracy, to an established Church?" Better, far better that, than to run into anarchy, pass through the fierce fires of infidelity and licentiousness, and then end in a stern military despotism. But neither is necessary. The form of a Government is not the important point; it is the principles.

Republicanism has not saved us from tyranny and oppression, and monarchy has not deprived England of freedom. The cruelty of any king is tender mercies to the cruelty of an unbridled multitude. It is not the shape which the Government has taken that is our danger; nay, that arrangement of wheel within wheel, of a State Government exercising sovereign powers within a General Government, has been our preservation, the very ark of our safety.

It is the principles which lie at the foundation of a Government and which will flow out from that Government and pervade every department of civil and social life, that is our peril. Poland was a monarchy, but the principle of equality among the nobles produced precisely the like consequences as those which have sprung from the principle of equality here.

The remedy is not in any change of Government, but in the modification of principles, which, having the prestige of authority, have influenced the whole spirit of the people, and have rendered irreverence, insubordination, presumption, recklessness, of the very essence of the national character. Like Laocoon and his children, we have been enfolded and crushed by the serpents which have issued from our own altars.

We must go back to the principles of the Bible, if we would find our permanent remedy, and reject as infidel any faith in man's virtuous self-government, any idea that society or government can exist without due classification. Subordination reigns supreme in Heaven, and it must reign supreme on earth. Subordination, not inferiority; they are very different things.

The one is the obedience and the reverence of duty; the other of degradation. The one finds honor and glory in being true and faithful to its position; the other has no merit, because it fills but its own proper place. The one has sublime examples in the subordination of the Church to Christ, in the subordination of the Son of God to his Almighty Father; the other has its illustrations only in the natural gradation of created things. Without this discrimination between subordination and inferiority, there can be no highly civilized society. It is the support of all authority, the true moral principle of all order in social life.

When the Spartan youths all rose upon the entrance of an old man into their assembly, they exhibited the true meaning of subordination, and honored themselves while they displayed the high principles of their civilization, Pagans though they were.

In this country there is nothing to keep man in check except the principles which he himself may lay at the foundation of his government, and which may extend their influence through all the phases of social life. Military power is the arm of despotism for preserving order. We know, except in war, no such instrument. We are dependent upon the people themselves for the preservation of order, and unless they shall be trained to be the guardians of law, there can be no law.

When the very principles upon which a Government and its civilization rest lead inevitably to disorder and to irreverence, how can you look for the virtues which are the only support of any Government? You may as well expect grapes from thorns or figs from thistles.

The remedy for all this lies not in any change in the form of our Government, but in persuading ourselves, who are the people, to surround ourselves once more with Constitutional arrangements, which shall be a bulwark against our own capricious or passionate impulses, and which shall give the lie to any demagogue who shall attempt to persuade us that we are capable at all times of governing ourselves, and that every one of us is the equal of his fellow.

We should at once endeavor to put it out of our own power to corrupt ourselves, by laying down fundamental propositions of the most conservative character, and adhering to them through good report and through evil report. If in this moment of our soberness and of our sadness, we could break up our old bottles, and put our wine into new bottles, framed out of stuff which has stood the experience of ages, we should have cause to bless this revolution all the days of our history.

"But as no man having drunk old wine straightway desireth new, for he saith the old is better," the question comes up by what means may these old principles be done away with and new ones be introduced? And I rejoice to say that already have our Governments, both State and Confederate, made some movements in the direction of Faith and of conservatism.

The recognition of God in our Constitution — would it had been a clear, plain recognition of Christ — is in itself a step almost equivalent to that which France made in her reaction from atheism to Christianity. We have scarcely realized, my Christian hearers, what was the position of the old Government in its relation to God. It was as atheistic as France in her worst days of wild revolution.

The Goddess of Reason, 'tis true, was not paraded through our streets and personified in the high seats of legislation under the form of an harlot, but God was as completely ignored and the perfectibility of man placed in his stead. No such thing is on record any where in the world, whether among barbarian or civilized people, that a nation had no recognized God!

We deem it the height of superstition, when we read of the Pantheon at Rome, in which were gathered all the Gods of all the nations, that honor might be done to all. But what was our country, as it stood under the old Constitution, but a Pantheon, in which every man worshipped his own idol and demanded the protection of the Government in his folly?

Thank God, we have washed out that stain, and if we have not yet distinctly proclaimed ourselves a Christian nation, we are at least a nation of Theists — men who recognize the presence of God in the affairs of the world. That is a point gained; a step out of darkness into light; and for that He may bless us and give us more light. We need it sadly upon our path, for we have to tread our way back, through peril and blood, to the great principles of faith and honesty, which underlie all well established Governments.

Already have our people willingly laid down upon the altar of their country some of the false principles which they had been tempted to try, and have evinced a willingness to distrust themselves. May the good work go on until our children shall regain what we have lost; until authority shall be reverenced, because it is ordained of God; until justice shall be made independent of either money or faction; until religion shall throw aside its mere spiritualism, and shall become the conservator of morals as well as a guide to Heaven.

It may be that the bloody war in which we are engaged is necessary for our purification. War is a fearful scourge, as God's word plainly tells us; but it may sanctify as well as chasten, it may purge out our old dross, even though it be through the fires of affliction. It may be our moral as well as our political safety.

The infidel principles which I have been discussing have, even in a century, struck deep root into the minds and hearts of our countrymen, and it requires an equally deep cautery to burn them out. Had our separation been a peaceful one, we should have gone on as before, trusting in what are called the principles of American independence, expecting to find permanent prosperity under the old popular doctrines of the land.

Our people had great faith in the form which freedom had assumed in this land, because they attributed to it the unexampled physical prosperity which encompassed them. Its evil principles had not yet been worked out to their perception, although discerning minds have long foreseen the coming catastrophe. This cruel war, together with the rapid crushing out at the North of all freedom of thought and of action, will enable them to understand clearly the effects of principles which would leave no checks and balances in a Government, and which make the multitude believe that their will should override all law and all constitutions.

It will be easier then, perhaps, to persuade them to drink the new wine, when they shall have seen the deleterious effects of the old. Besides this, war will necessarily, when it presses upon us with severity, as it is likely now to do, quell faction, break up party spirit, bring out patriotism, valor, self-denial, heroism, which, although they be worldly virtues, are far better than selfishness and a narrow-minded avarice.

It will stir up all the energies of the people, which were stagnating under the effects of indolence and isolation.

It will drive the islander from his sea-girt home, in which the winds and the waves were soothing him to sleep with their wild lullaby; it will bring the mountaineer from his lonely valley, where his mind was circumscribed by its crags and precipices, and it will mingle them with the great mass of the people, and out of the crucible will come a nation, with larger views, with nobler feelings, with energies high strung for all the purposes of national life.

And this people, thrown upon its own resources, will develop them by their own industry, and mingling through commerce with the world, will learn the value of virtues which they have hitherto permitted to slumber, will open their minds to perceive that other nations may teach them lessons not only of literature and science, but of freedom and government. And thus will they learn the true value of Liberty.

To use the rich language of Macauley: "At times she takes the form of a hateful reptile — she grovels, she hisses, she stings — but woe to those who in disgust shall venture to crush her. And happy are those who, having dared to receive her in her degraded and frightful shape, shall at length be rewarded by her in the time of her beauty and her glory."

# God, The Giver Of Victory And Peace

A THANKSGIVING SERMON

DELIVERED IN THE PRESBYTERIAN CHURCH

SEPTEMBER 18, 1862

RALEIGH, N. C.

By

REV. JOSEPH M. ATKINSON

# GOD, THE GIVER OF VICTORY AND PEACE

Weeping may endure for a night, but joy cometh in the morning. Psalm 30; 5: latter clause.

What a perfect picture of the providence of God and the experience of man! Alternation of good and evil, pain and pleasure, light and darkness, joy and weeping is the law of this lower world. In heaven where "transport and security combine," all is fixed, stable, everlasting; the experience of good is absolute, unmingled, unbounded. There shall be no succession, save of ever-growing felicities; no change, save of a continual rise from glory to glory.

> On all those wide extended plains,
> Shines one eternal day;
> There God the Son forever reigns,
> And scatters night away.

On earth, whether our state be one of joy or sorrow, we need to be reminded of this glorious prospect — in the one case to sober, in the other to cheer us. The mind takes the color of the passing time, and thinks it will ever be as now it is, and fancies it will always feel as now it feels. But we should know from the varied dispensations of God in the past, from what others and ourselves have undergone, and from the repeated testimonies of the inspired Word, how false this estimate of things!

This is signally illustrated in the recent history of our country. God had good reason to send sorrow; but when sorrow has done its appointed work — when, by the sadness of the countenance the heart has been made better, we may expect the darkened cloud to withdraw and a glorious burst of sunlight to appear, like that which even now

> "Flames in the forehead of the morning sky," flashes its gladdening rays from east to west, and calls our whole Confederacy to thanksgiving and praise.

It is in happiest accordance with the spontaneous impulse of a Christian people that the honored Chief Magistrate of these States, banded in a common brotherhood of love, of interest, of suffering and of mercies, has called us to grateful ascription and religious rejoicing.

On a memorable occasion, in the personal history of our Lord,[6] when the envious Pharisees rebuked the jubilant rejoicings of the disciples, He said, if these should hold their peace, the stones would immediately cry out. We might well look for a stern and audible rebuke from brute insensate things, if we should withhold our thankful tribute on this day to the God of our salvation. The Lord hath done great things for us, whereof we are glad. Bless the Lord, O, our souls, and forget not all His benefits.

At no distant day in the past, a dark cloud of uncertainty, of disaster, of wrath, overhung our whole Confederacy and discharged its collected fury on our devoted land. A series of unexpected and appalling reverses, beginning with the ill-fated battle of Somerset, followed in rapid succession by the capture of Roanoke Island, the loss of Newbern, Nashville, and of various intermediate points, and culminating in the surrender of New Orleans, the commercial emporium of the South, the evacuation of Norfolk and the blowing up of the Merrimac, had caused all faces to gather blackness.

Then the boldest was filled with apprehension. The most sanguine were tempted to despair. The head of every patriot was bowed in profoundest grief. Shall we not be permitted to hope that the heart of every Christian was bowed in humility, confession and supplication? We felt that vain was the help of man, and we cast ourselves on the fatherhood of God.

When brought to the lowest point of public depression and of conscious dependence, our deliverance was at hand, God poured the spirit of dauntless heroism into the hearts of a whole people — soldiers, legislators, leaders, alike. The generous resolution was taken to defend the Capitol of the Confederacy to the last extremity. From that moment our

---

[6] Luke 19: 40.

prospects began to brighten. Then came the successful repulse of the enemy at Drury's Bluff, flushed with anticipated triumph and glorying in imagined invincibility.

Again our coveted and hated capital was beleaguered by the most numerous and best appointed army of modern times, led by their most trusted and skillful generals. But day after day that mighty host was baffled and beaten back, like the surges of the sea raging against Gibraltar. Their strongest entrenchments were stormed. Their most costly munitions were captured or destroyed by the valor of our troops, animated, sustained and guided by the Lord of Hosts. The defense of Richmond was a prodigy, not only of human heroism but of Divine might.

From that day to this, our march has been an unbroken series of splendid successes, under the invisible presence of the pillar and the cloud. Shall we not henceforward ascribe all glory to the Lord of Hosts, while mindful of our inextinguishable debt of gratitude to those noble patriots and martyrs whom He employed for our defense?

When the eyes of the prophet's servant were opened, he beheld the mountain filled with chariots of fire and horses of fire. In the first great battle of Cortes against the Mexicans the enthusiastic invaders imagined that they saw St. James, the patron St. of Spain, leading their fiery forces on to victory.[7]

If our eyes could have been unsealed during those seven day's memorable battles before Richmond, we should doubtless have seen a more awful and a more glorious spectacle. We should have seen an angel, terrible as that which smote the host of Sennacherib, hurling back the multitudinous cohorts of our self confident invaders, filling their ranks with confusion, dismay and death. Weeping may endure for a night, but joy cometh in the morning.

---

[7] The same inspiring but imaginary vision, only in a form still more glorious, was again vouchsafed during the expulsion from Mexico. — Prescott's Conquest of Mexico, vol. ii. p. 341.

Never in the history of mankind has the wonder-working providence of God been more strikingly manifest than in the successive phases of this contest. We wholly misapprehend the real significance of this revolution if we fail to discern His hand and His counsel in all that has been done, or, with high providence, permitted to be done. For the present, not joyful but grievous, it has doubtless been a divine agency for the spiritual education of our people in the highest lesson of religious wisdom, akin to that painful economy by which Jehovah led his ancient people through the perils of the pathless wilderness to the possession of the promised land.

In the successive periods and phases of its progress, it has disappointed all probable anticipations; putting to shame the confident predictions of the wise and vindicating the superior sagacity of humble piety. Its principal agents were themselves even unconscious, before-hand, of the important part which they were designed to bear in the execution of the decrees of infinite wisdom.

So far as it may be permitted to man to interpret it, the great purpose of God would appear to have been to exalt his own glorious sovereignty in debasing the pride of material power and illustrating the supremacy of moral forces. In this point of view, its progress has been to us singularly instructive and cheering. Not only does it stand aloof from all vulgar revolutions, but from that which we have been taught to regard with almost superstitious veneration as the most wonderful and noble in the annals of our race; that by which, under the divine favor, we achieved our independence of the British crown and became the freest and most powerful people in the New World.

The course of Providential development in our first Revolution was essentially unlike what we have thus far witnessed in this. Compared with the former, the hand of God is more bare, more open, more visible, in that which is now in process of consummation. The personal history of one man is the record of that revolution. The portion of the life of Washington comprehended within the period, contains and exhausts the Revolution itself. He was not only the type and hero of the Revolution, but what was silently transacted in his thoughtful mind and conceived in his patriotic heart, and executed by his own individual prowess, constituted the sum of the Revolution.

Thus far at least there is no one man of whom this can be said. There is no one man to whom the glory of these splendid achievements can be so eminently ascribed. It is this circumstance which especially distinguishes it from our first Revolution. In consequence of his undisputed ascendancy Washington received among us, it is to be feared the glory which is due to God only, and other eminent patriots and statesmen of that day, Henry, Hamilton, Jefferson, Madison and Marshall, were unduly exalted and relied on. The illustrious men of that generation constitute a grand Pantheon, each having his own proper altar and his own particular worshippers.

It should indeed be to us a matter of grateful acknowledgement that God has raised up for us in this our time of need, able and godly leaders, like Lee, Jackson, Hill and others, whose character would confer honor on any cause, as their public services would shed luster on any age. But, perhaps, it is well for us that there is no one name with which the transcendent glory of this period of our country's history is too exclusively connected. Thus the apparent sphere of the Divine operation is enlarged, and our dependence on His favor, though not more immediate and absolute, is more conscious and visible.

In perfect consistency with this view, it may be affirmed as a uniform method of Divine Providence, springing, perhaps, from profound causes hidden in the nature of things and in the nature of man, that in all great Revolutionary movements, religious or political, the tendencies of the times should embody themselves in some one heroic individual whom all men are content to take as the type and representative of the whole period.

Thus Luther stands forth confessed as the representative of the German reformation, Calvin of the reformation in France, Zwingli of the Swiss, and Knox of the Scottish reformation. Passing now to the domain of civil Revolution, we recognize at once Napoleon, with his brilliant endowments, his indefatigable power of bodily endurance, his inexhaustible fertility of resource, his insatiable thirst of military glory and supreme indifference to human life as the incarnate genius of the great Revolution in France, near the close of the last and the opening of the present century.

At the mention of the American Revolution every eye turns at once to the majestic image of Washington, with his unsullied patriotism, his consummate prudence, his immeasurable, self-control, as the model of all natural and all civil virtues.

When we come to our own day, may we not hope that Jackson, the Christian hero, the man of piety and prayer, with a fervency of spirit, like David's in the sanctuary, and a martial ardor like David's in the field, has been graciously given us as the interpreter and impersonation of the Christian element and the Christian consciousness of this grand conflict?

We cannot but regard it as a singular mercy of God, that the men for the most part who are the chief agents of Providence in conducting this Revolution, should be in personal piety, in such perfect correspondence with its religious character; and that the recognition of God in his incommunicable glory as Supreme Disposer of all events, should be so universal among our Rulers and people.

So long as we shall deeply feel our dependence on God alone, and put our trust in Him, He will favor us, and our progress will be irresistible as the march of time. Faith is the principle of endeavor and endurance. It prompts energy and produces patience. In its relation to God, it waits and is dependent. They that believe shall not make haste. It says to the subject soul, stand still and see the salvation of God.

In its relation to man, it is daring and defiant; seemingly desperate, imprudent, wild and reckless. But when apparently most adventurous, it is in fact most guarded and most prudent; for it is animated by a sublime enthusiasm which links the feebleness of the creature with the almightiness of God. The great virtue, therefore, which the crisis demands, and, we trust, has called forth, is faith in God — the perennial source of patience, courage and hope.

We are prone to rebel against the dispensations of the Most High and murmur as did Israel of old. But how is faith in the Divine Providence vindicated even in time! How often within the limited sphere of our own personal concerns, have we seen that our own plans would have been our ruin, and that the events which appeared most disastrous when they occurred, were blessings in disguise.

It is the sovereign prerogative of God to bring good out of evil. Thus the awful catastrophe of our apostasy as a race is made the occasion of the eternal salvation of his elect, and of affording therein the most amazing illustration of His glorious attributes, to all intelligent creatures, throughout never-ending ages.

And doubtless, each inferior but to us perhaps, scarcely less mysterious evil, as the rupture of what once seemed to us the golden chain that bound together in firm concord this bright sisterhood of States, and in place of amity and peace, gave us the alarms and atrocities of war, will yet find means even out of this visible chaos, to cause a brighter and a more beautiful creation to emerge.

In that magnificent plea of Milton for the liberty of unlicensed printing, the glorious image of his beloved country rises up before him in poetic vision, and he exclaims, "Methinks I see in my mind a noble and puissant nation, rousing herself like a strong man after sleep and shaking her invincible locks; Methinks, I see her as an eagle mewing her mighty youth and kindling her undazzled eyes at the full midday beam; purging and unscaling her long abused sight at the fountain itself of heavenly radiance."

This picture and prophecy we would transfer to our own dear Southern land. Now, she is involved in the heat and dust and blood of the battle: Hereafter, she shall repose in victory and triumph and peace. Now she sits as a widow, forsaken of the nations: Hereafter she shall arise, radiant as a queen, resplendent as the day, crowned with immortal honor, in favor with God and man. Now, she is oppressed, but not overwhelmed; enveloped in flames, but not consumed; in peril, but not appalled; putting her trust under the shadowing wings of the Almighty. Weeping may endure for a night, but joy cometh in the morning.

She is now toilfully learning those precious lessons which she shall teach hereafter to oppressed and struggling nations; and to the proud and heartless Tyrants, who in other lands and in future clays, may seek to degrade the noble and enslave the free. She is now making for herself a name which shall be gratefully and admiringly murmured wherever freedom has a friend or the God of Providence a worshipper! The only proper view of this Revolution, is that which regards it as the child of Providence, who "maketh the wrath of man to praise Him and the remainder thereof He restrains."

The ends contemplated by men and the actions permitted, not approved by God, are in many cases, very unlike his ultimate designs. And we may say to our Northern oppressors, as Joseph to his cruel brethren, As for you, ye thought evil against us, but God meant it unto good. Gen. 50:20. All that was affirmed, and more than was imagined of the ulterior aims of those who inaugurated this atrocious war, has been already done or plainly indicated already.

Were we able to interpret aright the painful dispensations of the Almighty, we might find that our frightful series of reverses during the winter and spring, were as truly merciful in their intent as our recent splendid successes. It was a humiliating but needful part of our education as a people. It was a bitter medicine, but we hope it wrought a lasting cure.

It taught us our prostrate dependence on Him who, sitting on the circle of the Heavens, hath appointed to the nations of the earth the bounds of their habitation and rules with absolute sway over the councils of Cabinets and the event of battles. It was the indispensable condition of the exercise of virtues, without which no character is complete, whether of an individual or a whole people — virtues less obtrusive and less glaring than heroic prowess on the field of bloody strife, but not less magnanimous, less essential or less rare — the virtues of self-control, of patience, of fortitude and of hope.

It has served to exhibit a striking characteristic of our people, previously unknown, it may be, to themselves. I mean their marvelous recuperative energy. In a week after a defeat or disaster, they have seemed as resolute, as hopeful, and as eager as ever. In the presence of terrible calamity, under the pressure of heavy affliction they exclaim,

> "All is not lost; the unconquerable will
> And resolution never to submit or yield,
> And what is more, not to be overcome."

Another quality conspicuously evinced in the progress of this contest has been the singular unselfishness of the great body of our troops, many of them belonging to the best families of our Southern country, born in affluence, nurtured in ease and honor; yet entering the ranks and serving with "proud submission" — with "dignified obedience," under men in every way inferior to themselves, but invested by lawful authority for a temporary purpose with the right and the place of command.

The true history of this war will show that nobler instances of knightly courtesy, of generous valor and of chivalrous emprise, have not been found among the best and bravest of our officers, than among the men subject to their authority.

I have spoken thus far of the gallantry of our soldiers and the patriotism of our people, but assuredly not with the design of giving the supreme glory to them. They have been but instruments in the hand of a higher power; channels through which the Divine goodness has streamed forth upon us.

For the singular preservation of the precious lives of our leaders and troops exposed beyond all former precedent; for the signal victories vouchsafed to our arms over an arrogant and exulting foe; for the patriotic unity which has animated all classes and both sexes; for the spirit of moderation, of firmness and of humanity which has marked the policy and conduct of our rulers, our fervent thanks are due to that benign Providence who alone bestowed and inspired it all.

The glorious deliverances which we have so often experienced heretofore, so far from exhausting the Divine bounty, may under an economy of grace, be turned into an argument for still greater mercies hereafter. When the stripling David armed only with a sling and pebbles from the brook, went forth to meet the giant of Gath, the thought of ancient deliverances kindled his courage. And David said, Moreover, the Lord that delivered me out of the paw of the lion and out of the paw of the bear, He will deliver me out of the hand of this Philistine.[8]

There ought to be not the spirit of carnal rejoicing and self-complacent boasting among us now, but great solemnity of heart and great tenderness of walk. We should humble ourselves even in the hour of victory, before the eternal Majesty of Heaven and earth, whose right hand and holy arm hath gotten Him the victory.

If, by ingratitude and unbelief, we provoke Him to depart from us, our failure and ruin will not be more deserved than dreadful. The brilliant successes with which His favor has crowned our arms and gladdened our hearts, will be like a single star or a small cluster of stars in a firmament of gloom — a bright chapter in a volume written within and without in characters of mourning, lamentation and woe.

This contest is not ended. Infuriated by defeat, our enemies are more rancorous and implacable than ever. They are summoning new levies of hundreds of thousands, to effect, if possible, the subjugation of our people and will resort to every device which cruelty, sharpened by malice and mortification, can suggest to effect their purpose. In these circumstances we look to that God who delivered David and Israel, and while we celebrate His past goodness, hopefully invoke His future favor.

Some trust in chariots and some in horses, but we will remember the name of the Lord our God. Not unto us, not unto us, but unto thy name, give glory for thy mercy and for thy truth's sake. Weeping may endure for a night, but joy

---

[8] 1 Samuel; 17: 37.

cometh in the morning. Abiding in such a posture of spirit as this, may we not hope that what He hath so auspiciously begun He will carry on to a glorious consummation?

A conflict waged in self-defense for all that man holds dear, and consecrated by the martyr-blood of the best men in these Confederate States — by the solemn voice of all our religious convocations, of all Christian churches and above all by the visible favor of Almighty Power, cannot but terminate happily. We should learn, therefore, to exercise a cheerful trust in God and cherish perfect unity among ourselves.

And amid all the excitements of war, let us not cease to feel that a people's spiritual interests are their supreme interests; especially in a time of political convulsion, when so many moral and social bonds are relaxed or broken. He, therefore, who at this crisis does most for his own soul and the souls of others, does most for his country; and he who by his conduct or teaching lowers the standard of Gospel piety, is an enemy not only to religion but to liberty.

There are times when extraordinary energies should be put forth by the servants of the Most High. Whenever men are profoundly agitated by a political convulsion or by a war, such as that which is now raging throughout our extensive borders, vice of all kinds abounds. Satan and his agents are active and vigilant. At such a time the people of God should evince a corresponding energy.

Never were Christians called to more diligence, self-denial, courage, benevolence and industry than at this solemn juncture; and it is, at such a time as this, that God and all good men are most fruitfully active. In a contest like this every man must serve his country according to his several ability and in his appointed sphere. Every man must find the place and the duty suited to him, and to which he is suited.

None can be more important than practical prayerful labor for the religious welfare of our heroic soldiers; directly seeking their salvation by preaching to them — by writing and distributing Tracts and Hymns and Bibles — by praying for them — and by tender sympathy with them in the trials and temptations to which they must be inevitably exposed.

If God should breathe over THESE CONFEDERATE STATES the spirit of devotion, of humility, of dependence and of faith, it would be better than any victory in the field, however brilliant — for it would be at once a proof of His favor and a pledge of our prosperity.

Instructed by the calamities of war, we shall estimate more highly the blessings of peace. We hardly ever value as we ought uninterrupted prosperity, or estimate as we should any good while it is ours. The evils of this trying period will not be lost to us, if they shall impress upon us all an adequate sense of the preciousness of peace and bring the policy of our Rulers and the temper of our people into perfect harmony with the spirit of the Gospel, peace on earth, good will to men.

Such have been the gallantry and patriotism of our troops in the field, and such the charity and courage of our women in anticipating and ministering to their wants, that we may pursue our chosen policy of peace with all nations without the imputation of effeminacy or cowardice.

After the lapse of a few years, we trust that we shall look back upon these trying times as on a troubled dream, and in the secure enjoyment of peace repeat, with even more solemn and tender emphasis than on this day of thanksgiving and praise. Weeping may endure for a night, but joy cometh in the morning.

The martyred dead have taken possession of this Southern soil for the Southern people. It was theirs originally, by the gift of God, and they have bought it anew by their blood. This land will be endeared to us and to our posterity, because it is the earthly resting-place of our immortal dead.

It was the boast of the ancient Greek, as his eye wandered over his beautiful and beloved land, that every hill bore the tomb of a hero or the temple of a God. But more noble dust mingled not with the soil of Attica than that which reposes in the bosom of our own dear native land. It surely lends attraction to heaven, viewed with reference to our present constitution, to think that there we shall behold and converse with the best and loveliest we have known on earth.

If Socrates could talk of transports of joy at the prospect of seeing Palamedes, Ajax and other heroes of antiquity in a future world — how should the Christian feel when he looks forward to an everlasting abode, not a transient meeting with the saints of all ages — with his Christian friends who have fallen in his defense — and with Christ Himself, the Author and Finisher of our faith.

If he hoped for felicity in comparing his experience with theirs — how shall we rejoice in reviewing dispensations of Providence now impenetrably dark, or imperfectly understood, but then shining in the light of Heaven. The past and the future meet in the memory of the dead.

The sweetest and brightest link in the chain that stretches back over the past, binds us to the dead; and that chain stretches forward to eternity and attaches itself to the Throne of the living God. Thus death joins on to life; and all that is sacred in memory connects itself with all that is inspiring in hope. Weeping may endure for a night, but joy cometh in the morning.

# Our Cause In Harmony With The Purposes Of God In Christ Jesus

A SERMON
Preached in Christ Church, Savannah,
On Thursday, September 18th, 1862,

BEING THE DAY SET FORTH BY THE

### President of the Confederate States
AS A DAY OF
PRAYER AND THANKSGIVING

**FOR OUR MANIFOLD VICTORIES, AND ESPECIALLY FOR THE FIELDS OF MANASSAS AND RICHMOND, KY.**

BY THE

Rt. Rev. STEPHEN ELLIOTT, D. D.,
Rector of Christ Church, and Bishop of the Diocese of Georgia.

"Why do the heathen rage, and the people imagine a vain thing?" Ps. 2:6

Savannah
1862

### To the Clergy of the Diocese of Georgia

Whereas THE PRESIDENT OF THE CONFEDERATE STATES did, on the 4th day of September, issue his proclamation setting apart Thursday, the 18th day of September inst., as a day of Prayer and Thanksgiving to Almighty God, for the great mercies vouchsafed to our people, and more especially for the triumph of our arms at Richmond and Manassas, in Virginia, and at Richmond, in Kentucky, and did invite the people of the Confederate States to meet on that day at their respective places of public worship, and to unite in rendering thanks and praise to God for these great mercies, and to implore him to conduct our country safely through the perils which surround us, to the final attainment of the blessings of peace and security.

Now, therefore, I, Stephen Elliott, Bishop of the Protestant Episcopal Church of the Diocese of Georgia, do recommend to the Clergy of said Diocese, to open their several places of worship on Thursday, the said 18th day of September, and to unite with their congregations in thanksgiving and praise to Almighty God for all His mercies, and especially for our signal and manifold victories over the invaders of our country, according to the following form:

Morning Prayer as usual to the "Venite Exultemus." Instead of the "Venite," let the Psalm of Praise and Thanksgiving after victory, to be found in the "Forms of Prayer to be used at Sea," and beginning "If the Lord had not been on our side, now may we say," be said or sung.

For the Psalter — Psalms 136, 144, 146.

GLORIA IN EXCELSIS.

First Lesson — 2 Chronicles: Ch. 20 to V. 31.

THE TE DEUM.

Second Lesson — 1 Timothy: Ch. 6 to V. 17.

Before the General Thanksgiving introduce the Collect for Victory, to be found in the "Forms of Prayer to be used at Sea," beginning "O, Almighty God, the Sovereign Commander of all the world," changing "this happy victory" into "these happy victories," and "this great mercy" into "these great mercies," wherever the words may occur.

Introduce, likewise, the "Collect for Peace and Deliverance from our Enemies," to be found among the occasional thanksgivings.

It not being a Litany day, the Litany will not be said. The Prayer set forth by the Bishop to be used during the continuance of the war, will also be omitted upon this occasion.

# A Sermon

### PROVERBS 24:17-18.

"Rejoice not when thine enemy falleth, and let not thine heart be glad when he stumbleth:"

Lest the Lord see it, and it displease him and he turn away his wrath from him."

ON the 16th day of last May, in the moment of our bitterest adversity, when our honored Chief Magistrate had called the people of THESE CONFEDERATE STATES to supplication and prayer, at the close of the sermon preached upon that occasion, I was bold to utter the following sentiments:

"In my opinion the real troubles of our enemies are just about to begin. They find themselves now, with the heats and sickness of summer coming upon them, with the water courses preparing to dry up, with their armies in a hostile country far from their base of operation, in the face of determined and exasperated enemies, led by some of the best generals of the continent, with the wail of Europe beginning to swell upon the breeze, and their work not half done.

Truly their position is one not to be envied; and in the midst of their exultation and feasting the handwriting is upon the wall of their palace. For a few weeks more their successes may seem to continue, but the summer's sun shall not have passed away, ere we shall find ourselves freed from their power, and rejoicing in present deliverance. And what is more, we shall be forced to confess that the Lord hath done it in the face of all the nations."

A few weeks after these utterances were made, commenced that series of victories which culminated on the 30th day of August, one day before the summer's sun had finished its course, in the battles of Manassas and Richmond, freeing us from the power of our enemies, and causing us to be gathered together today, through all the wide extent of our Confederacy, that we may offer the sacrifice of thanksgiving and of praise to Almighty God for our present deliverance.

I reproduce these words today, not to claim for myself any spirit of prophecy, but because the conclusions then enunciated were deduced, through a train of reasoning, from premises distinctly laid down in the word of God, and acted upon again and again in his dealings with the nations, and also because I desire to gain credit with you for opinions which I shall utter today, and which may be of vast importance to you in the future.

When a man's judgment has been more than once strikingly confirmed, his views deserve attention and ought to receive it. And knowing how loth man is to admit God's hand in any of the affairs of the world — how set he is to rest altogether in secondary causes and secondary agencies — how he will move, if possible, in the lower atmosphere of sense and of worldliness, I would fortify myself, in this way, in behalf of ulterior conclusions, which I derive from the same infallible book of wisdom and of knowledge, the Holy Scriptures.

To some they will prove unpalatable, because they will not smack of peace — to others they will seem visionary, because they will deal with spiritual influences which the world admits not into its calculations — by many they will be deemed humiliating, because they will rest our success and our security upon causes distinct from our own valor or wisdom or merit, but they appear to me to be in entire accordance with God's purposes, and to furnish adequate reasons for a condition of things which seems to the world inconsistent with the Christian principles that ought to control this country and this people.

My purpose is to justify the ways of God to man, even when those ways have been forced, by the blindness and perverseness of human nature, to pass through seas of blood and over the ruined and desolated hearthstones of multitude.

If the affairs of the world are regulated at all by God, we cannot suppose that the destiny of a great Christian nation, such as these United States were, would be disregarded by him or unaffected by his control.

It was rapidly becoming, at the moment when this civil convulsion began, a mighty power in the earth, a controlling element in the progress of the world. A century more would have made it not only the mightiest nation of modern times, but would have exalted it to an equality with the greatest Empires which have ever swayed the earth.

Vast then must have been the interest which was permitted to shatter it while yet ascending to its greatness; heinous the sin which could deserve such a punishment as is now scourging it from its one ocean to the other. We can find that interest only in the institution of slavery which was the immediate cause of this revolution.

We can find the sin only in that presumptuous interference with the will and ways of God, which, beginning in an overmuch righteousness, coalesced rapidly with infidelity, and ended in a bold defiance of the word of God, and of the principles of his moral government.

As the world draws towards its end, the hand of God becomes more visible in its affairs. Even in human arrangements where a scheme or a policy is complicated, ordinary men can understand but little of them in their beginning or during much of their progress. But when they draw near to their consummation, the purpose becomes more evident, the converging movements more perceptible, the final result more clear and determined. The last touches are those which harmonize the discordant features of the plan and pronounce it the work of a great and persistent mind.

It can then be seen what was the meaning of each arrangement — what the intent of every act, however unintelligible when first they flashed upon the perception. And so with the mighty and sublime work of God upon earth. We cannot understand it as it progresses, because our finite minds cannot comprehend the policy of an infinite will.

The Bible reveals to us what it is, tells us through what agencies it is to be produced, introduces us to the beings who are working it out, gives us a chart of the future as well as a history of the past, but nevertheless our limited vision is embarrassed amid the complicate movements of the world, and the numberless causes which combine to produce a single effect.

We perceive that it is going on; at long intervals of time we can trace backward its persistent though interrupted course, but we cannot conceive what the future steps are to be, nor how such confusion as often reigns upon earth can be tending to the production of an ultimate harmony. But as the period approaches when God's economy of grace is to be consummated, then are we permitted to gather up all the interlacing threads and to distinguish the glorious pattern which the Almighty Artist has been working out through the instruments which he is wielding, and has been wielding for ages.

That work is the regeneration of a fallen world, and that regeneration is to be wrought out through the preaching of the gospel to every creature, through his opening all the Continents of the earth to the influence of the religion of Jesus Christ. When this shall have been accomplished, when the gospel shall have been preached as a witness to all the world, then will the end come, and Christ shall be set upon his Holy Hill of Zion.

If we examine the religious condition of the world, keeping this purpose in our view, we will perceive that paramount Christian influences are steadily at work every where else except in Africa.

Europe is Christian in its entire length and breadth, that is, has had the gospel preached as a witness to all her various kingdoms and empires. America has been re-peopled altogether from Christian nations, and the cross is adored over all her wide area, save where the rapidly expiring Indian tribes yet break its continuity.

England, France, and Russia are fast casting over Asia the spell of their vast political power, and the old worship of Brahma and the moral teachings of Confucius and the imposture of Mohammed are tottering to their fall.

Australia is peopling under the auspices of Great Britain, and wherever she goes, her Church goes with her. Africa alone is uninfluenced by Christianity, and whence is that influence to proceed?

Tis true, that here and there, along her outward limits, Christian Churches have planted their feeble settlements, and Christian missionaries have devoted themselves in faith to the service of the Lord. But they have gone, for the most part, only to die, and have made no impression upon that vast interior which swarms with life and knows no religion save that of Nature, or the fraudulent devices of man.

How, then, is that dark spot upon the world's surface to be enlightened? Who is to pierce those pestilential regions and preach the everlasting Gospel, even though it be only for a witness? And echo answers who? for all have attempted it, and all alike have failed. The self-denying missionaries of Rome — men who have gained a foothold in all other regions — have tried it, but have been swept away before the flood of barbarism and incivility.

The highly educated missionaries of the English Church have tried it, and neither their knowledge, nor their devotion, nor the prestige of English power, have availed any thing against climate and disease. The indomitable missionaries of the Moravian Church have tried it until Sierra Leone has been a very Golgotha to them.

The enterprising missionaries of the American Churches have tried it, and while their previous knowledge of the

African in this country had, in a measure, prepared them their work, they too have failed, because the Caucasian blood has not been able to bear the enervating heats and destructive fevers of the torrid zone. Whence, then, is their regeneration to come, for come it must, if the Bible be the word of God, ere the present economy of things shall terminate?

We are driven to look for it from some agency which shall able, through national affinities, through a like physiological structure, through a oneness of blood and of race, to bear the burden of this work, and ultimately, in God's own time, to plant the gospel in their Father-land, after they themselves shall have been prepared, through a proper discipline, for the performance of this duty. And I find this agency in the African slaves now dwelling upon this Continent and educating among ourselves.

I see here the instruments whom God is preparing, in his own inscrutable way, to cooperate with the other instruments who are at work upon the other Continents to bring in the kingdom of our Lord and Saviour Jesus Christ, and it is this conviction, and not any merit in ourselves, which makes me confident that we shall be safely preserved through this conflict.

Most of you are looking to other causes for our success and our preservation, to the valor of our troops, to the skill of our generals, to the extent of our territorial surface, to foreign influence, to the power of commerce and of trade. I am looking to the poor despised slave as the source of our security, because I firmly believe that God will not permit his purposes to be overthrown or his arrangements to be interfered with.

He has caused the African race to be planted here under our political protection and under our Christian nurture, for his own ultimate designs, and he will keep it here under that culture until the fullness of his own times, and any people which strives against this divine arrangement will find that it is running against the thick bosses of Jehovah's buckler.

Those who have looked at slavery superficially, have permitted themselves to be moved away from scriptural decrees by such trivial things as are the necessary accompaniments of all bondage, and have rashly yielded to their sensibilities the conclusions which ought to be drawn exclusively from the word of God. They have passionately decided that God could have nothing to do with an institution bearing upon its face the evils and miseries which attend the enslavement of any people.

They seem strangely to forget that he kept his own chosen people — the descendants after the flesh of that Abraham whom he called his friend — the children of that Jacob whom he surnamed a Prince with God — in bondage to Egypt for four hundred years, until they were disciplined to go forth and become a nation among the nations.

What cared He, in his stern, unbending preparation of a people educating for divine ends and for immortal purposes, for such trivial things as slavery, as toil, as the sufferings of a subject race? There were they kept under the yoke until he saw fit to break it and to carry them, a humbled and prepared people, into the land which had been marked out for them as the scene of their future glory — a glory of spiritual triumphs.

Will man learn nothing from the past? Shall God unveil his purposes and his dealings to his sight, and will he forever turn away besotted and without perception? With this treatment by God of his own chosen people full in their view, with a clear perception of the necessity of a people, of African lineage, to be disciplined and educated for the work of the Lord, will Christian nations be yet so blinded by their passions, and so deceived by their sensibilities, as to combine to overturn a divine missionary scheme, and blot it out from the face of the earth?

But it will be all in vain, and the Church of the future will see and confess that as Egypt was the land of refuge and the school of nurture for the race of Israel, so were these Southern States first the home and then the nursing mother of those who were to go forth and regenerate the dark recesses of a benighted Continent.

The great revolution through which we are passing certainly turns upon this point of slavery, and our future destiny is bound up with it. As we deal with it, so shall we prosper, or so shall we suffer. The responsibility is upon us, and if we rise up, in a true Christian temper, to the sublime work which God has committed to us of educating a subject nation for his divine purposes, we shall be blessed of him as Joseph was, and he will say to us,

"Blessed of the Lord be thy land, for the precious things of Heaven, for the dew, and for the deep that coucheth beneath, and for the precious fruits brought forth by the sun, and for the precious things put forth by the moon, and for the chief things of the ancient mountains, and for the precious things of the lasting hills, and for the precious things of the earth and fullness thereof, and for the good will of him that dwelt in the bush."

But if contrariwise, we shall misunderstand our relations and shall assume the dominion of masters without remembering the duties thereof, God will "make them pricks in our eyes and thorns in our sides, and shall vex us in the land wherein we dwell."

It is very curious and very striking, in this connection, to trace out the history of slavery in this country, and to observe God's providential care over it ever since its introduction. Strange to say, African slavery, upon this Continent, had its origin in an act of mercy. The negro was first brought across the ocean to save the Indian from a toil which was destroying him, but while the Indian has perished, the substitute who was brought to die in his place, has lived, prospered and multiplied.

When the slave trade had become so hateful to all civilized nations, because of the horrors which accompanied it, that with one consent it was abolished and put under the ban of the world, that which was supposed to have dealt a fatal blow to slavery proved its salvation and rapid increase.

The inability any longer to procure slaves through importation, forced upon masters in these States a greater attention to the comforts and morals of their slaves. The family relation was fostered, the marriage tie grew in importance, and the eight hundred thousand slaves who inhabited these States at the closing of our ports in 1808, have, in the short space of fifty years, grown into four millions!

When slavery was once again endangered by the very scanty profits which were yielded to the planters by their old staples of indigo and rice, articles of only partial consumption, God permitted a new staple to be introduced — men called it an happy accident — the staple of cotton, which seems to have no limit to its consumption, and which cannot be increased too fast for the wants of the world.

When the border States, which could not profitably grow this staple, were calculating the value of the slave institution for themselves, and were actually debating, in conventions, its speedy extinction, a sudden and unexpected value was given to their old staples of wheat and tobacco — men called it again an happy accident — and the slave rose once again into importance, and God used self-interest to check the disposition towards emancipation.

When the false philanthropy of Europe was making many converts to its views, even in the Southern States, and earnest minds were deeply agitated upon the question of the sinfulness of slavery, God permitted a Christian nation to try the experiment of emancipation upon a small scale — to try it in the face of the world — and the wretched and ruinous result of idleness, of dissipation, of anarchy which followed in the most fertile and beautiful Islands of the globe, satisfied our people that it was the veriest mistake ever made by a wise nation.

When, in these still more recent times, the institution was denounced as unscriptural, and contrary to the spirit of Christianity, and the finger of scorn was pointed at us and we were unchurched for our adherence to it, and were called to bear the shock of opinion striking upon us from the Christian world, such an host of writers from every department of literature sprang into the arena — statesmen, economists, philosophers, divines, as if raised up by God — and refuted those calumnies so overwhelmingly, that the public mind became settled to an unusual degree, and we were prepared to contend for it as for one of our most sacred domestic relations.

God protected it at every point, made all assaults upon it to turn to its more permanent establishment, caused the laws of nature to work in its behalf, furnished new products to ensure its continuance and, at the same time, ameliorate its circumstances, made its bitterest antagonists to furnish arguments against its destruction, and raised up advocates who placed it, through reasoning drawn directly from the Bible, upon an impregnable basis of truth and necessity, connecting it, as we have shown you, with sublime spiritual purposes in the future.

And, finally, when the deeply-laid conspiracy of Black Republicanism threatened to undermine this divinely-guarded institution, God produced for its defense within the more Southern States an unanimity of sentiment, and a devoted spirit of self-sacrifice almost unexampled in the world and has so directed affairs as to discipline into a like sympathy those border States which were not at first prepared to risk a revolution in its defense.

We have been gathered together today by a proclamation of our President to return thanks to Almighty God for a series of brilliant victories won by our gallant soldiers over the invaders of our soil.

Most fervently do we thank Him for his presence with us upon those fields of terrible conflict, for skill of our commanding generals, for the heroism of our officers of every grade, for the valor and self-sacrifice of our soldiers, for the glorious results which have followed upon the success of our arms. Most devoutly do we praise and bless His holy name, this day, for the deliverance of our country from the polluting tread of the enemy and for the punishment which he has seen fit to inflict upon those who vainly boasted that they would devour us.

We give all the glory to Him, while we cannot forget the living heroes whose inspired courage led them triumphant over fields of desperate carnage, nor the martyred dead who have poured out the gushing tide of their young and noble life-blood for the sacred cause which carried them to the battle field. But battles, at last, even with all the dazzling halo which surrounds them, are but fields of slaughter, unless made illustrious by the principles which they involved or by the spirit which animated and ruled over them.

The meeting of barbaric hordes upon fields of blood, of which history is full, where men fought with the instinct and ferocity of beasts, simply for hatred's sake or the love of war, is disgusting to the noble mind, and carries with it no idea save that of brutality. We could not thank God for victories such as those, and therefore, in keeping this Holy Festival our thankfulness must rest more upon the cause for which he has called us to arms, upon the spirit which has accompanied it, and upon the guardianship which he has established over us, than upon the mere triumphs of the battlefield.

We do not place our cause upon its highest level until we grasp the idea that God has made us the guardians and champions of a people whom he is preparing for his own purposes and against whom the whole world is banded. The most solemn relation upon earth is that between parent and child, because in it immortal souls are committed to the training of man not only for time but for eternity. There is no measure to its sublimity, for it stretches upwards to the throne of God and links us with immortality.

We tremble when we meditate upon it and cry for divine help when we weigh its responsibilities What shall we think, then, of the relation which subsists between a dominant race professing to believe in God and to acknowledge Christ and a subject race, brought from their distant homes and placed under its charge for culture, for elevation and for salvation, and while so placed contributing by its labor to the welfare and comfort of the world. What a trust from God!

What reliance has he placed upon our faithfulness and our integrity! What a sure confidence does it give us in his protection and favor! His divine arrangements are placed in our keeping. Will he not preserve them? His divine purposes seem to be intermingled with our success. Will he not be careful to give us that success and just in the way that he shall see to be best for us?

His purposes are yea and amen in Christ Jesus and cannot be overturned by man. It places our warfare above any estimate which unspiritual minds can make of it. While many other motives are urging us to the battle-field and we rush forward to defend our liberties, our homes, our altars, God is super-adding this other motive — the secret of his own will — is making it to produce within us, unconsciously perhaps to ourselves, a power which is irresistible.

Our conscience in this way is thus made right towards God and towards man; our heart is filled with his fear and his love; our arm is nerved with almost super-human strength, and we have reason to thank him, not only for what he has done for us, but for what he has restrained us from doing for ourselves and others from doing for us. This noble cause has made him our guide and our overruling governor, and we are moving forward, as I firmly believe, as truly under his direction, as did the people of Israel when he led them with a pillar of cloud by day and of fire by night.

Next to the cause in which we are engaged, we have to thank God for the spirit of our people and of our armies. Such a contest as this which we are waging could never have been carried on successfully without such an entire devotion as pervades the States of this Confederacy.

Although shut in from the rest of the world, and deprived of all our accustomed luxuries and many, even, of our comforts; although cut of from intercourse with those we love in foreign lands, many of whom are near and dear to us; although forbidden even to know what is going on in science or literature or art, although stripped of all legitimate commerce and trade; although, in some of the professions, debarred from all business and all means of profit; although left with the ruling product of the country incapable of sale, save when a speculative demand within our own borders may arise for it, there is yet heard no murmur, no complaint, no disaffection, but all are willing to bear and to suffer for the cause's sake.

God has given us a willing mind and we cheer each other on in faith and trustfulness. And not only to the sterner sex has God given this enduring temper, but the attitude of woman is sublime. Bearing all the sacrifices of which I have just spoken, she is moreover called upon to suffer in her affections, to be wounded and smitten where she feels deepest and most enduringly.

Man goes to the battle-field but woman sends him there, even though her heart strings tremble while she gives the farewell kiss and the farewell blessing. Man is supported by the necessity of movement, by the excitement of action, by the hope of honor, by the glory of conquest.

Woman remains at home to suffer, to bear the cruel torture of suspense, to tremble when the battle has been fought and the news of the slaughter is flashing over the electric wire, to know that defeat will cover her with dishonor and her little ones with ruin, to learn that the husband she doted upon, the son whom she cherished in her bosom and upon whom she never let the wind blow too rudely, the brother with whom she sported through all her happy days of childhood, the lover to whom her early vows were plighted, has died upon some distant battle-field and lies there a mangled corpse, unknown and uncared for, never to be seen again even in death.

Oh! those fearful lists of the wounded and the dead! How carelessly we pass them over, unless our own loved ones happen to be linked with them in military association, and yet each name in that roll of slaughter carries a fatal pang to some woman's heart — some noble, devoted woman's heart. But she bears it all and bows submissive to the stroke. "He died for the cause. He perished for his country. I would not have it otherwise, but I should like to have given the dying boy my blessing, the expiring husband my last kiss of affection, the bleeding lover the comfort of knowing that I kneeled beside him."

This is the daily language of woman throughout this Confederacy, and whence could such a spirit come but from God, and, what is worthy to produce it but some cause which lies beyond any mere human estimate. And when we turn to our armies, truly these victories are the victories of the privates.

God forbid that I should take one atom of honor or of praise from those who led our hosts upon those days of glory — from the accomplished and skilful Lee — the admirable Crichton of our armies — from the God-fearing and indomitable Jackson, upon whose prayer-bedewed banner victory seems to wait — from the intrepid Stuart, whose cavalry charges imitate those of Murat, from that great host of generals who swarm around our country's flag as Napoleon's Marshals did around the Imperial Eagle, but nevertheless our victories are the victories of the privates.

It is the enthusiastic dash of their onsets, the fearless bravery with which they rush even to the cannon's mouth, the utter recklessness of life, if so be that its sacrifice may only lead to victory, the heartfelt impression that the cause is the cause of every man, and that success is a necessity.

What intense honor do I feel for the private soldier! The officers may have motives other than the cause, the private soldier can have none. He knows that his valor must pass unnoticed, save in the narrow circle of his company; that his sacrifice can bring no honor to his name, no reputation to his family; that if he survives he lives only to enter upon new dangers with the same hopelessness of distinction; that if he dies, he will receive nothing but an unmarked grave, and yet is he proud to do his duty and to maintain his part in the destructive conflict.

His comrades fall around him thick and fast, but with a sigh and tear he closes his ranks and presses on to a like destiny. Truly the first monument which our Confederacy rears, when our independence shall have been won, should be a lofty shaft, pure and spotless, bearing this inscription: "TO THE UNKNOWN AND UNRECORDED DEAD."

But we have reason to thank God today, not only for what he has given us the heart to do, but for what he has restrained us from doing, and restrained others from doing in our behalf. If the premises upon which I have rested all my reasoning be correct, then is the unity of the slave institution, in this country, a matter of vast importance. And I think I can perceive how God has been working for us to produce that result by restraining us from any premature invasion of the border States, and in the meantime disciplining them for his ultimate purpose.

Those States were not prepared, a year ago, to receive an invading or protecting army, whichever you may please to call it. They had been, for years, under influences adverse to our institution of slavery, and at one period appeared to be fast approaching to Free-soilism, with its resulting demagoguism and corruption.

An eloquent statesman, now gone to his rest, had come into public life at a period when the mad fervor of the French revolution had inclined men to think that liberty, as they termed licentiousness and anarchy, was the greatest blessing bestowed by God upon man, had himself strongly imbibed that feeling and did much to impress it especially upon Kentucky and Maryland.

From him, too, for he was their political idol, those States had conceived a profound veneration for the Union, and had not been borne along by that tide of discontent which was every day swelling through the more Southern slave States, and making them realize that the Union was a curse and not a blessing, a means used for destruction and not for security.

Those States rather favored the earlier steps of Federal encroachment. The tariff of duties for protection, the system of internal improvement by the National Government, the idea of a strong central system were fostered in those States and found eloquent advocates and a strong and oft times a dominant party.

To these influences were united those views of philanthropy, which, taking shape in England, under Wilberforce and his adherents, found a ready home in this land of freedom, as it loved to call itself, and gave rise in the one State to the Colonization Society, and in the other, to a scheme of gradual emancipation. It is but a little while since those States began to recognize any danger from the encroachments of the Federal Government, or could perceive any lasting mischief to grow out of Free-soil principles.

They were not ripe, therefore, for action when we acted, and although many of the young and ardent, who had imbibed the reactionary spirit in favor of State sovereignty and of slavery, rushed with ardor to our banner, the men of the old school, of the Whig regime, of the philanthropic party, conceived it to be a causeless rebellion, and were as ardent for the Union as the most devoted Republican of the North.

It was a struggle between the young and the old, between the new doctrines and those of the past, between traditions circling around idolized names and mischiefs which were gradually forcing themselves upon the public mind. It required a year of Black Republican legislation, unmodified by the conservative Southern element and a year of Black Republican domination, to turn the scale fully in our favor.

God wisely kept us back, by his inscrutable guidance, from invading those States a year ago, and we can now understand why the first battle of Manassas went so strangely and mysteriously unimproved, and why defeat so thickly pursued us in the West. It was that the presence of Northern armies might discipline the people for a thorough union with the South and might bring them more heartily into the support of the institution he was protecting.

And when he perceived that the effect had been produced, he led us back to that very field of Manassas where we had paused in the full career of victory, and placed us under almost the identical circumstances of triumph, as if He said to us in words,

"A year ago, my people, I placed my bit in your mouths and restrained you from advancing to a work not then prepared to your hand, but now I have made it ready and the hearts of the people are willing in the day of my power. Onward to your work, and gather in to the arms of your Confederacy the utmost verge of slavery, that the world may see that I am the God who disposes all things according to the purpose of my will."

We have great cause, moreover, to be thankful to Almighty God that he has restrained the powers of Europe from any interference in our behalf, and has permitted us to gain these glorious victories under his auspices alone. It was highly important for our future to prove the strength of our institutions and to convince the world that the African with us was not a source of weakness or an object of fear, but was a comfort and a help.

And in no manner could this have been so fully demonstrated as by leaving us to struggle alone with the mighty power which has been endeavoring to crush us, while this people was in the midst of us, almost equal in numbers and unrestrained by the presence of armies. Tis true that in some districts they have flocked to the banner of freedom, which they consider equivalent to idleness, just as children would rush after any new thing or boys would be tempted by a holiday. But nowhere has any disaffection manifested itself or any hatred to the white race been developed.

They have mingled freely in all our counsels, have been restrained in no unusual degree, have been permitted to go in and out very much as they pleased, have followed their masters to the field and been faithful to them in danger, in suffering and in death. They have shown themselves a docile, and, in many instances, a most affectionate race, and have sadly disappointed those who counted upon their alliance and co-operation.

This circumstance has already impressed itself not only upon Europe, but upon our very antagonists, and they have been forced to confess that the slave was not as ready to embrace freedom as they had supposed him.[9] The

---

[9] Mr. Lincoln's proclamation, for general emancipation, which has appeared since this sermon was delivered, is a strong proof of this position, for surely the invading armies of last winter and spring, did not wait for any proclamation, but acted out the principle without any instructions from Washington. As our Lord has taught us all to pray "Lead us not into temptation," would it not be well for or the State Governments, in view of this proclamation, to order all slaves to be removed within our military lines, and to provide the planters with the means of doing it, under certain conditions? The loss of property to individuals and of wealth to the State will otherwise be very great this winter.

interference of European powers could have done us no service and might have done us great mischief, and what, at one time, we considered injustice and selfishness, has turned out for us the richest mercy.

We can now say confidently to the world, "God has protected us in the hour of our necessity and has made this people, whom you calumniated and vilified as an oppressed and down-trodden people, to honor us in the face of all the nations, and to refute for us the slanders of politicians and the lies of hypocrisy. They have adhered to us in our difficulties, have borne with us our poverty, have comforted us in our sorrows, have never once lifted their arms against us and now testify to the world that our culture has changed them from savages into servants, from barbarians into men of Christian feeling and Christian sympathy."

I cannot see, as yet, the termination of this war, because I do not think that all the moral results have been produced which are to come out of it. We have yet much trouble before us and many trials to endure ere it shall be ended. God does not permit his creatures, especially those who are bound to him in the bond of the Christian covenant, to be slaughtered as they have been slaughtered in this war without meaning to produce effects adequate to the punishment.

If the armies which have been brought into the field have at all approached in numbers what they have been officially reported to be, then I cannot be far wrong when I affirm that already, in the brief space of eighteen months, a quarter of a million of human beings have been swept away by disease, by wounds and by death upon the battle field.

What a terrible reckoning! It cannot be for nothing! And it must go on until England shall be convinced that slavery, as we hold it here, is essential to the welfare of the world, until the North shall find that her fanaticism was a madness and delusion, until we ourselves shall learn to value the institution above any estimate we have ever placed upon it, and to treat it as a sacred trust from God, until all shall acknowledge, with one consent, that it is a divinely guarded system, planted by God, protected by God and arranged for his own wise purposes in the future of him, with whom one day is as a thousand years, and a thousand years as one day.

And above all do I believe that this revolution will not have finished its work until punishment shall have been rolled back upon that fountain of evil whence have sprung all these bitter waters. I cannot conceive any thing more hateful to God than the infidelity which has reveled in the Eastern States for the last forty years, having its center and its seat in the modern Athens, as the Bostonians have proudly called their city.

And if, as the Apostle said, the mark of the Athenians was that they spent their time in nothing else but either to tell or to hear some new thing, and to plant altars to unknown Gods, well has the name been chosen for themselves. For all that time has Christ been dishonored and discrowned; for all that time has impious reason been exalted with a quiet superciliousness above the word of God; for all that time has every accursed heresy been spewed out of the mouths of men who called themselves the ministers of God.

Nothing was too monstrous to be uttered, nothing too vile to be listened to. One would affirm that Christ was a philosopher good enough for his day, the legitimate successor of Plato and of Aristotle, but that the present times required a Christ more advanced in philosophy, and especially in the philosophy of abolitionism. Another would declare that there was no objective God, but that God was whatever each man conceived him to be within himself, that is, that man was the creator of God and not God the creator of man.

Another would impiously cry out against the God of the Bible, because he, was a slave-holding God, and against Christ, because he was a slave admitting Christ, and against the Bible because it tolerated and affirmed the system. The Holy Ghost was utterly discarded and sinned against, until the great mass was given up to delusion and a lie.

And out of this defiled nest have flown the birds of evil omen who have scattered discord and confusion over the land. At present they seem to be reaping money — the fruit which they love, but which the Bible calls the root of all evil — from the seed of their planting. War is filling their coffers and they are riding upon the highest wave of prosperity.

But although our arm may not reach them, God is upon their track and ere this conflict is ended, will bring them to repentance and remorse or else punish them in the day of his wrath. "Be sure your sin will find you out," is a law which never goes unfulfilled.

And therefore is it that I have placed at the head of my sermon the words of the wise Solomon, that we may all this day draw the proper distinction between exulting over an enemy and offering praise and thanksgiving to God for his wrath. "Rejoice not when thine enemy falleth, and let not thine heart be glad when he stumbleth: Lest the Lord see it and it displease him and he turn away his wrath from him."

Let us not, by any improper exultation, turn away God's wrath from our enemies, and especially from these wretched infidels, the harbingers of war, of woe, and of anarchy. Let our thanksgiving be one of deep solemnity and deep humility, looking upon God's movements in our behalf with awe and waiting for him to inflict his wrath, in his own good time, upon his own revilers and the despisers of his son. He will arrange it all and if you will watch upon his wrath you will say, "Great and marvelous are thy works, Lord God Almighty; just and true are thy ways, thou King of saints."

# God's Providence In War

A SERMON

DELIVERED

BY

REV. J. W. TUCKER

TO HIS CONGREGATION
IN
FAYETTEVILLE, N. C.

On Friday, May 16th, 1862.

FAYETTEVILLE:

1862

# SERMON

"I form the light, and create darkness: I make peace, and create evil: I the Lord do all these things."
— Isaiah 45:7.

We have met together in obedience to the proclamation of our beloved President, to supplicate the blessing of God upon our arms. Our Chief Magistrate in making this call to prayer, and this congregation in cheerfully responding to it, alike recognize the hand of God in the origin and progress of this conflict.

As a Christian people, we look not to fortune nor to accidents for help in this hour of our country's peril, but to the God of battles and of nations. The reason is apparent: If the teaching of the Bible, and the revelation of the Christian religion be true, there is no such thing as fortune; there can be no accidents. An accident is an effect without a cause; fortune is an act or a series of acts, without an agent.

But it is an axiom in Philosophy, and a first principle in all religion, that there can be no effect without a cause; no acts without responsible agents as their authors. What is generally regarded as accident and fortune, are those effects, the causes for which are unknown, and those acts, the agents producing which are unseen.

But are we to conclude that because we are ignorant of the cause producing a certain class of effects, that therefore, they have no cause? or that as the agent in a certain series of actions is unknown to us, that they must of necessity be acts without an agent? We certainly cannot pretend that we know all the causes, and are acquainted with all the agents operating in God's vast empire. There can be then no such thing as fortune or accidents — everything is of providence and under the control of God.

Every power in nature and man works for God. Every thing that happens, comes to pass by the permission or the decree of God. All acts are provided for in God's plan and over-ruled by his providence, for the advancement of his glory and the well being of his people. It will not do to say that God cannot prevent men from acting as they do without destroying their moral agency, and that therefore, sin is in the world, not by the permission, but in defiance of all the perfections of God.

We pray to God to prevent the wickedness of men, every day, without destroying their moral agency. Every prayer we address to God asking him to succor our friends in temptation; to bring them to repentance; to give our enemies better hearts and change their purposes of wickedness towards us, is a request for him to do the very thing that it is here assumed he cannot do.

He certainly controls some men in perfect harmony with their moral liberty. Every good man is an illustration of this. He lives and acts under constant divine influences and attains his highest freedom under this divine control. If God may, and does thus control some men without infringing upon their moral agency, why may he not thus control all men? As every thing is either decreed or permitted by God, he certainly has a purpose in all he permits or decrees.

No intelligent or rational being would act or permit others to act without a purpose. It is a mark of intelligence not to act without a motive or reason for acting. Whenever God, who is the supreme, the infinite intelligence, acts, in decreeing that others shall act, or in permitting them to act, he has a purpose for doing so.

This being true, it is evident that God has a plan and a purpose in reference to all nations, revolutions and wars. All these things are brought about in accordance with the divine plan, and in fulfillment of the divine purpose, which was drafted in the mind of God before the world was called into being. He has a providence in all national revolutions. He directs, controls, governs and regulates them. They are made to subserve his purposes, to advance his glory, and to promote his cause.

1st. This is clearly taught in the Bible — "Is there evil in the city and the Lord hath not done it. I form the light and create the darkness: I make peace and create evil: I the Lord do all these things." "All things work together for good to them that love God: to them who are the called according to his purpose."

2d. Men have universally believed this. The heathen nations who have no revelation, and are therefore, guided alone by the light of nature and their own moral and spiritual intuitions, recognize God's providence in all social convulsions and national revolutions. They consult their oracles in reference to wars; they ask God to give them victory on the day of battle, and turn away from them the ruin of defeat. In the hour of victory they return unto him thanksgiving, and offer sacrifices in token of gratitude.

Christian nations act under the influence of the same conviction, in appointing days of national humiliation, fasting and prayer for the blessing of God upon their arms. Is this universal faith without a foundation in truth? Does the race act under the influence of a falsehood? That which is universal is natural; that which is natural is divine — "The voice of nature is the voice of God."

3d. Without this sort of divine control, there could be but little providential protection afforded us. It would afford us but little protection, to save us from the storm and tempest, the flame and the flood, pestilence and famine, and then turn us over without protection to the tender mercies of wicked men and devils. What sense of security could we have under God's providence, if it was confined to the material world, and the whole sphere of its operations was circumscribed to the domain of matter.

God's providence is in this war. It must be so if he watches o'er the destiny of men and nations. It was the purpose of no party to bring on this war. All parties tried to prevent it. No one believes, that had all the slave States seceded at once, that there would have been any attempt at subjugation, coercion, or the reconstruction of the Union by force of arms. But the simultaneous secession of the whole South was the plan of the original secessionist. They advocated it as a peace measure; as the only measure that could secure permanent peace, and prevent a bloody war, either in or out of the Union.

The war was not desired nor planed by the Union men, either North or South; they deprecated it; it was what they feared — the evil they labored long to prevent; they refused even to consider the question of secession, lest it should result in a bloody war. They pleaded and begged for a compromise, but it was unavailing. The very means they used to prevent it, was the very means that resulted in bringing it about.

The manifestation of this strong union feeling confirmed Lincoln in his purpose to put down what he is pleased to term the rebellion by military power. This called forth his proclamation, and this proclamation brought on the war. The Black Republican party North did not desire war; they used all the power of the government to prevent, yet their efforts to prevent it kindled its baleful fires from the banks of the Potomac to the shores of the Rio Grande.

In the South we should not criminate each other in regard to the origin, progress and rapid development of this conflict. We all labored, earnestly, honestly, to prevent it, yet that providence which "shapes our ends, roughhew them as we may," overruled these very means to bring it about for some wise purpose. We are in the midst of it, and we should all try, unitedly and earnestly, to fight through it. American society being what it was, no earthly power could have prevented it.

God in his providence did not prevent it, though the whole American people earnestly prayed for him to do so. Though we cannot understand it, we cannot question that it is to answer some wise and benevolent purpose in the progressive development of God's great plan for the elevation of the nations and the salvation of the world.

God is with us in this conflict; we think he is on our side in this struggle. We believe this, first, because our cause is just; we have acted and still act purely on the defensive; we have asked nothing but the rights secured to us in the constitution — the privilege of self-government Having failed to secure this in the Union, we proceeded to come out of it, either in the exercise of the natural right of revolution or the legal right of secession. I care not which you call it:

whether natural or legal, it was identically the same sort of State action that took us out of the Union, that was used to place us in it. If it was a legal process when used to place us in the Union, it was equally a legal process when employed to take us out of it.

We went in by Sovereign State action; we came out in the same way. Whether in doing this we exercised a natural or a legal right, or both, I care not. It was right if the privilege of self-government is right; and the conflict necessary to the defense of this action, is, as far as we are responsible for it, a righteous conflict.

It is not of our seeking; we could not avoid it. It has been forced upon us. The fires of fanaticism had been slowly consuming the foundation of our government for years, until at last the nations of the earth were startled in horror by the throes of a political earthquake, that shook into ruins the proudest Temple of Liberty that the sun of heaven ever shone upon.

We saw the war cloud as it began to rise slowly but surely; and we used every means in our power to arrest it. Statesmanship, compromise, legislation were all employed, but in vain. It at last covered our political sky with the blackness of darkness, and broke upon us in a fearful storm of fire and blood. Our cause is just, and God will defend the right.

Second, God is on our side — is with us in this conflict — because we have had reverses. "Whom the Lord loveth he chasteneth, and scourgeth every son whom he receiveth. If ye are without chastisement, then are ye bastards and not sons." The wise and affectionate father will punish, correct and chastise the children of his love for their good.

This principle of the divine administration applies to nations as well as individuals. This must be so because the nation is constituted of individuals. God was evidently with his chosen — the people Israel; but he suffered them to endure the bondage of Egypt. He afterwards brought them out of Egypt with a high hand and an out-stretched arm; but he suffered them to meet with sad reverses in the wilderness.

He was evidently with his own chosen nation — the Jews; but they were often defeated in battle by the armies of the surrounding nations.

God has without question been with his church in every age of the world; but he has found it necessary to preserve his people with the salt, and purify them by the fires of persecution. God was with our Revolutionary fathers in their struggle for independence; but he suffered them often to be defeated in their seven years conflict with the mother country; but the eagle bird of Liberty gathered strength while rocked by the storms and tempests of a bloody Revolution. So

Second, God has sent our reverses for our good. They were necessary to humble our pride; to stop our foolish and absurd boasting, and to make us feel the importance of the conflict in which we are engaged. They have tried our patriotism, and have shown to the nations of the earth that it is as pure as the gold which has been tried by the hammer and the fire.

Third, Our victories indicate the presence of God with our armies in this conflict. Who can read the reports of the battles of Bethel, Bull Run, Manassas Plains, Ball's Bluff, Springfield, Shiloh and Williamsburg, without being convinced that God gave us the victory, and that to him we should render thanksgiving for the glorious triumph of our arms. Every soldier who moved amid the perils and dangers of these bloody conflicts, must feel that the "Lord of host is with us; and the God of Jacob is our refuge."

Fourth, Another evidence that God is with us is seen in the remarkable preservation of the lives of our troops under circumstances of the greatest apparent danger. The bombardment of fort Sumter is a miracle and a mystery. The result can only be accounted for by admitting divine protection.

Nor was God's protecting providence less evident in the bombardment of the forts of Hatteras, Port Royal, Roanoke Island and Number Ten, than it was in the result at Sumter. In every case there was employed the most formidable armament that the world has ever known, from which there was thrown into our forts a storm of shot and shell, without a parallel in the history of warfare. And yet, ah! mystery and miracle of providence! not fifty of our men were killed in all the engagements.

So signally has God manifested his approbation of our cause by the protection of our troops under circumstances of the greatest peril, and most appalling danger, that it should make our whole people grateful to him as the great Giver of all good and the kind Preserver from all evil.

We will close by a few practical remarks:

1st. There is nothing in the present aspect of things, nor in the late reverses to our arms, to cause us to doubt our final success and ultimate victory. The loss of our cities and towns, on the sea-board and large rivers, is the natural result of going into this conflict without a navy; with a people that at present probably has the most formidable navy in the world.

We have not had the time nor the material for the construction of a navy; but as ours is an agricultural, and not a manufacturing and commercial society, our strength and national vitality is not in our large cities, on the ocean, but in our rich and fertile fields in the interior These places are not our whole country; the loss of them is not the loss of our country, nor does it render our cause hopeless.

We have got an army of five hundred thousand men in the field, well equipped, well drilled, well armed and constituted of as good fighting material as any in the world; an army that has never been whipped by the same number of men on any field; an army composed of the heroes of Bethel, Manassas, Ball's Bluff, Springfield, Shiloh and Newbern. Such an army in an open field and fair fight can never be vanquished. Then why should we fear? Doubt of success in a just cause with such an army, and the God of nations and of battles on our side! If, as a people, we deserve to be free, ultimate failure in such a cause and under such circumstances with such an ally, is impossible.

2nd. We must have confidence in our government and in our army. There may have been errors in administration, but neither our President nor his cabinet profess to be infallible; they are but men — with all the infirmities of men. We should expect them to commit errors. We should not look for perfection. The fact is the government under all the circumstances, has been a remarkable success. The severe criticism in which we sometimes indulge, in regard to the action of our generals, and the valor of our troops, is irrational, unjust and ungrateful. We are incompetent to criticise the actions of our generals, for two reasons —

First. We know nothing about the science or the art of war, therefore we should not give a criticism on a subject of which we are totally ignorant. But even if we had military talent, and military training and experience, we, at home know nothing of the circumstances and necessities under which they act. To form and express an opinion, disapproving their course, is to show our own ignorance, and to treat them with great injustice, by condemning them unheard. They understand it — we do not; they know the facts — we do not; they are responsible — we are not; they make the sacrifices, and face the dangers — we stay at home; therefore good sense, modesty, justice and gratitude should make us careful how we censure them.

When Johnson evacuated Harper's Ferry, the whole country rang with complaints at the movement; but we now know that it was that movement that gave us the victory at Manassas When General Albert Sidney Johnson fell back from Bowling Green and Nashville, the whole family of croakers were loud in their censure; but it was that movement that gave us the victory of Shiloh. Now with these facts before us, we should be careful how we complain of our government, our generals, and our troops.

Judging of the present by the past, we should infer that the falling back from Yorktown, the evacuation of Norfolk, and the withdrawing our troops from New-Orleans, are movements of as much strategy as those which have been attended with such fine results. These men, with brave hearts and strong arms, stand as a wall of fire between the invading foe, and our homes, our property, and our loved ones; and for this we owe them a debt of eternal gratitude. Shall we repay their sacrifices for us and ours with a want of confidence?

We should pray to God to give success to our cause, and triumph to our arms. God will defend the right. We may approach him then in full assurance of faith; with strong confidence that he will hear and answer and bless us. Prayer touches the nerve of Omnipotence; prayer moves the hand that moves the world; prayer is the rod in the hand of faith, that extracts the fiery curse from the burning bosom of the dark storm-cloud, and turns from our country and our homes the thunder-bolts of divine wrath. Prayer will convert darkness into light — our night into glorious day — our defeat into victory — our disasters into triumphs — our sorrow into joy — our weakness into strength — our feebleness into might.

Our cause is sacred. It should ever be so in the eyes of all true men in the South. How can we doubt it, when we know it has been consecrated by a holy baptism of fire and blood. It has been rendered glorious by the martyr-like devotion of Johnson, McCulloch, Garnett, Bartow, Fisher, McKinney, and hundreds of others who have offered their lives as a sacrifice on the altar of their country's freedom.

Soldiers of the South, be firm, be courageous, be brave; be faithful to your God, your country and yourselves, and you shall be invincible. Never forget that the patriot, like the Christian, is immortal till his work is finished. You are fighting for every thing that is near and dear, and sacred to you as men, as Christians and as patriots; for country, for home, for property, for the honor of mothers, daughters, wives, sisters, and loved ones.

Your cause is the cause of God, of Christ, of humanity. It is a conflict of truth with error — of the Bible with Northern infidelity — of a pure Christianity with Northern fanaticism — of liberty with despotism — of right with might. In such a cause victory is not with the greatest numbers, nor the heaviest artillery, but with the good, the pure, the true, the noble, the brave. We are proud of you, and grateful to you for the victories of the past. We look to your valor and prowess, under the blessing of God, for the triumphs of the future. Then

> "Strike till the last armed foe expires,
> Strike for your altars and your fires,
> Strike for the green graves of your sires;
> God and your native land."

Women of the South. We know your patriotism, your bravery, your nobleness of soul. It is not your privilege to fight. You can not move amidst the dangers, the perils, the blood and the carnage of the battle-field, beside your fathers, brothers, husbands and lovers. But you can do a work quite as important. You can gird them for the conflict, and with words, looks, glances and smiles, cheer them on to victory and to glory. Every letter you write them from home, should be filled with "thoughts that breath and words that burn," that will catch and kindle from man to man, and heart to heart, until all along our lines shall blaze with a martyr's courage and zeal for country and for home.

You can also, by your fortitude, patience, courage and strength of spirit, shame into silence the fearful, trembling terror-stricken, craven-hearted men in our midst, who are constantly predicting our failure in the glorious struggle in which we are engaged.

They absorb all the rays of light, and reflect none — they act as non-conductors in the social chain, that arrest the flow of the currents of patriotism through society — their influence is like the blighting frost upon the flowers. It blasts the hopes of the timid and chills the hearts of the desponding. By destroying confidence in the stability of our government, in the success of our arms, and the ultimate triumph of our cause, they prepare the way, to the extent of their influence, for the ruin of the country by the destruction of our credit and the depreciation of our currency.

Wise men, if they cannot be made brave should be taught silence. They should not be suffered to do us harm by their cold comfort, and damn our cause by faint praise.

You can also pray for God's blessing and protection on the loved ones who are absent. Every home should be a sanctuary — every dwelling a Bethel — every spot an altar, from which prayer should be offered for our country, and for our loved ones who are braving the dangers of the battle field for us, and all we hold dear.

# A Fast-Day Sermon

PREACHED IN THE

CHURCH OF SUGAR CREEK

MECKLENBURG COUNTY, N. C.

February 28th, 1862

## BY REV. R. H. LAFFERTY
PASTOR

FAYETTEVILLE

1862

## SERMON

"Up, sanctify the people, and say, Sanctify yourselves against tomorrow: for thus saith the Lord God of Israel, *There is* an accursed thing in the midst of thee, O Israel: thou canst not stand before thine enemies, until ye take away the accursed thing from among you." — Joshua 7:13.

GOD had made many precious promises to the children of Israel. And in the fulfillment of these promises he did lead them out from the land of Egypt, and the power of their oppressors, by a mighty hand and an out-stretched arm; and he established them securely in the land of their fathers, a land flowing with milk and honey. But in the attaining of these great promised blessings they had many powerful enemies to meet, they had many battles to fight.

They had taken God for their leader, and had committed their cause unto him who judgeth righteously. Hence, there was a peculiar obligation resting upon them to obey God, their leader. And just as long as they abide by the commands of Jehovah and obey orders, their enemies fall before them; but the moment they forget the covenant, commit sin, and disobey God, they are not able to stand before their enemies, but are filled with terror and dismay.

They came to Jericho, a strongly fortified city, and it fell before them an easy prey; "And they utterly destroyed all that was in the city, both man and woman, young and old, and ox, and sheep, and ass, with the edge of the sword. And they burnt the city with fire, and all that was therein; only the silver and the gold, and the vessels of brass and of iron, they put into the treasury of the house of the Lord," as God had commanded them.

The next place of attack was the city Ai. Joshua sent men to view it, and they report that about two or three thousand men will be sufficient to go up and smite Ai; "for they are but few." Accordingly about three thousand men of Israel went up against Ai, but they could not stand before their enemies, they were smitten, and fled: "wherefore the hearts of the people of Israel melted and became as water." This is a sad disappointment to Joshua and the elders of Israel, and they prostrate themselves "to the earth before the ark of the Lord," expressive of their deep grief.

And Joshua cries out, "O Lord, what shall I say, when Israel turneth their backs before their enemies. For the Canaanites and all the inhabitants of the land shall hear of it, and shall environ us round, and cut off our name from the earth: and what wilt thou do unto thy great name?" Joshua is at a loss to know why it was that he and Israel, who professed to put their trust in the Lord, had met with such a signal defeat.

God reveals to him the cause of his defeat. "*Israel hath sinned,* and they have also transgressed my covenant which I commanded them; for they have even taken of the accursed thing, and have also stolen, and dissembled also, and they have put it even among their own stuff." "Therefore the children of Israel could not stand before their enemies, but turned their backs before their enemies, because they were accursed: neither will I be with you any more, except ye destroy the accursed from among you."

"Up, sanctify the people, and say, Sanctify ourselves against tomorrow: for thus saith the Lord God of Israel, *There is* an accursed thing in the midst of thee, O Israel: thou canst not stand before thine enemies, until ye take away the accursed thing from among you." It is now folly for the children of Israel to go out to battle, for uninterrupted disaster and defeat will follow them, until they expel that from their midst which has offended God.

In taking Jericho, the specific command was that the city, together with all that it contained, should be utterly destroyed, except "all the silver, and gold, and vessels of brass and iron," which were to be consecrated unto the Lord; and were to be brought into the treasury of the Lord.

But among the hosts of Israel there was one covetous man, and for his sin they all suffer. Achan, the son of Carmi, the son of Zabdi, the son of Zerah, of the tribe of Judah, was the transgressor. His confession shows the supreme wickedness of his heart in endeavoring to enrich himself by robbing God, and breaking his commands. "When I saw among the spoils a goodly Babylonish garment, and two hundred shekels of silver, and a wedge of fifty shekels weight, then I coveted them, and took them; and, they are hid in the earth in the midst of my tent, and the silver under it."

This transgressor and all that appertained to him were taken out and destroyed, Israel was purged of his sin, God returned to them in mercy, and their enemies were easily vanquished. The great lesson taught by all this is, that if Israel take God for their leader, they must implicitly obey him, and if they trust in him for deliverance, that trust must not only be nominal but real.

We, my hearers, citizens of these Confederate States, are engaged in a terrible war, in self defense. It is a war, not of our seeking, but forced upon us. In the commencement of these difficulties we used every means that honor and religion demand, to avoid hostilities. We sent our Commissioners again and again to the Capital of the United States for the purpose of adjusting our affairs in a friendly manner. They were spurned from the throne, treated with contempt, insult, and with *dark, dark duplicity*.

We sought not the blood, the soil, nor the treasures of our enemies: we only asked them to let us alone, and permit us to work out our own destiny, as a people. We plead for this inalienable privilege and right. This was peremptorily denied us. We then arose in the defense of our own soil, and in the protection of our homes, and committed our cause into the hands of God who judgeth righteously. God favored our cause in a remarkable manner, and gave us as signal deliverances as he gave to the children of Israel.

We have declared that we put our trust in God, and therefore virtually have declared that we would obey God, turn from sin, and hate covetousness, as a people, and as individual citizens. This has been our position from the beginning. It is a solemn position; for it secures to us the chastising rod of God if we disobey him, or violate his commandments.

Recently our cause has not prospered, our army has again and again been defeated, the enemy has triumphed. We may well ask, why is this? Has God forsaken us, and given us over to the power of our enemies? I answer, no. But God may in these adverse providences be saying to us as he said to Joshua, "Israel hath sinned," "there is an accursed thing in the midst of thee: thou canst not stand before thine enemies, until ye take away the accursed thing from among you."

In view of these disasters, and under a sense of dependence upon God, our most worthy and beloved President, Jefferson Davis, has recommended that the people throughout these Confederate States observe this day, as a day of fasting, humiliation and prayer, and that we confess our sins, and implore the guidance and protection of God. This then is our professed business in the Sanctuary today.

It is a matter of vast importance that we look at our sins, and mourn over them with a godly sorrow. I will at this time notice some of those sins over which we should mourn today, and for which God may be chastising us as a people.

## I. INGRATITUDE TOWARDS GOD FOR HIS MANY FAVORS, SPIRITUAL AND TEMPORAL

God has showered down upon us many blessings; he has given to us a pleasant land, a goodly heritage, and has caused our cup to run over. He has given us an open Bible, Sabbath, Sanctuaries; all the means of grace. Perhaps no people has been more highly favored; and we ought to have been a people overflowing with gratitude to God, the giver. But this has not been the case with us. To too great an extent we have forgotten God, and in our prosperity we have said, I shall never be moved.

The signal deliverances which our army and our country received drew forth expressions of thankfulness to God, and professions of gratitude for the special divine interposition which we had experienced. But it must be admitted that this has been followed, if not accompanied, with a boastful self-relying spirit, which is the very opposite of that spirit which prompts true gratitude.

Our true condition is just this; we are not only frail, ignorant, helpless creatures, but we are sinful creatures, and as such deserve not, and have not, any claim upon the favorable notice of God. God might in justice deliver us up to the power of our enemies, and, employ them as agents, with all their malice, in chastising us for our sins. He might in justice send pestilence and famine throughout our land. But he has not thus dealt with us. Not because we have not deserved all these things, but because of his unmerited mercy.

We may then say with the prophet, "It is of the Lord's mercies that we are not consumed, because his compassions fail not." This ought to be the sentiment of our hearts; and in view of God's undeserved deliverances and benefits, and of civil and religious blessings, even in the midst of revolution, we should be humble in the very dust before God, and gratitude should fill our souls. But we have failed to do this, our humility has been a feigned humility, and we have to a great extent forgotten the hand that has been holding, leading, defending, and feeding us. This is ingratitude.

God is now chastising us for our sins, and by the disasters with which our army has recently met, he is saying to us, "there is an accursed thing in the midst of thee: thou canst not stand before thine enemies, until ye take away the accursed thing from among you." Let us get low before God today, let us, not feignedly, but truly, confess our sins, and do it with the firm resolve that, by his grace assisting us, we will forsake sin, and cleave unto the Lord. "Let us search and try our ways, and turn again to the Lord. Let us lift up our heart with our hands unto God in the heavens."

And let us be careful to cherish that gratitude which ought ever to accompany a sense of our dependence and sinfulness, and of God's goodness manifested towards us.

## II. CONVERTING THE BOUNTY OF GOD INTO A CURSE

About a year ago fears were entertained that the cause of our Confederacy might suffer much from a scarceness of bread. Supplies from abroad were completely cut off: the blockade was upon us. Indeed our enemy made his boast that he would soon *starve us out*. Consequently the public journals all over the land, at an early day, exhorted and urged our people to give special attention to the cultivation of corn and other grains and vegetables, necessary for food both for man and beast. The timely advice was heeded, labor to an unusual extent was put forth in this direction, and many prayers were offered up for a fruitful season.

God answered these prayers, and blessed the husbandman with an overflowing harvest; so that according to the general estimate, a sufficiency was produced last year to feed our Confederacy for two years. Thus God turned the counsel of our enemies into foolishness, and quieted the fears of our people.

In view then of our circumstances, of our fears of the marked blessing of God, and of that gratitude that ought to fill our hearts, there was a special obligation resting upon us to garner every bushel of corn, and sacredly use it in feeding our people while engaged in the sacred work of defending our homes, securing our rights, and expelling the invader from our soil.

But instead of this, to our utter astonishment and mortification, as soon as the harvest is gathered, we see, all over the land, a thousand distilleries in full blast, converting that which was given to sustain and strengthen our people into something worse than a deadly poison. No sooner than our prayers are answered, God's bounty received, and our fears of starvation dissipated, than we turn round and destroy the bounty, and in that destruction produce that which wherever it goes secures imbecility, distress and death.

Whether the making of whiskey is right or wrong in itself considered is a question which I will not stop to consider, as that is not the point now before me; but I do assert, that, in our present peculiar condition, our people could not adopt a more suicidal course, or more efficiently aid our enemies, than by converting the bread that God has given us into whiskey, and thereby securing a famine. When our corn is converted into ardent spirits its nutritious properties are forever destroyed, and these properties cannot be brought back, although the salvation of our country might hang suspended upon the attempt.

If Joseph, and the people of Egypt, had destroyed the surplus corn of that country during the seven years of plenty, famine and extinction must have been the inevitable result in the years of scarceness that immediately followed. And although they might have had their store houses filled to overflowing with spirituous liquors of the choicest quality, yet they could derive no relief or nourishment from these. They could not be a substitute for corn.

So when the year of scarceness comes to us we will not be able to subsist long upon our corn converted into whiskey, however abundant it may be. And what will we do? We cannot procure our supplies from abroad, for the enemy is besieging us, and we surely cannot have the impudence to go and seek relief from God, after grossly insulting him by deliberately destroying the bread with which he had so liberally furnished us.

We should look at this insult now, and with shame and contrition confess it before God, and forsake it. It is an accursed thing in the midst of us, and we cannot stand before our enemies, until we remove this accursed thing from among us.

### III. THE INTEMPERANCE OF OUR LAND AND ARMY

There can be no doubt, in the mind of any one, who takes a glimpse at the places of general concourse, that intemperance is on the increase in our land. Let any one visit our court-yards and depots, or take a seat in our cars, and he will see the evidence around him that we are becoming an intemperate people.

View our citizens as they assemble to consult respecting our common safety and defense, and how many are there entirely disqualified by intoxicating drink for calm deliberation? Witness our soldiers as they pass to the scenes of deadly strife, or return on furlough to their homes, and how many of them seem to think it an absolute necessity to be armed with the bottle or the jug, and boldly draw from it until they are completely drunk! And are these things to continue?

Is it so, that the more the enemy presses upon us, and our dangers increase, we will seek relief and comfort from the intoxicating bowl? Intemperance is a great sin in the sight of God, and it is especially so in those who profess to put their trust in him. Is it not an insult offered to God to ask or to expect him to bless and cooperate with drunken soldiers, and intemperate commanders!

God's displeasure must rest upon such a practice. "No drunkard shall inherit the kingdom of heaven." "Woe to the crown of pride, to the drunkards of Ephraim. The crown of pride, the drunkards of Ephraim, shall be trodden under feet." Now if these things be so, ought there not to be great searching of heart to see if this be not that "accursed thing in the midst of us" which displeases God, and causes us to flee before our enemies? The sin of Achan brought the displeasure of God and defeat to the entire camp of Israel. And one drunken commander or soldier may bring down the displeasure of God and secure the defeat of our entire army.

If there ever was a time in the history of our country when virtue, temperance, calm determined resolve, and wise deliberate counsel, ought to be exercised, this is that time. The grog shops throughout the land ought to be closed, the distillery fires extinguished, and our people from the highest to the lowest practice true temperance. We might then expect God to go forth with our arms. But let intemperance continue and increase, and the result must be increasingly disastrous.

Babylon of old was taken when the King was in a state of intoxication. And although a powerful enemy was beating at the gate of that renowned city, yet Belshazzar and his thousand lords did not hesitate to engage in a drunken carousal; then it was that Babylon was entered and fell an easy prey to the invading foe. And we know not but some, perhaps rainy of our recent disasters have had their secret remote origin in intemperance or intoxication.

It is my deliberate opinion that our people must abandon the free use of intoxicating drinks, or intoxicating drinks will prostrate us under the power of our enemies, and be our ruin. Let us then confess before God, mourn over, and forsake that sin, which must be a reproach to any people. Let us ask forgiveness of our God, and plead with him to return to its again, and again go forth with our armies, and give them, not the mad reckless daring produced by ardent spirits, but the courage undaunted of the true Christian patriot. Then one will chase a thousand, and two will put ten thousand to flight.

### IV. THE PROFANENESS OF OUR PEOPLE

Intemperance and profaneness are near of kin. They often go hand in hand. Profaneness is a habit inexcusable, in past days regarded as impolite, and is certainly highly displeasing to God. It is a disregard of the authority of God, and an irreverent use of the sacred titles of the Ruler of the Universe. It tramples under foot a plain command: "Thou shalt not take the name of the Lord thy God in vain: for the Lord will not hold him guiltless that taketh his name in vain."

The teaching of Christ is very plain on this point. "Swear not at all; neither by heaven; for it is God's throne; Nor by the earth; for it is his footstool; neither by Jerusalem; for it is the city of the great King. Neither shalt thou swear by thy head, because thou canst not make one hair white or black. But let your communication be, yea, yea; nay, nay; for whatsoever is more than these cometh of evil."

It is an excuse that will not be valid at the court of heaven, that we have become so accustomed to swearing that we do not know often when we take God's name in vain. This only enhances our guilt, and it exhibits the dreadful wickedness of sin in leading us to disobey God until we can do it without a thought. But does any one doubt that profaneness prevails in our land?

This doubt may be soon dissipated. Take your seat, if you please, in a large popular hotel in one of our cities. The large promiscuous crowd are all strangers to you. You are amazed to find that oaths are belched forth on the right hand and on the left. You fix your eye upon one whose dress and general bearing is that of the true gentleman. Your instinctive thought is, surely here is one who will not swear. He soon enters into conversation. He becomes a little excited; and presently you are satisfied that you have been somewhat deceived, for he too employs the dialect of hell.

He intersperses freely his assertions and conversation with oaths. But this practice is not confined to the promiscuous crowd, but prevails all over the land, and has found its way, to an alarming extent, into our army. Our soldiers swear; and may I not in truth say, that many of our officers are profane.

In view of these things, and in the knowledge of these things, must not the solemn question arise in the serious reflecting mind, how can God go with our army, and crown their efforts with victory, while that army, professing to trust in him, curse and blaspheme his holy name?

It would have produced amazement in heaven and earth too, if God had blessed, defended, and crowned with victory Joshua and the hosts of Israel, while they were disobeying him, and taking his name in vain.

So we may not be astonished at the recent defeats of our army, When we remember the holiness of God, and the veracity of God, and that he has declared that he "will not hold him guiltless that taketh his name in vain." The prospects before us are gloomy. Not simply because we have a powerful malignant enemy with which to contend. This is but a small part of my fear or dread, for it is easy for God to save by many or by few. But it is because we have offended God by our sins. Profaneness stalks abroad. Even our boys and servants are rapidly coming up to the stature of perfect men in profanity. They too can swear.

God declares by his prophet Jeremiah, "Because of swearing the land mourneth." Is not this an accursed thing in the midst of us, a fatal moral disease all over the land, securing the displeasure of God, and by his judgments causing the land to mourn? And may it not be true that we cannot stand before our enemies until we are purged of this daring sin? Let us with humility confess it, let us mourn over it, and let us forsake it that we may find mercy.

And if my voice could reach the ear of all our beloved soldiers, I would earnestly and affectionately say to them, soldiers, if you would have the blessing of God, if you would be shielded by God's power in the day of battle, and if you would be able to stand victorious before your enemies, revere God, obey his commandments, fear an oath. You then have God with you, and you can sing as the saints have ever delighted to sing, "God is our refuge and strength, a very present help in trouble." "The Lord of hosts is with us; the God of Jacob is our refuge."

## V. THE SPIRIT OF EXTORTION.

Under ordinary circumstances, when commerce is uninterrupted, supply and demand will generally fix just prices in the market. But at such a time as this, when commerce is broken up, when our harbors are blockaded, and the necessaries of life are monopolized, there cannot be free trade, and a healthful competition, but the consumer is at the mercy of the seller.

The seller has the consumer now entirely in his power. If he asks and receives a fair price, he is dealing uprightly with his neighbor; but if he asks and receives an enormous price, more than he knows the article to be worth, he is dealing unjustly with his neighbor, and is taking from him that to which he has no righteous claim. And it alters not, in the least, the case, to say, that he voluntarily gave the enormous price; it was a willingness produced by necessity; and advantage was taken of this necessity. This is extortion.

It has its origin in an undue love of gain. It is a practice that is pointedly condemned in God's word, and is classed among the blackest crimes: "Be not deceived; neither fornicators, nor idolaters, nor adulterers, nor effeminate, nor abusers of themselves with mankind, nor thieves, nor covetous, nor drunkards, nor revilers, nor *extortioners*, shall inherit the kingdom of God."

God brings this as a heavy charge against the children of Israel: "Thou hast greedily gained of thy neighbors by extortion, and hast forgotten me, saith the Lord God." God expresses his displeasure and anger for such conduct, by Saying, "Behold, therefore, I have smitten my hand at thy dishonest gain which thou hast made." Ez. 22:12-13.

Extortion then is a sin upon which God frowns and fixes the token of his displeasure. But the question here arises, is this sin practiced in our land? I answer that it is. The evidence of this is found in the fact of the exorbitant price at which many articles are held and sold. It is practiced not only upon our citizens and soldiers, but likewise upon our government. There are those who are determined to grow rich by the war; they are ready to take advantage of any needy pressing demand for the necessary articles of life, and they perseveringly wring, if possible, from government with a death grasp the very last dollar. Such sin approximates, perhaps transcends the sin of Achan.

Achan took the wedge of gold from the spoils of Jericho, and thus supposed that he was enriching himself; but these enrich themselves by dishonest gain, taken, not from an enemy, but from fellow-citizens, and from that government that is throwing over them the aegis of its protection; and this too at a time when every nerve is strained in self-defense, and in beating back the invading foe.

The rebuke of the prophet Elisha to his servant Gehazi is a fitting rebuke for them: "Is it time to receive money, and to receive garments, and olive-yards, and vineyards, and sheep, and oxen, and men servants, and maid-servants?" 2 Kings 5:26. Is it a time to set the heart upon riches, and go in their pursuit, when the enemy is at the door, and our soil is invaded? Surely each one ought to be satisfied with moderate gains, and be willing to sacrifice even these for the common good.

In view then of that utter abhorrence which God has for extortion, and in view of the undoubted fact that it is largely practiced through this land, we should speedily humble ourselves at the feet of our offended Sovereign, confess our guilt, and turn to him by righteousness. The spirit of extortion must be supported by the spirit of justice and of honesty, if we would have God smile upon us and our country's cause.

If we would have the protection of heaven, we must seek it by hating covetousness, loving mercy, and walking humbly with our God. We must seek it, by withdrawing our sympathies and our confidence from every one who engages in this dishonest business, and thus keep ourselves back from being partaker of this sin; and we must seek it by sanctifying ourselves, by "washing our hands in innocency."

## VI. NOT OFFERING OURSELVES AND OUR SONS FREELY FOR THE DEFENSE OF OUR COUNTRY.

War is a business not to be sought or desired. But when our peaceful homes, these sacred spots of earth, are invaded, every instinct of our nature, and every principle of Christianity urge us forward to their protection and defense, even unto blood. So it is of our States. They are each the sacred home of a great family, where each member has secured to him rights and privileges, and where each one has duties to perform.

Our General Government is the Confederacy of these great families or States for their mutual safety and well-being. There are mutual interests, mutual benefits, and mutual obligations. And when our country is invaded, as it now is, it is a duty which we owe our families, our country, and the world, to arise and meet the invading foe. And although it may touch the most tender chord of our hearts to part with our sons and send them away to the tented field, yet our affection for them is not to keep them back from offering themselves for the defense of our country.

The present is no time for hesitation or for shrinking back from the stern obligations that now look us in the face. The plain teaching of God's providence and his word is to gird on the weapons of warfare and go forth to the deadly charge. "Cursed be he that doeth the work of the Lord deceitfully, and cursed be he that keepeth back his sword from blood."

When Israel, on a certain occasion, had a great battle to fight it was expected that all would be present and meet their obligation, and share in the dangers. But there were those who would not forego the ease and the comfort of home, but continued their ordinary business, and left their brethren to fight their battle and "jeopard their lives unto the death in the places of the triumphal song they are very sarcastically rebuked for their indifference to their country defense. "Why abodest thou among the sheepfolds, to hear the bleatings of the flocks? For the divisions of Reuben there were great searchings of heart."

And the inhabitants of a certain place refused to go and aid in fighting their country's battles, but they were marked as cursed of God. "Curse ye Meroz, said the angel of the Lord, curse ye bitterly the inhabitants thereof; because they came not to the help of the Lord, to the help of the Lord against the mighty."

There are then times when it is our duty to offer ourselves and our sons freely, and go forth to battle, and show ourselves valiant to fight. When Israel did this their song was, "Praise ye the Lord for the avenging of Israel, when the people willingly offered themselves. My heart is toward the governors of Israel, that offered themselves willingly among the people.

Have we willingly and freely offered ourselves and our sons? Or have we not rather to too great an extent been remaining at home, "to hear the bleatings of the flocks," and have left our army and our country to be overrun by an aggressive powerful foe?

It is well for us to look at the point before us, and the issue of this deadly strife. It is not the reestablishment of the old Federal Government. This is now placed beyond a possibility. But it is the independence of THESE CONFEDERATE STATES, or subjugation.

This is the only issue, this the only question now to be settled. And what is subjugation? I reply, it is that of being reduced to a state of vassalage, we become tributary States, and will be obliged to pay tribute to our conquerors. What then is the duty which we owe our children, our country, and our God, in view of such an issue as this? Evidently freely to offer ourselves and defend our country even to the last bitter end, and adopt the sentiment of the patriots of former times, "give me liberty, or give me death."

I fear that we have not sufficiently entered into the merits of this momentous question that our country is now discussing and settling at the point of the bayonet, and the cannon's mouth. And while our countrymen, our fellow-citizens, have been suffering and bleeding, and dying, for our defense and safety, we have been too indifferent of the great interests at stake.

God is rebuking us for this in our recent disasters, and is saying to us, "there is an accursed thing in the midst of thee," and is leading us to feel that we have erred in not more freely offering ourselves, and is perhaps impressing many a mind with the solemn denunciation, "Cursed be he that keepeth back his sword from blood."

Our interests, our obligations, and our dangers, are mutual, and therefore we cannot, without guilt, refuse to take any part in that strife and struggle in which our country is now engaged. Your affections may be strong, as they ought to be, for your fathers, husbands, brothers, or sons, but this is no valid reason why you should not be willing that they should go and perform that duty which God in his providence has imposed upon them, and to which our country is loudly calling them.

Let us make the sacrifice, however costly; it will only enhance in our estimation, the sacred boon of independence when once achieved, and will lead us to watch and defend it, in all coming time, with undying care.

## VII. IN NOT PLACING OUR ENTIRE TRUST IN GOD, AND IN FAILING TO MAKE DAILY SUPPLICATION UNTO HIM FOR HIS BLESSING.

We are obliged to believe from the teaching of God's word that individuals and nations are safe who put their trust in the Lord. "O Lord of hosts, blessed is the man who trusteth in thee." "They that trust in the Lord shall be as Mount Zion, which cannot be removed, but abideth for ever." Trust in God implies confidence in him, and at the same time implies a sense of our dependant helpless condition.

It likewise implies a pledge on our part, that we will honestly endeavor to obey God, and have respect to all his commandments. And this trust is not confined to the hour of danger and calamity, but is carried with us along all the paths of life.

We as a people profess to put our trust in God. Now what is the nature of this professed trust, and the fruits which it produces? Do we feel our weakness, and our ignorance, and are we impressed with a sense of the great truth that "vain is the help of man?" I am persuaded that, to a certain extent, these things are so; but I greatly fear, that we are not honestly taking God for our portion, and sincerely endeavoring to keep his commands.

If we throughout THESE CONFEDERATE STATES had the spirit and humble reliance upon God which Jehoshaphat, King of Judah and his people had, when their enemies invaded their soil, how soon might peace be established throughout all our borders.

"And Jehoshaphat feared, and set himself to seek the Lord, and proclaimed a fast throughout all Judah. And Judah gathered themselves together, to ask help of the Lord; even out of all the cities of Judah they came to seek the Lord."

Now notice the humble, helpless, and confiding spirit manifested in the prayer offered up. "And now, behold, the children of Ammon and Moab and Mount Seir, whom thou wouldest not let Israel invade, when they came out of the land of Egypt, but they turned from them, and destroyed them not; Behold, I say, how they reward us, to come to cast us out of thy possession, which thou has given us to inherit. O our God, wilt thou not judge them? for we have no might against this great company that cometh against us; neither know we what to do; but our eyes are upon thee."

"And all Judah stood before the Lord, with their little ones, their wives, and their children," expressive of their hearty assent to every sentiment uttered in this prayer. Here we see that entire trust which in God's sight is so acceptable; and the result was that the enemy became their own destroyers, and God's people stood still, by his command, and beheld the salvation which to wrought. "And the fear of God was on all the kingdoms of those countries, when they had heard that the Lord fought against the enemies of Israel. So the realm of Jehoshaphat was quiet; for his God gave him rest round about."

We must then as a sinful, helpless people come and cast ourselves upon the arm of our God, to whom we have referred our cause; and to this point I believe that God will bring us by the defeats that are overtaking us. Then God will appear for us as our deliverer.

If we are placing our entire trust in God we are betaking ourselves unto prayer. Are we doing this? Is the spirit of prayer increasing in our land? Perhaps both these questions must in truth be answered in the negative. Prayer constantly should be made unto God, both in our army and over the land, as a people professing Christianity cannot reasonably expect to succeed without this.

When Israel was engaged in war with Amalek, the whole battle turned upon the point, whether Moses held up his hand or let down his hand, expressive of looking to God and trusting in him for victory, or failing to look to him and withdrawing that trust. "And it came to pass, when Moses held up his hand, that Israel prevailed, and when he let down his hand, Amalek prevailed."

Now may it not be true, that we have failed to hold up our hand daily in importunate prayer, pleading with God to prosper our cause, and go forth with our army? And if this be true, we may not be astonished that we are not able to stand before our enemies, but are defeated and thrown into confusion. There is something wrong in our midst, sin is at the door, and we may be sure our sin will find us out. God requires of us more than the bare profession that we trust in him.

Israel made such professions, but they were never saved from the power of their enemies, until they searched out their sins, and brought forth fruits meet for repentance. So we must exhibit our trust in God by turning away from sin, and having respect to all the statutes of the Lord. Let us then now turn to the Lord, from whom we have grievously departed, "with fasting, and with weeping, with mourning; and let us rend our hearts and not our garments." Let our repentance and humility be genuine and not hypocritical, and God will be gracious to us as a people, and cause us to praise him yet, for his signal deliverances.

In conclusion, I will add that there are two things on which I have no doubt. First. That God will chastise us for our sins. God chastises nations as well as individuals. And we may be well assured that our ingratitude, our folly in converting the blessings of God's hand into a curse, our intemperance, our profanity, and our covetousness, will bring down upon our heads the corrections of our Heavenly Father.

These corrections may be severe; they may be protracted; and they may be varied. But they will come, until we are brought to confess our sins, turn from them, and trust in God with the whole heart. "God cannot be deceived, and he will not be mocked." If we have taken him for our God, and have committed our cause unto him, and at the same time have forsaken his law, walked not in his judgments, broke his statutes, and kept not his commandments, he will visit our transgression with the rod, and our iniquity with stripes, until we are brought to feel that it is an evil and a bitter thing to sin against God.

God has commenced this work. O that we were wise, that we might speedily confess our sins and forsake them, that the uplifted rod might be turned away.

Secondly. That our cause will eventually triumph. All over the land there is the consciousness that ours is a righteous cause. Our warfare is the sacred work of defending our homes from the polluting touch of the invader. God has given us the assurances of his in favor in those signal victories which he has granted unto us. And although our arms have recently been defeated, and disasters have overtaken us, yet we are not to sink down in despondency and gloom, but we are to betake ourselves to the throne of grace, as we do this day, and there confess our guilt, seek the Divine guidance and protection, and renewedly place our trust in God.

And the time will come, I have no doubt of it, when these Confederate States will come out from that furnace through which they are now passing, and will take an enviable position in the family of nations, as the most complete exponent upon earth of a free government, and will have inscribed upon their banner in brilliant undying characters, to be seen and read by the latest generation, *"God is our Helper."* Amen.

# Shiloh

A Sermon

Preached by

Rev. John Lansing Burrows
Baptist Minister

1862

# A SERMON

"The Lord appeared again; in Shiloh." — I Sam. 3:21.

SHILOH, is henceforth to be one of precious names in the history of THE CONFEDERATE STATES. With it will be associated as with those other names, derived from the Holy scriptures, Bethel and Manassas, the idea of victory — God given victory.

The etymological import of all these names is impressively significant. Bethel signifies "the place or house of God." "the place where God reveals himself." And this sweet name we are permitted by the Providence of God, to associate with our first victory; by which we may fondly hope, the Lord intimated His ultimate purpose of delivering us from the wrath and oppression of our foes.

If God favors the right cause, and the name is at all indicative of His efficient revealing of his own power and grace, then our enemies had reason to dread assailing us near any place with such a name as Bethel.

Manassas signifies, "causing to forget." When Joseph gave this name to his first born son in Egypt the reason is thus given, "God hath made me forget all my toil and all my father's house."

And after the wonderful battle which bears that name, we flattered ourselves that we might forget the toils and struggles that led to it, and anticipate henceforward rest and peace. We said, "it is Manassas" and now we will forget our toils and the wrongs we have suffered in what we were accustomed to call the house of our fathers. And alas for us! Manassas did cause us to forget, too guiltily, that our strength and dependence were in God. In our exultation we forgot our trust, in our pride we forgot the humility which God loveth.

Too much like the fourteenth king of Judah, who was named Manasseh we set up idols in the temple of the Lord and worshipped images of our own making. Like him too we have been scourged of the Lord by the hands of our enemies and driven for a season out of at least a portion of our rightful territories. And like him to, I trust many of us in our calamities, have renounced our false dependencies, repented of our wanderings, renewed our allegiance and covenant with Him, and regained His protecting favor. May no future Manassas again cause us to forget and practically repudiate our God.

And now we have, *Shiloh*. There are two prominent philological meanings which the learned have given to this name. We will dwell for a little upon both, hoping that we may find in either a good omen for our cause. One meaning insisted upon by many critical authorities is, "The Desired," "The Asked or," "The Longed for."

How beautifully appropriate is this meaning of the word "Shiloh" to us. It is the Desired, the Longed for. This victory we have been praying! for earnestly, devoutly tearfully, in the closet, at the family altar, in the church, and in our daily prayer meetings. He who heareth the cry of His children, hath listened in pity to our importunities and hath given us Shiloh — what we have desired and prayed for.

Brethren, is there not a connection between the prayers of God's people and the victory we have gained. Why do we pray if we do not believe it? We may not be able to trace the cord, which prayer casts up, to encircle the arm of Jehovah, and then draw down its might upon the head of our oppressors. Its end may fly beyond our scope of vision, be lost in the distances which sight cannot pierce. We are conscious of the effort, and we see the results, and we will be contented to remain in ignorance of the intervening processes and agencies.

There are arachnidan insects which are said to be capable or spinning a long, slender thread, out upon a current of air, which wafts it upward until it fastens itself to the ceiling of a room or the limb of a tree, thus forming a ladder up which the tiny creature climbs to its desired position. We have like power by prayer.

The burdened heart throws out its cords, which, wafted upward by the spirit's breath, fasten themselves upon the hand of God, and draw us up to Him or draw that hand down to us. All over this land, Christians have prayed in penitent earnestness, have gotten hold of the arm of Jehovah, and brought it down upon our enemies heads. What we longed for has been granted. We prayed for it and God has given us Shiloh — the desired, the asked for. What an encouragement to beg for still greater favors.

We need more interpositions of God's hand. He is trying our faith and perseverance. Will our humility and profound sense of dependence stand the test of victory? Oh! shall we not, encouraged, faith-strengthened by attaining the longed for, implore larger mercies — for the defeats or our foes are mercies to us. Let us not fail to acknowledge his interference and give Him the glory — but the more faithfully walking in His commandments and clinging to His strength, press on to the great end, desired and longed for.

But the study of learned Expositors has discovered another meaning of the name. They call Shiloh, "The Tranquilizer," "The Pacification," "The great author of Peace." May we not hope that in this sense, Shiloh may be the beginning of a series of successes which shall bring peace to us. It is a sad illustration of the ruin wrought by sin that man never attains peace but through strife. Even the innocent child must have its struggle with death, before entering upon the rest of heaven.

The convicted sinner must pass through a desperate warfare with himself before he can attain to the peace of God. The saint knows in his own inner experience that strife precedes peace. And the nations have gained peace only through battles. Though this may not be the struggle that shall result in peace to the convulsed nation, yet there must come a battle which will decide the great contest. With or without the name that battle will be the Shiloh — the procurer of peace.

It cannot require many such contests to convince our enemies that their ambitious and tyrannical purposes are impracticable; that they must settle these controversies as prudence and wisdom would have settled them at first, without violence and murder. We are fighting for peace. We want peace for ourselves and we are anxious to live in peace with our neighbors and the world.

Oh! what joy it would bring to our suffering and distracted land, if this etymological signification of the name Shiloh, could be answered, and that bloody battle field prove the Pacificator from which should issue the negotiations which sooner or later must come, that shall result in the recognition of our indisputable right to self government, in the cessation of hostilities and the restoration of peace. We hail with joy the omens which this name suggests and will pray that they may be fulfilled.

With these remarks suggested by such auspicious names, let us pass to a more particular discussion of the text. *The Lord appeared again; in Shiloh.*

I. It is first implied that the Lord had appeared before. "Again" involves the idea of a previous revealing of Himself.

This was true as it related to the history or Israel. Again and again had Jehovah restored to them His favor, so often forfeited by their rebellion and guilt. So has it been with this nation. Infinitely beyond our deservings has the Lord revealed to us His favoring mercies. Our remorseless enemies, confident and boastful of greater numbers and superior resources, have been reluctantly compelled to admit over again the divine apothegm, "The battle is not always to the strong."

God has appeared for us, and our marshaled forces, contemned and ridiculed, as too few and weak for effective resistance to such numbers and might — as dissolute and ragged and ignorant and miserably armed — have held the braggart foe at bay for more than a year. Through God's favor we have driven his efficiently equipped armies from many a battle field and at this hour hold them in check at all their selected points of assault.

We cannot attribute these mercies, to greater numbers, to ampler resources, to more effective implements of war, to superior drill and discipline, for in all we have been inferior. To what then shall we attribute it? The text is the answer — "The Lord hath appeared" for us.

How applicable to us also as individuals is this text. To you, sinner, the Lord hath often appeared, in his providence checking your rebellious depravity, taking from you the objects behind which you hid yourself from His claims — by afflictions teaching you His sovereignty and the need for His favor — and by mercies appealing to your gratitude, obedience and love. In his gospel, through a pious father's instructions and a mother's prayers, through the teachings of your youth, by the voice of conscience and by the call of His Spirit, God hath often appeared and revealed His will to you.

In the long catalogue of means of grace by which he would draw you to himself has He manifested Himself. And to you too, child of God, has He often appeared drawing you from sin, forgiving your wanderings, comforting you in sorrows, answering your prayers, delivering you from temptations and perils. We have each of us many reasons gratefully to own, "the Lord hath appeared unto me."

II. The text implies further, than there are *intermissions of these revealings of God's favor.* There are spaces between then, and again. When I say "again" the Lord has come, I intimate that He has been absent from my soul — I mean that His favor has been withdrawn. Like Job, I cry, "Oh that I knew where I might find him." "Behold, I go forward, but He is not there, backward, but I cannot perceive Him, on the left hand where he doth work, but I cannot behold Him, He hideth himself on the right hand that I cannot see Him." Even the gracious soul often mourns the hidings of His face. These are the most distressing phases in the Christian's experience.

And if the careless transgressor will only examine into his own experiences, he to may convince himself that God draws nearer to him at some times than at others. There are seasons when he hears no call of God's voice, scarce any complaints of that divine monitor within his own conscience, seasons during which he can sin almost without any alarm or compunction. How sad your condition when God withdraws from you, when He leaves you to your own follies and unchecked wanderings.

Do I speak to any now, who seem to themselves to be thus forsaken of God, who can transgress His laws with impunity, who can press down the broad road, without terror or remorse. You can look back to the time when God appeared and spoke to you, and clearly proffered to your soul forgiveness and favor. Oh, wretched state when He withdraws these tokens of His presence and grace.

Through such a period too we seem to have passed in our recent national experience, for God deals with nations as with individuals. One reverse after another has humbled us, and called us back to the true source of strength and success. We bear with sad depression of soul the names of Roanoke and Newborn, of Henry and Donaldson. What has driven Him from us? The cause was as essentially righteous at Roanoke as at Bethel, at Donaldson as at Manassas. Why then have we been humbled before our enemies?

Perhaps in His sovereignty God sees that unmixed prosperity will not be best for our future good. He who disciplines His servants by affliction, thus preparing them for usefulness on earth and for the blessedness of Heaven, He who has sanctified his church by trials and tracked her pathway by the, blood of her martyrs, He who made "even the Captain of our salvation perfect through sufferings," leads infant nations too through disasters, to more solid and permanent prosperity than they could otherwise obtain.

Without some such reverses, we should be proud, self-exultant, boastful, self reliant. We should say in our independence, "Is not this great Babylon that we have built?" "Our own hands have gotten all this." God is jealous of His own glory. He will not give his praise to another. He will, I believe, lead us to independence of the northern government, but he will not leave us in independence of Himself. If we abandon our trust in Him, He will abandon us to our own resources, and make our enemies His rod for our chastisement.

III. Still further the text suggests *the renewed appearing of the Lord*, "He appeared again." Oh, with what rapture does the abandoned saint hail once more the light of His smile. When after a season of withdrawal, in some hour of despondent yet earliest prayer, the Lord lifts up upon the spirit, the light of His countenance, it is like the darting of bright sunbeams through a storm-fraught cloud.

Among the happiest hours of the Christian's life are those in which he thus regains the conscious favor of the Lord, a sweet assurance of forgiving love, an admission to that intimacy of communion with his Heavenly Father, in which he can in filial love confess his wanderings and implore restoration, in which he hears the forgiving, re-adopting voice that owns him as a child, and whispers peace and comfort to his soul. This is a blessedness unknown to the world.

And sometimes too the Lord renews his calls to the impenitent Sinner. After seeming to have left him for a season He again visits him by some providence, by some call of warning, or threatening, or promise, awakens him to a sense of his danger and guilt, and presses upon his soul the claims of Jesus Crucified. Then again is the time of his visitation. Neglect it and to you, as to Jerusalem, Jesus may say, "Oh that thou hadst known, even thou at least in this thy day the things that make for thy peace."

When God does thus draw near to you sinner, then "give all diligence to make your calling and election sure." It may be the last call, of Jesus to your soul. Do you not feel that you ought now to settle the great controversy between God and yourself, and become a devout and true hearted disciple of Jesus? Oh, yield and meet with a submissive heart to the visits of God.

And may we not too, hope and believe that to our struggling nation, "the Lord hath appeared again; in Shiloh?" We have prayed for victory. One victory has been granted. In this one instance the longed for has been granted.

It may not yet be as decisive in its immediate results as we had hoped, it may not prove directly the Peace bringer, and yet we may I expect it to have all important bearing upon the issues of the great struggle. We may hope and pray that it may be the first, in this campaign, of a series of triumphs that will prove to our enemies the hopelessness of their ambitious and nefarious schemes, that will compel the surrender of our invaded territories, that will inaugurate, the negotiations that shall result in peace.

Oh! it is right for us to rejoice in such a victory and to strike the timbrel in gratitude and praise, as did Miriam upon the shores of the Red Sea over the overthrown and destroyed Egyptians.

And yet, not without grief and sympathy with the suffering and the bereaved, can we rejoice over a victory. Many of our brave sons have poured out all the blood of their hearts in struggling for the triumph.

Many are yet groaning in pain from the wounds that torture them. There is trembling in many a home not yet reached by the intelligence of the fate of the loved that were in the battle. There are widows made desolate; weeping today over groups of children left fatherless, for whose support and welfare they are now to struggle and toil alone. Many a father groans, "Joseph is not, and Simeon is not, and ye will take Benjamin away also."

Among the lost we mourn most deeply the fall of the gallant leader of the army, not because his life in itself was more precious than that of others, but because our cause has lost the wisdom and skill that long years of study and experience had accumulated in a single mind. Nor will we withhold the sigh of compassion from the slaughtered of our enemies.

We may weep even for the guilty malefactor who dies by sentence of the law, while we would not arrest that sentence. We regret the anguish and sorrow which our foes have brought upon themselves, by their wicked inroads into the territories of a people who have doubtless as good right to govern themselves, and to choose their own rulers, as any other people on the earth which God has made for all. Sad, amid such carnage and grief, we may and ought to be, even while exultation and praise for the victory thrills our souls.

But the most cheering association of all that connects itself with this victory is, that God has revealed Himself as our shield and defense. "THE LORD appeared again; in Shiloh." Can we take the praise to ourselves? I would withhold none of the honor due to our brave sons for their fidelity and courage. They deserve our gratitude and praise; all the rewards and honors which a grateful country can bestow. But they were the willing agents through whom GOD wrought.

Let its not offend Him by denying or doubting His interposition and aid. An army comparatively poorly clad and poorly armed, has met and mastered an army of at least equal numbers, said to have been one of the best equipped and prepared for battle that the world has ever seen. What with such differences, has turned the victory to our side?

After admitting the operation of all secondary causes, what other conclusion can we reach than this — the God of battles favored our cause? Now, let us keep God on our side by recognizing and praising Him — by self-distrust; and confidence in Him — by obedience and love. Let us remember — "When thy brethren go up to battle then keep thee from every wicked thing."

# The Word of God a Nation's Life

A Sermon

Preached before

the

Bible Convention of

THE CONFEDERATE STATES

Augusta, Georgia

March 19th, 1862

by

Rev. George Foster Pierce

Bishop of the Methodist E. Church

1862

# A SERMON

> "That he might make thee know, that man doth not live by bread only, but by every word that proceedeth out of the mouth of the Lord doth man live." — Deuteronomy 8:3

"The things which were written aforetime, were written for our learning, that we, through patience and comfort of the Scriptures, might have hope." The narratives of the old Testament are not to be regarded as simple paragraphs in general history — mere links connecting, in consecutive order, the events of the olden time, but as embodying great principles in human society and in the divine administration, vital alike to the well-being of the one and the uniformity of the other.

God is always the same; and the Bible, while it records the actions of men, is really the history of God, and as "with Him there is neither variableness nor shadow of turning," we learn from His past procedure what we may expect as to His present and future government.

This fact being fully apprehended, we have a key to the dispensations of Providence, and need not greatly err in interpreting current events or in speculations as to the future. While in the Mosaic economy, there were many statutes, local and temporary, having their origin and use in what was peculiar to an introductory dispensation, yet among them are laws of universal and permanent obligation — principles ordained of God for all time, and perpetuated for the instruction of mankind, in the lasting records of the Church.

Government is an institution of Heaven: the powers that be are ordained of God. It is true, the Scriptures do not designate any particular form of government as best — nor are they eclectic as between the various theories which have challenged the suffrage of mankind; but as the condition precedent to the divine blessing, the duties of rulers and subjects are distinctly defined, and conformity to them urged by all that is precious in a nation's hopes, and by all that is fearful in the just judgment of Almighty God.

It is true, that many features of the Jewish polity were rudimental, introductory, and intended to teach the great lessons of dependence and obedience, as well as to meet for the time being the local necessities of tribes and families. Patriarchal supremacy, the subordinate authority of the chiefs of clans, and, under them, the heads of houses were all necessary to local government, but were wholly inadequate for general purposes.

Similarity of institutions was too feeble a bond of unity, and the elements of discord and disintegration were too strong to be neutralized by the perpetually diluting memories of a common descent and the traditional marvels of Egypt, the wilderness and the land of Canaan. Before their settlement in the Land of Promise, the children of Israel, however distinct as a people, were not a *nation* in the organic sense of that word; and their governmental condition was elementary, and the *forms* of authority were simple — yet sufficient for order and prompt action.

While the law did not abrogate these institutions, and the theocracy to be inaugurated did not supersede them, God was all the time educating them to broader views of their destiny, and to more exalted conceptions of their spiritual relations, and of the high functions they were to perform as a chosen people among the nations of the earth.

The disciplinary process by which the Jews were conducted through their singular history from bondage to national independence, power and prosperity, looked to two grand objects — one of which has been largely overlooked in our perusal of the historic records of the Old Testament.

One purpose, and the primary one, was to train up a people to a nationality, favorable in the plans of Providence for the introduction of Messiah's kingdom: the other and the collateral one, secondary in order, yet vastly important to mankind, was, that taking the *Jew* as the type of his race, God might develop the sources of weakness and danger — the probable points of departure from the true and the right way — the temptations most likely to corrupt and deteriorate — the elements of decay, overthrow and extinction.

The Jews, with all their folly, ingratitude and perverseness, were fair specimens of human nature; and an impartial record of individual experience or national history, would show pride, unbelief, and forgetfulness of God in forms as revolting and under circumstances as provoking, as any furnished by Ephraim or Judah.

Moses, in the address of which the text is a part, exhorts the children of Israel to obey all the commandments of the Lord their God — reminds them of the way along which they had been led, of the affliction which they had endured, and the deliverances wrought for them — interprets for them the program of divine Providence, and declares the ulterior object to have been that they might know, that "man doth not live by bread only, but by every word that proceedeth out of the mouth of the Lord doth man live."

The lowest construction which these words will bear — and doubtless the doctrine is true — is, that man's animal physical life is not sustained by bread alone, but by any thing that God may appoint and sanctify for nutriment; that His blessing first gave the earth its fertility and continues it, and if He were to command the air to sustain us, it would be equally obedient.

But the text has a higher meaning. It teaches that not only our being, but our well-being depends upon conformity to the divine word — that life, in its lowest gradation, as predicable of man, is not sustained by the natural law of adaptation of means to ends, and can neither be developed, prolonged nor made happy, outside of the will and word of the Lord — that bread, though ordained as the staff of life, does not nourish by virtue of its chemical properties, but by the blessing of the Lord — that the transgression of the divine law, by intemperance — excess in the use of what God supplies or allows — poisons, destroys, entails disease and death; that life is to be regarded not as a physiological fact, but a moral endowment, deriving its dignity and value from its religious use, the moral appropriation of its powers, its spiritual relations, and its possible eternal sequences.

The words, "man liveth," though a simple form of speech, are nevertheless compound in their signification. "Man" is a generic term, and stands for the race; "liveth" is concrete, and includes man as an individual being, as a member of the community, as a citizen of the country; and the whole comprehension of the phrase is, that man, considered as an independent personality; that human society, in its aggregate; the church, as an ecclesiastical organization; the State, as a body politic, are all under the same general law of dependence, subjection and obedience, as the condition of life, honor, prosperity and perpetuity.

We have assembled under very peculiar circumstances. As a people, we are in the midst of revolution. Our secession from the old Federal Union, and the inauguration of a new Confederacy, have not only dissolved the political ties which connected us with the Northern States, but have broken up our religious societies, our benevolent institutions, and thrown us upon new organizations to meet our responsibilities as a Christian people to the world around us.

It has seemed to me appropriate, therefore, to waive, in the discussion of the subject chosen, the special views and individual applications which the words would justify and even demand under ordinary circumstances, and to content myself in a brief discourse upon a few leading ideas, as they apply to society and the State.

The chapter opens with the implied doctrine, that the test of true allegiance to God, and the security of a quiet and peaceable life in all godliness and honesty, is in universal obedience to the divine commandments.

This is a broad, perhaps a startling proposition; but it is the starting point of all sound and safe reasoning on the question of duty, either personal, social or political. Obedience, to be sincere, must be entire. Neither God's authority nor man's real interests, will allow of any limitation.

All religion consists in recognizing the law and glory of our Maker — submitting to duty because it is His will, and not because it is a decision of our reason. The authority of the divine statute must be most solemnly regarded; otherwise, outward conformity is no proof of inward loyalty. To prevent delusion, this thought must be borne in mind, or the sacrifices we make to our own pride and selfishness may assume the name and claim the reward of religious service.

While the will of God is absolute and binding, even when the reasons of its enactments do not appear, still to manifest the nature and perfection of His government, He has been pleased to declare the benefit of His laws, and these appeal so strongly to our instincts and our solicitations of interest, as to constrain our admiration and homage, and, under powerful impressions of reverence and fear, we sometimes resolve upon and pledge fidelity and service.

But God, who knows the latent propensity of evil in our nature, may often address us as he did the children of Israel, when they vowed to do all that he had commanded. "The people have well said all they have spoken; O, that there were such an heart in them, that they would fear me, and keep all my commandments always that it might be well with them and their children forever!"

To prove them, to know what was in their hearts, whether they would keep his commandments or no, He humbled them, suffered them to hunger and thirst, led them through a variety of difficult circumstances, favored them with many miraculous deliverances. They were thwarted and they were indulged, disappointed in their expectations and surprised by their mercies, punished for their sins that they might be admonished, and pardoned that they might be encouraged.

But they were slow to learn the lessons of Providence. Distrust, murmuring, ingratitude, disobedience, marked all their history. Failing in the fundamental principle of submission and reference to God, they sought out many inventions. To say nothing now of the evil leaven of pride, self-will, the imitation of the multitude to do evil, which permeated their domestic life and social manners, very soon forgetting all the precautionary counsels of Moses, all the wonders of their own marvelous annals and their peculiar covenant relations, the practical recognition of their invisible King became an abstraction — a tradition without authority and a fable without a moral.

They sought to live by bread alone, to prosper without virtue, to fight without divine warrant, and to conquer without celestial aid. The word of the Lord was buried amid the rubbish of their desecrated temple. The altars, the high places, every green tree, the enthroned abominations of the heathen, revealed a nation of backsliders and idolaters, and finally of captives and exiles.

To conserve a nation, that word of the Lord so often announced in the Bible, "THE LORD REIGNETH," must be recognized, acknowledged, practically believed. Incorporated in the Constitution, confessed by the chief magistrate, re-echoed by subordinate rulers, pervading the legislation of the country, presiding over public opinion, it will be a safe-guard in revolution, a guide in peace, a Pharos, beaming light and hope upon the future.

Political morality would never have been deemed a thing of no concern, an article of barter, bandied about the market places of the land, if men had not first imagined that the Most High did not regard the actions of men and administer justice among the nations. A perverted public sentiment, largely tinctured with atheism, which excludes God from the affairs of earth, and confines Him, (if it admit His existence at all,) to heaven and heavenly things, is a fruitful source of venality and corruption in high places and low places, of insubordination, of commercial fraud and infidelity to contracts, of impious legislation and wide-spread contamination.

Our republican fathers wisely separated the Church from the State; their degenerate successors madly separated the State from Heaven. It has been the fashion to theorize and decide on politics, as if Christianity were not a superior, supreme law, and as though God had abandoned his book and his rights to the chances of a doubtful contest. Statesmanship has become an earthly science, a philosophy without religion, and a system of expediency without a conscience. In discussing systems of finance, commerce, tariffs, international relations, who insists on moral causes, on the dependence of the nations on Him who turns the seasons round, dispenses the changes and destinies of governments, and cannot, and will not be forgotten, without rebuke and judgment?

Loose and licentious notions of liberty are the legitimate out-growth of ignoring the supremacy of God. Vicious maxims in trade become current; capital is invested in enterprises which war against morality; vice puts on the livery of fashion and becomes bold by patronage; the administration of justice grows lax, in morbid sympathy with a false philanthropy; unpunished crime gangrenes society; and deified wealth rides over principle and merit and talent, and a hollow, heartless selfishness holds carnival over the wreck of every virtue.

The voice of the multitude, the example of the great, the power of money, constitute an inquisition so virulent and overbearing that reproof is dumb; the testimony of the Church is paralyzed, and, if from the wilderness which popular sin has made, there comes out some fearless prophet of Heaven, threatening the wrath to come, society, demoralized by indulgence and blinded by long impunity, rains upon his honest head the epithets, *bigot, enthusiast, fanatic, hypocrite,* and rushes on unchecked to its doom.

Men may philosophize, speculate, declaim, but God *will* reign. He never abdicates or dies. His glory He will not give to another. We are not our own, but men under authority. *In morals we have no rights of legislation.* We have a Master in heaven. His title to reverence is indisputable; His claim to homage and obedience inalienable. We *must* render to God the things which are God's.

If we would be a Christian nation, what the law commands or allows must never contravene the behests of Heaven. Nations have a sort of collective unity, and between rulers and people there is a reciprocal responsibility, and if there be connivance in evil, each is amenable for the guilt of the other.

If the executive, or legislative, or judicial department bring the law or policy of the country into conflict with the revealed economy of God, the people should remonstrate, vindicate the divine right, exhaust the remedies in their power, and, if they cannot reform, at least fix the burden where it belongs. If the people grow corrupt — impious, and claim the natural right to do moral wrong, then the government must set itself to honor God, by becoming a terror to them that do evil. Rulers must not bear the sword in vain, if they would fear God and live by his word.

The Church, too, must cease to shrink before the cant of those godless demagogues, who, when the good seek to array public opinion against vice, and to bring law into harmony with the Bible, preach liberty of conscience, all the more vociferously because they have long since ceased to have any conscience or rule of life, save selfish indulgence.

Her testimony against evil must be clear, intrepid, meek but firm, patient but unwearied. The insane cry of popery and priest-craft must no longer smother the thunders of the pulpit; and the theory of a Christianity which converts people without a change of heart or life — liberal enough to let men do as they please for the sake of their name and their money — which grants indulgences for sin rather than be thought uncharitable, relaxes by an apocryphal canon the stringent, inexorable rules of purity and self-denial, must be met, routed, exiled; and the sacramental host must know, that if they would drink of the river whose streams make glad the city of God, then must they fulfill the commission of His lips.

The impregnation of government, law, art, commerce, civilization, with her own pure, gentle, peaceable, loving sentiments, is the predicted triumph of Christianity: and we approximate the glory of that millennial age, when we honor the divine word by believing its promises, fearing its threatenings, adopting its counsels, practicing its morals; when we magnify the Lord and exalt His name; when we recognize His providence, beseech His aid, deprecate His wrath, by confession, petition and reformation. I am glad that our young Republic acknowledges God in her Constitution and calls on Him to witness the rectitude of her aims and objects.

I am glad that our President, in several official acts, "seeing, that we have no might against the great multitude coming upon us," has sought to turn the eyes of the people to the Lord their God; and that, in his late inaugural, he concludes with an earnest appeal to God, and a thrilling declaration of his own abiding trust in the justice and mercy of the Lord Almighty. I am glad that the people have responded again and again to the call to fast and pray with unwonted earnestness and universality.

Amid much that is discouraging to the pious, in view of abounding iniquity, these national acts, interpreted by Scriptural examples, inspire hope that God will vouchsafe to the intercessions of the faithful few our deliverance and liberty. O, my countrymen, let us reverence the Lord of Sabaoth, and let us remember that our country is to be preserved and perpetuated, not by science, wealth, patriotism, population, armies or navies, but by every word that proceedeth out of the mouth of the Lord.

"Hear me, Asa and all Judah and Benjamin: the Lord is with you while ye be with Him, and if ye seek Him, He will be found of you; but if ye forsake Him, He will forsake you."

Another word of the Lord, by which society is to be improved and the nation exalted to healthy, happy life, is His statute on the religious training of the young. On this subject, for a series of years, the policy of the country has been wrong and growing worse. The testimony of the Church has been timid, wavering and inconsistent. In relation to it, the commandment of the Lord is explicit.

The admonitions and counsels of the Bible are frequent, earnest and pointed, but a proud and petulant philosophy, full of conceit and flippant maxims, has corrupted both opinion and practice, and circulated ideas full of deadly poison, blighting to character and fatal to all government. The primal cause of well nigh all the evils which afflict society, is to be found in defective family discipline, example and instruction, and in a nearly total disregard of the injunctions of the Bible, the word of the Lord upon this subject. To train up a child in the nurture and admonition of the Lord, is a lofty commission, a moral duty of the highest grade, next in responsibility to our personal salvation.

To fulfill it in perfection, requires the highest order of intellect and the deepest work of grace. According to the capacity given, or that might be acquired, every parent is bound by the most solemn considerations, both personal and relative, temporal and eternal, to do what he can in developing the immortal mind committed to his charge into the highest style of character.

Admitting the intrinsic difficulties of the task, I can not forbear remarking, that the embarrassments most complained of chiefly arise from substituting the Divine by human plans — the sternness of authority, arbitrary, imperious, and passionate; turbulent temper, venting themselves in petulance and scolding; an indiscriminate use of the rod, or the bribery of weak compliances or irredeemable and unredeemed promises, or the postponement of all effort till the day of salvation is gone; and all these in the face of God's word, which says: "Fathers, provoke not your children to wrath;" "forbear threatening;" "put away lying;" "be not hasty in thy spirit to be angry;" "he that loveth his son chasteneth him betimes."

The Bible not only gives specific instruction in all these things, but is itself the best instrument of discipline. Its doctrines are to be taught, its principles explained, its motives urged, its promises applied, its threatenings announced. "And thou shalt teach them diligently unto thy children, and shalt talk of them when thou sittest in thy house and when thou walkest by the way, and when thou liest down, and when thou risest up."

For, says the Psalmist, God "established a testimony in Jacob, and appointed a law in Israel, which he commanded our fathers, that they should make them known to their children: that the generation to come might know them, even the children which should be born: who should arise and declare them to their children: that they might set their hope in God, and not forget the works of God, but keep his commandments." How wise, how benignant, how conservative this statute!

A father dies without a will: the division of his estate is settled by the arbitrament of law; but if he failed to communicate the knowledge of God, who shall supply his omission, or make up to the wronged or defrauded child his lost heritage? How natural and beautiful the Divine plan for transmitting truth! Every parent a historian and preacher; every habitation a temple; every path a school-house; every bed a pious retreat, where age sinks to rest with the language of piety on its lips, and youth is hushed to repose by the music of love in the words of heaven.

Oh! if the people would live by every word that proceedeth from the mouth of God, what families! how happy; what children! how lovely; what churches! how pure; what a nation! how great, and wise, and strong, having God so nigh in all that we call upon Him for.

What a departure from the word of the Lord must that be, which has accredited people with religion — *Bible religion* — and yet allowed them to live in the neglect of a primary duty, integral to personal piety, essential to Church progress, fundamental to public order and national greatness! Verily, the bread which we have been using may continue breath and being, but it is scanty, husky fare, and will fill the land with moral skeletons, tattered, hungry prodigals, too feeble to stand in virtue's ways, and too far off to return to our Father's house.

If we would have our sons as plants, grown up in their youth; our daughters as corner stones, polished after the similitude of a palace; if we would enjoy the fatness, the sweetness, the wine of life, we must live by every word of God. We must come back to the law and to the testimony, and renouncing and denouncing all the pert infidel sayings of the times, all the cant of irresolution, the pleas of sloth, the pretences of a mock humility, set ourselves to realize that prophetic scene, bright with celestial promise — "and all thy children shall be taught of the Lord, and great shall be the peace of thy children."

It is due to the subject, and appropriate to the occasion, to say that the whole education of the country should be Christian. During the formative period of life, it is obviously the will of God, and to the interest of society, that the rising generation should be taught the knowledge of God, the mind developed in the light of the Bible, and the heart guarded from the contagion of bad example, and trained under a system decidedly evangelical. Science and religion should be united in indissoluble wedlock.

The sanctities of the parental roof and the memories of pious instruction, should be perpetuated in the schoolhouse, the academy, the college. The interests at stake are too precious to be jeoparded by any omissions, or lapses, or intervals of neglect. The infidel policy of leaving the youthful mind unbiased and free, is unsound in principle and impracticable in fact.

It is a stratagem of the enemy of souls, too shallow to deceive a thinking man, and ought to spring the good to an instant occupancy of the ground, and a tenacious holding of it, by all the arts of love and mercy, the most assiduous pains-taking care, and the most devout supplications to God for needed help. The Christian denominations of the land have been seeking to do somewhat in this direction; but they have largely modified their plans, to forestall the charge of sectarianism, and escape the apprehended edge of reproach from their enemies.

What! is it sectarian to teach a youth to fear God, to do right, to love the country! Sectarian, to urge patriotism, benevolence, personal purity, by the sanctions of revealed religion! My brethren, if we would live by the word of the Lord, we must no longer compromise our duty to God and the country, by diluting our systems of education to suit carnal taste and worldly wisdom. We must prepare for the future.

The conflict for dominion between light and darkness is progressing — the crisis is at hand. We must come up to the help of the Lord against the mighty. The young should be enlisted as conscripts of the Kingdom. Catechisms, Sunday schools, family religion, pastoral care, religious education, should all be levied upon, pressed into service, if we would save the landmarks of morality from the inundations of vice, and draw over the nation the shield of Omnipotence.

Put the Bible in every house, an evangelical teacher in every school, a man of God in every pulpit — stir up, vitalize, intensify every agency for good in the Church; multiply by faith and prayer revivals of religion; seek, O seek, the instruction and conversion of the young and then, when this terrible war is ended and peace reigns in all our borders, we shall have a state of society so bright, beautiful and blest, that time shall have no emblem of it in the past but Eden, and eternity no type in the future but heaven.

This history of the past, as well as the suggestions of the text, constrain me to add one more illustration of the general truth I have been expounding. The life of a nation, in the sense of stability, honor, credit, prosperity, depends largely upon the moral character of its rulers. Nor are these results regulated by merely natural causes.

History, sacred and profane, attests that God's blessing is upon the good, and His curse sooner or later upon the bad. In the political creed of this country, a man's morals, his relations to God, have scarcely been thought of in his elevation to office. Party, party-service, order in rotation, have often determined the candidate, and, albeit he was the victim of notorious vices, the wire-worker reckoned advisedly upon rallying the strength of the party to his support, through his affinity with the vile on the one hand, and the unscrupulous devotion of all the rest to the platform, on the other.

We are the victims today of this ungodly traffic in vice, of unscriptural theories of government, of selfish schemes of power, of the fanatical ambition to enthrone an idea born in the seething brain of a pseudo-philanthropy, which boldly avows that the Bible is a lie if it does not teach its creed, and God to be rejected if He does not endorse it.

The word of the Lord is, "provide out of all the people able men that fear God." "The wicked walk on every side, when the vilest men are exalted." "When the wicked beareth rule, the people mourn." On the other side, a ruler "is a minister of God for good" — "a terror to evil doers, and a praise to them that do well." "Righteousness exalteth a nation, but sin is a reproach to any people," especially when sin is exalted, honored, enthroned in the high places of the land.

In the divine administration, rulers are contemplated as the head and representatives of the people, even in hereditary governments; and it must be eminently so in an elective one. It is to be remembered, therefore, that the people must share in the judgments which the sins of rulers provoke. When these proud transgressors challenge the Divine Being by their reckless impiety, the retribution is often sudden and overwhelming, as when He smote Herod with worms; or a gradual blight, a living death, as in the days of Jeroboam, the son of Nebat, who made Israel to sin.

One mode of divine punishment, (and perhaps the most to be dreaded,) is to abandon a people to corruption, leave the disease to work its course without check, permit them to fill up the cup of their iniquity, and, when sin puts on the glare of renown and the robes of office, and dances in festal gaiety under the patronage of the great — when the floodgates are open, the impediments are gone, and pollution rolls like a flood — then, the clouds of wrath brew in the heavens above, and the Dead sea makes ready her grave beneath.

Another mode is, to make the people mourn their folly, through the passions of their rulers, and then come wars, taxes, oppression, waste of blood and treasure; or the clouds of heaven are sealed and the parched earth responds not to the tiller's toil; mildew blights the ungathered harvest, pestilence wastes population, or the red rain of battle drenches the land with sorrow, and captivity is the doom of the nation.

We are beginning a new career. God help us to avoid the errors of the past, and, throwing off the shackles of parties, conventions and platforms, to abide by the word of the Lord. Let us have a Christian nation in fact as well as in name, that God may be as a wall of fire round about this young Confederacy, and a glory in the midst of her.

There is one other departure from the word of the Lord, common to the policy of the country, adopted and pursued by well nigh all, which demands and deserves rebuke. I mean the greed of gain, the deification of money. The subject is too large for discussion now, but a word to the wise will not be amiss.

In this very chapter, Moses admonished the people against the self-same evil into which we have sadly run, and notifies them that the only security against the temptations of an all-surrounding abundance, was to remember, fear and obey God.

"Beware, lest when thou hast eaten and art full, and hast built goodly houses and dwelt therein; and when thy herds and thy flocks multiply, and thy silver and gold is multiplied, and all that thou hast is multiplied; then thine heart be lifted up, and thou forget the Lord thy God." Alas! this is the crime and the curse of America. We have prospered, grown rich, luxurious, proud, and have said in our hearts, "my power and the might of my hand hath gotten me this wealth."

The history of the world confirms the testimony of the Bible as to the moral dangers of accumulated treasure. Wealth is favorable to every species of wickedness. Luxury, licentiousness of manners, selfishness, indifference to the distresses of others, presumptuous confidence in our own resources — these are the accompaniments of affluence, whenever the safe-guards of the Divine word, both as to the mode of increase and the proper use, are disregarded.

As to the higher forms of character and civilization, unless regulated and sanctified by Scripture truth and principle, *opulence* has always been one of the most active causes of individual degeneracy and of national corruption. Under the influence of its subtle poison, moral principle decays; Patriotism puts off its nobility and works for hire; Bribery corrupts the judgment seat, and Justice is blinded by gifts; Benevolence suppresses its generous impulses, and counts its contributions by fractions.

Religion, forgetting the example of its Author and the charity of its mission, pleads penury, and chafes at every opportunity for work or distribution; Covetousness devours widows' houses and grows sleek on the bread of orphans;

Usury speculates on providence and claims its premium, alike from suffering poverty and selfish extravagance.

Extortion riots upon the surplus of the rich and the scrapings of the poor, enlarges its demand as necessity increases, and, amid impoverishment, want and public distress, whets its appetite for keener rapine and with unsated desire, laps the last drop from its victim and remorselessly sighs for more.

The world counts gain as godliness, prosperity as virtue, fraud as talent; and *money*, MONEY, MONEY, is the god of the land, with every house for a temple, every field for an altar, and every man for a worshipper. The Church, infected by popular example, adopts the maxims of men, grades the wages of her servants by the minimum standard, pays slowly and gives grudgingly, and stands guard over her treasures, as if Providence were a robber, and they who press the claims of Heaven came to cheat and to steal.

Whenever the conservative laws of accumulation and distribution, as prescribed in the Bible, are ignored, then not only does the love of money stimulate our native depravity, but the hoarded gain furnishes facilities for uncommon wickedness.

The attendant evils are uniform. They have never failed in the history of the past. When commerce, manufactures and agriculture pour in their treasures, then, without the counteracting power of Scripture truth and Gospel grace, they infallibly breed the sins which have been, under God, the executioners of nations. Such is the suicidal tendency of unsanctified wealth, that the greater the prosperity of a people the shorter the duration.

The virulence of the maladies superinduced destroy suddenly, and that without remedy. Now mark how apposite, how prophetic, how descriptive, the word of the Lord: *"They that will be rich fall into temptation and a snare, and into many foolish and hurtful lusts."* "He that *maketh haste* to be rich shall not be innocent." "He that *hasteth* to be rich hath an evil eye." How these passages rebuke the spirit of speculation, the greedy desires, the equivocal expedients, the high-pressure schemes of the people!

"Lay not up for yourselves treasures upon earth." "Charge them that are rich in this world, that they be not highminded nor trust in uncertain riches." O, ye who make, and save, and hide, and hoard, hear ye the word of the Lord: "Your riches are corrupted, and your garments are moth-eaten; your gold and silver is cankered, and the *rust* of them shall be a witness against you, and shall eat your flesh as it were fire." O ye who strut and shine in plumage plucked from the poor and needy, "ye have received your consolation;" "weep and howl for the miseries that shall come upon you."

One of the moral secrets of this *wretched* war, as we *call* it, (perhaps it may turn out to be *merciful*,) in my judgment, is, to arrest the corruption of prosperity — to unsettle, agitate, break loose the people from their plans and hopes — dethrone their *cotton idol*, and, by upheaving the incrustations imposed by long years of peace and security, to let into our darkened minds the light of truth and ventilate the dormant conscience.

Infatuated by the love of the world, sensualized, fast-rooted in our pride and forgetfulness of God, the Spirit of grace has been shut out, the hearts of men were impervious, through the power of dominant, over-mastering habit, and the preaching of the Gospel as fruitless as would have been the tinkling of a cymbal.

The Church has been sliding into the world: the broad Scriptural lines of demarcation were well nigh passed. Piety had grown thin, meager, unreal. Christian manhood was merged in a mawkish spirit of compliance — a supple, sickly liberality, ready to break down the last barrier to the encroachments of fashion and the demands of an ungodly age. We needed reform. The shocks and vibrations of war's terrible batteries were necessary to shake the drowsy, stagnant atmosphere, to change the currents of thought, to break down the dominion of old ideas, and set us free from the selfish policy of the past.

To this end, God has "stirred up our nest," pushed us out from our resting places, unhinged the whole machinery of life, and called us to privation, sacrifice and peril. Oh, that this bitter discipline, this fiery ordeal, may prepare us for a liberty, better regulated, and a religion more spiritual, active and useful.

Hear now "the conclusion of the whole matter." The sum of this teaching is, that man liveth not by bread only, not by natural means, not by human philosophy, not by expediency, by time-serving — the shifting policy of earth; but, that, if we would be good, prosperous, useful, happy, safe, we must live by every word of God. My brethren, we are not mere life-time creatures, born to graze over the world like the beasts of the field, or to flit about in gaiety and song like the birds of the air; but subjects of discipline, spirits on probation, where great deeds are to be done, heroic sacrifices to be made, the distresses of others to be relieved, and our generation to be served by the will of God.

The earth we inhabit is not a mere physical frame-work, but a theatre of religion, of devotion to Christ and service to man. Breath, digestion, growth, sumptuous fare, titles, names, rank, power — these are not life, but semblances, mockeries, all. No, no; life is a boon of grace, the gift of God, capable of high achievement and noble destiny. To save our souls and to serve our race — this is our task; and to fulfill it is "life and health and peace,"

Love to God and man is our highest dignity, the divinest charity, the surest preparation for duty and death. While the wise, and rich, and mighty glory in their possessions, let us give all for "the pearl of great price." While the wavering minds of an unbelieving world toss restlessly upon a sea of doubt, let us hold fast by the oracles of God, the sure word of prophecy and promise. Precious Bible! Here is treasure which never waxes old. Here is knowledge without decay, truth which endureth forever.

From it, comes all pure morality; out of it, proceeds all the sweet charities of life. In it, is the motive power that is now reforming, and by and by will achieve the reformation of our race. The old man, leaning upon his staff and tottering to the tomb, reads it and thanks God he was born to die. The gray-haired matron soothes her sorrows by its record of love, and the light of her hope, kindled by its inspiration, projects beyond the desolations of death. Childhood and youth pillow their heads upon its truth in nature's last struggle, and die with their fingers between its promise-freighted leaves.

In the house of mourning, its footstep is noiseless as an angel's wing, and its power to cheer more potent than an angel's tongue. At the grave of the buried, it chants the hymn of hope, preaches the patience of faith to mourning friendship and stricken love, exhales and crystallizes the tears of sorrow, and gems the crown of life with these transfigured mementos of earthly suffering.

To devise a plan for giving this Book of books to the world, is the object of our meeting. Under present circumstances we can do but little. Our country is in trouble. War is upon us. We can, however, consult and pray, renew our expression of faith and love, strengthen the bonds of unity, and make ready for the future. It is a time for preparation.

Let us provide a treasury for the gifts of the Lord's people, organize for effective action when peace shall come, give the New Testament at least to our soldiers, and show to the Churches and the world that we covet the eulogy pronounced by our Lord upon Mary, when he said, "she hath done what she could."

Let us declare our will and purpose to cooperate with the other associations of Christendom in the work of printing, publishing and circulating the sacred Scriptures without note or comment: and may God speed the holy work and hasten the day when the Bible shall be the creed of every people, the text-book of every statesman, the constitution of every nation, the joy and excellency of all the earth.

# OUR DANGER AND OUR DUTY

BY

# REV. JAMES H. THORNWELL, D. D.
COLUMBIA, S. C.

## OUR DANGER AND OUR DUTY

The ravages of Louis XIV in the beautiful valleys of the Rhine, about the close of the seventeenth century, may be taken as a specimen of the appalling desolation which is likely to overspread the Confederate States, if the Northern army should succeed in its schemes of subjugation and of plunder.

Europe was then outraged by atrocities inflicted by Christians upon Christians, more fierce and cruel than even Mahometans could have had the heart to perpetrate. Private dwellings were razed to the ground, fields laid waste, cities burnt, churches demolished, and the fruits of industry wantonly and ruthlessly destroyed.

But three days of grace were allowed to the wretched inhabitants to flee their country, and in a short time, the historian tells us, 'the roads and fields, which then lay deep in snow were blackened by innumerable multitudes of men, women, and children, flying from their homes. Many died of cold and hunger; but enough survived to fill the streets of all the cities of Europe with lean and squalid beggars, who had once been thriving farmers shopkeepers.'

And what have we to expect if our enemies prevail? Our homes, too, are to be pillaged, our cities our property confiscated, our true men hanged, and those who escape the gibbet, to be driven as vagabonds and wanderers in foreign climes. This beautiful country is to pass out of our hands.

The boundaries which mark our States are, in some instances, to be effaced, and the States that remain are to be converted into subject provinces, governed by Northern rulers and by Northern laws. Our property is to be ruthlessly seized and turned over to mercenary strangers, in order to pay the enormous debt which our subjugation has cost.

Our wives and daughters are to become the prey of brutal lust. The slave, too, will slowly pass away, as the red man did before him, under the protection of Northern philanthropy; and the whole country, now like the garden of Eden in beauty and fertility, will first be a blackened and smoking desert, and then the minister of Northern cupidity and avarice. Our history will be worse than that of Poland and Hungary.

There is not a single redeeming feature in the picture of ruin which stares us in the face, if we permit ourselves to be conquered. It is a night of thick darkness that will settle upon us. Even sympathy, the last solace of the afflicted, will be denied to us. The civilized world will look coldly upon us, or even jeer us with the taunt that we have deservedly lost our own freedom in seeking to perpetuate the slavery of others.

We shall perish under a cloud of reproach and of unjust suspicions, sedulously propagated by our enemies, which will be harder to bear than the loss of home and of goods. Such a fate never overtook any people before.

The case is as desperate with our enemies as with ourselves. They must succeed or perish. They must conquer us or be destroyed themselves. If they fail, national bankruptcy stares them in the face; divisions in their own ranks are inevitable, and their Government will fall to pieces under the weight of its own corruption.

They know that they are a doomed people if they are defeated. Hence their madness. They must have our property to save them from insolvency. They must show that the Union cannot be dissolved, to save them from future secessions. The parties, therefore, in this conflict can make no compromises. It is a matter of life and death with both — a struggle in which their all is involved.

But the consequences of success on our part will be very different from the consequences of success on the part of the North.

If they prevail, the whole character of the Government will be changed, and instead of a federal republic, the common agent of sovereign and independent States, we shall have a central despotism, with the notion of States forever abolished, deriving its powers from the will, and shaping its policy according to the wishes, of a numerical majority of the people; we shall have, in other words, a supreme, irresponsible democracy.

The will of the North will stand for law. The Government does not now recognize itself as an ordinance of God, and when all the checks and balances of the Constitution are gone, we may easily figure to ourselves the career and the destiny of this godless monster of democratic absolutism.

The progress of regulated liberty on this continent will be arrested, anarchy will soon succeed, and the end will be a military despotism, which preserves order by the sacrifice of the last vestige of liberty. We are fully persuaded that the triumph of the North in the present conflict will be as disastrous to the hopes of mankind as to our own fortunes.

They are now fighting the battle of despotism. They have put their Constitution under their feet; they have annulled its most sacred provisions; and in defiance of its solemn guaranties they are now engaged, in the halls of Congress, in discussing and maturing bills which make Northern notions of necessity the paramount laws of the land.

The avowed end of the present war is, to make the Government a government of force. It is to settle the principle, that whatever may be its corruptions and abuses, however unjust and tyrannical its legislation, there is no redress, except in vain petition or empty remonstrance.

It was as a protest against this principle, which sweeps away the last security for liberty, that Virginia, North Carolina, Tennessee and Missouri seceded, and if the Government should be reestablished, it must be reestablished with this feature of remorseless despotism firmly and indelibly fixed. The future fortunes of our children, and of this continent, would then be determined by a tyranny which has no parallel in history.

On the other hand, we are struggling for constitutional freedom. We are upholding the great principles which our fathers bequeathed us, and if we should succeed, and become, as we shall, the dominant nation of this continent, we shall perpetuate and diffuse the very liberty for which

Washington bled, and which the heroes of the Revolution achieved.

We are not revolutionists — we are resisting revolution. We are upholding the true doctrines of the Federal Constitution. We are conservative. Our success is the triumph of all that has been considered established in the past. We can never become aggressive; we may absorb, but we can never invade for conquest, any neighboring State.

The peace of the world is secured if our arms prevail. We shall have a Government that acknowledges God, that reverences right, and that makes law supreme.

We are, therefore, fighting not for ourselves alone, but, when the struggle is rightly understood, for the salvation of this whole continent. It is a noble cause in which we are engaged. There is everything in it to rouse the heart and to nerve the arm of the freeman and the patriot; and though it may now seem to be under a cloud, it is too big with the future of our race to be suffered to fail.

It cannot fail; it must not fail. Our people must not brook the infamy of betraying their sublime trust. This beautiful land we must never suffer to pass into the hands of strangers.

Our fields, our homes, our firesides and sepulchres, our cities and temples, our wives and daughters, we must protect at every hazard. The glorious inheritance which our fathers left us we must never betray. The hopes with which they died, and which buoyed their spirits in the last conflict, of making their country a blessing to the world, we must not permit to be unrealized.

We must seize the torch from their hands, and transmit it with increasing brightness to distant generations. The word failure must not be pronounced among us. It is not a thing to be dreamed of. We must settle it that we must succeed. We must not sit down to count chances.

There is too much at stake to think of discussing probabilities — we must make success a certainty, and that, by the blessing of God, we can do. If we are prepared to do our duty, and our whole duty, we have nothing to fear. But what is our duty? This is a question which we must gravely consider. We shall briefly attempt to answer it.

In the first place, we must shake off all apathy, and become fully alive to the magnitude of the crisis. We must look the danger in the face, and comprehend the real grandeur of the issue. We shall not exert ourselves until we are sensible of the need of effort.

As long as we cherish a vague hope that help may come from abroad, or that there is something in our past history, or the genius of our institutions, to protect us from overthrow, we are hugging a fatal delusion to our bosoms. This apathy was the ruin of Greece at the time of the Macedonian invasion. This was the spell which Demosthenes labored so earnestly to break.

The Athenian was as devoted as ever to his native city and the free institutions he inherited from his fathers; but somehow or other he could not believe that his country could be conquered. He read its safety in its ancient glory. He felt that it had a prescriptive right to live.

The great orator saw and lamented the error; he poured forth his eloquence to dissolve the charm; but the fatal hour had come, and the spirit of Greece could not be roused. There was no more real patriotism at the time of the second Persian invasion than in the age of Philip; but then there was no apathy, every man appreciated the danger; he saw the crash that was coming, and prepared himself to resist the blow. He knew that there was no safety except in courage and in desperate effort.

Every man, too, felt identified with the State; a part of its weight rested on his shoulders. It was this sense of personal interest and personal responsibility — the profound conviction that every one had something to do, and that Greece expected him to do it — this was the public spirit which turned back the countless hordes of Xerxes, and saved Greece to liberty and man. This is the spirit which we must have, if we, too, would succeed.

We must be brought to see that all, under God, depends on ourselves; and, looking away from all foreign alliances, we must make up our minds to fight desperately and fight long, if we would save the country from ruin, and ourselves from bondage. Every man should feel that he has an interest in the State, and that the State in a measure leans upon him; and he should rouse himself to efforts as bold and heroic as if all depended on his single right arm.

Our courage should rise higher than the danger, and whatever may be the odds against us, we must solemnly resolve, by God's blessing, that we will not be conquered. When, with a full knowledge of the danger, we are brought to this point, we are in the way of deliverance, but until this point is reached, it is idle to count on success.

It is implied in the spirit which the times demand, that all private interests are sacrificed to the public good. The State becomes everything, and the individual nothing. It is no time to be casting about for expedients to enrich ourselves.

The man who is now intent upon money, who turns public necessity and danger into means of speculation, would, if very shame did not rebuke him, and he were allowed to follow the natural bent of his heart, go upon the field of battle after an engagement and strip the lifeless bodies of his brave countrymen of the few spoils they carried into the fight.

Such men, unfit for anything generous or noble themselves, like the hyena, can only suck the blood of the lion. It ought to be a reproach to any man, that he is growing rich while his country is bleeding at every pore.

If we had a Themistocles among us, he would not scruple to charge the miser and extortioner with stealing the Gorgon's head; he would search their stuff, and if he could not find that, he would find what would answer his country's needs much more effectually. This spirit must be rebuked; every man must forget himself, and think only of the public good.

The spirit of faction is even more to be dreaded than the spirit of avarice and plunder. It is equally selfish, and is, besides, distracting and divisive. The man who now labors to weaken the hands of the Government, that he may seize the reins of authority, or cavils at public measures and policy, that he may rise to distinction and office, has all the selfishness of a miser, and all the baseness of a traitor.

Our rulers are not infallible: but their errors are to be reviewed with candor, and their authority sustained with unanimity. Whatever has a tendency to destroy public confidence in their prudence, their wisdom, their energy, and their patriotism, undermines the security of our cause. We must not be divided and distracted among ourselves.

Our rulers have great responsibilities; they need the support of the whole country; and nothing short of a patriotism which buries all private differences, which is ready for compromises and concessions, which can make charitable allowances for differences of opinion, and even for errors of judgment, can save us from the consequences of party and faction. We must be united.

If our views are not carried out, let us sacrifice private opinion to public safety. In the great conflict with Persia, Athens yielded to Sparta, and acquiesced in plans she could not approve, for the sake of the public good. Nothing could be more dangerous now than scrambles for office and power, and collisions among the different departments of the Government. We must present a united front.

It is further important that every man should be ready to work. It is no time to play the gentleman; no time for dignified leisure. All cannot serve in the field; but all can do something to help forward the common cause. The young and the active, the stout and vigorous, should be prepared at a moment's warning for the ranks.

The disposition should be one of eagerness to be employed; there should be no holding back, no counting the cost. The man who stands back from the ranks in these perilous times, because he is unwilling to serve his country as a private soldier, who loves his ease more than liberty, his luxuries more than his honor, that man is a dead fly in our precious ointment.

In seasons of great calamity the ancient pagans were accustomed to appease the anger of their gods by human sacrifices; and if they had gone upon the principle of selecting those whose moral insignificance rendered them alike offensive to heaven and useless to earth, they would always have selected these drones, and loafers, and exquisites.

A Christian nation cannot offer them in sacrifice, but public contempt should whip them from their lurking holes, and compel them to share the common danger. The community that will cherish such men without rebuke, brings down wrath upon it. They must be forced to be useful, to avert the judgments of God from the patrons of cowardice and meanness.

Public spirit will not have reached the height which the exigency demands, until we shall have relinquished all fastidious notions of military etiquette, and have come to the point of expelling the enemy by any and every means that God has put in our power.

We are not fighting for military glory; we are fighting for a home, and for a national existence. We are not aiming to display our skill in tactics and generalship; we are aiming to show ourselves a free people, worthy to possess and able to defend the institutions of our fathers. What signifies it to us how the foe is vanquished, provided it is done?

Because we have not weapons of the most approved workmanship, are we to sit still and see our soil overrun, and our wives and children driven from their homes, while we have in our hands other weapons that can equally do the work of death?

Are we to perish if we cannot conquer by the technical rules of scientific warfare? Are we to sacrifice our country to military punctilio? The thought is monstrous. We must be prepared to extemporize expedients. We must cease to be chary, either about our weapons or the means of using them.

The end is to drive back our foes. If we cannot procure the best rifles, let us put up with the common guns of the country; if they cannot be had, with pikes, and axes, and tomahawks; anything that will do the work of death is an effective instrument in a brave man's hand. We should be ready for the regular battle or the partisan skirmish.

If we are too weak to stand an engagement in the open field, we can waylay the foe, and harass and annoy him. We must prepare ourselves for a guerrilla war. The enemy must be conquered; and any method by which we can honorably do it must be resorted to. This is the kind of spirit which we want to see aroused among our people. With this spirit, they will never be subdued.

If driven from the plains, they will retreat to the mountains; if beaten in the field, they will hide in swamps and marshes, and when their enemies are least expecting it, they will pounce down upon them in the dashing exploits of a Sumter, a Marion, and a Davie. It is only when we have reached this point that public spirit is commensurate with the danger.

In the second place, we must guard sacredly against cherishing a temper of presumptuous confidence. The cause is not ours, but God's; and if we measure its importance only by its accidental relation to ourselves, we may be suffered to perish for our pride.

No nation ever yet achieved anything great that did not regard itself as the instrument of Providence. The only lasting inspiration of lofty patriotism and exalted courage is the inspiration of religion. The Greeks and Romans never ventured upon any important enterprise without consulting their gods. They felt that they were safe only as they were persuaded that they were in alliance with heaven.

Man, though limited in space, limited in time, and limited in knowledge, is truly great, when he is linked to the Infinite as the means of accomplishing lasting ends. To be God's servant, that is his highest destiny, his sublimest calling. Nations are under the pupilage of Providence; they are in training themselves, that they may be the instruments of furthering the progress of the human race.

Polybius, the historian, traces the secret of Roman greatness to the profound sense of religion which constituted a striking feature of the national character. He calls it, expressly, the firmest pillar of the Roman State; and he does not hesitate to denounce, as enemies to public order and prosperity, those of his own contemporaries who sought to undermine the sacredness of these convictions.

Even Napoleon sustained his vaulting ambition by a mysterious connection with the invisible world. He was a man of destiny.

It is the relation to God, and His providential training of the race, that imparts true dignity to our struggle; and we must recognize ourselves as God's servants, working out His glorious ends, or we shall infallibly be left to stumble upon the dark mountains of error.

Our trust in Him must be the real spring of our heroic resolution to conquer or to die. A sentiment of honor, a momentary enthusiasm, may prompt and sustain spasmodic exertions of an extraordinary character; but a steady valor, a self-denying patriotism, protracted patience, a readiness to do, and dare, and suffer, through a generation or an age, this comes only from a sublime faith in God.

The worst symptom that any people can manifest, is that of pride. With nations, as with individuals, it goes before a fall. Let us guard against it. Let us rise to the true grandeur of our calling, and go forth as servants of the Most High, to execute His purposes. In this spirit we are safe. By this spirit our principles are ennobled, and our cause translated from earth to heaven.

An overweening confidence in the righteousness of our cause, as if that alone were sufficient to insure our success, betrays gross inattention to the Divine dealings with communities and States.

In the issue betwixt ourselves and our enemies, we may be free from blame; but there may be other respects in which we have provoked the judgments of Heaven, and there may be other grounds on which God has a controversy with us, and the swords of our enemies may be His chosen instruments to execute His wrath. He may first use them as a rod, and then punish them in other forms for their own iniquities.

Hence, it behooves us not only to have a righteous cause, but to be a righteous people. We must abandon all our sins, and put ourselves heartily and in earnest on the side of Providence.

Hence, this dependence upon Providence carries with it the necessity of removing from the midst of us whatever is offensive to a holy God. If the Government is His ordinance, and the people His instruments, they must see to it that they serve Him with no unwashed or defiled hands.

We must cultivate a high standard of public virtue. We must renounce all personal and selfish aims, and we must rebuke every custom or institution that tends to deprave the public morals. Virtue is power, and vice is weakness.

The same Polybius, to whom we have already referred, traces the influence of the religious sentiment at Rome in producing faithful and incorruptible magistrates, who were strangers alike to bribery and favor in executing the laws and dispensing the trusts of the State, and that high tone of public faith which made an oath an absolute security for faithfulness.

This stern simplicity of manners we must cherish, if we hope to succeed. Bribery, corruption, favoritism, electioneering, flattery, and every species of double-dealing; drunkenness, profaneness, debauchery, selfishness, avarice, and extortion; all base material ends must be banished by a stern integrity, if we would become the fit instruments of a holy Providence in a holy cause.

Sin is a reproach to any people. It is weakness; it is sure, though it may be slow, decay. Faith in God — that is the watchword of martyrs, whether in the cause of truth or of liberty. That alone ennobles and sanctifies.

'All other nations,' except the French, as Burke has significantly remarked, in relation to the memorable revolution which was doomed to failure in consequence of this capital omission, 'have begun the fabric of a new Government, or the reformation of an old, by establishing originally, or by enforcing with greater exactness, some rites or other of religion.

All other people have laid the foundations of civil freedom in severer manners, and a system of a more austere and masculine morality.'

To absolve the State, which is the society of rights, from a strict responsibility to the Author and Source of justice and of law, is to destroy the firmest security of public order, to convert liberty into license, and to impregnate the very being of the commonwealth with the seeds of dissolution and decay.

France failed, because France forgot God; and if we tread in the footsteps of that infatuated people, and treat with equal contempt the holiest instincts of our nature, we, too, may be abandoned to our folly, and become the hissing and the scorn of all the nations of the earth.

'Be wise, now, therefore, O ye kings! be instructed, ye Judges of the earth. Kiss the Son, lest He be angry, and ye perish from the way, when His wrath is kindled but a little. Blessed are all they that put their trust in Him.'

In the third place, let us endeavor rightly to interpret the reverses which have recently attended our arms. It is idle to make light of them. They are serious — they are disastrous. The whole end of Providence in any dispensation it were presumptuous for any one, independently of a special revelation, to venture to decipher. But there are tendencies which lie upon the surface, and these obvious tendencies are designed for our guidance and instruction.

In the present case, we may humbly believe that one purpose aimed at has been to rebuke our confidence and our pride. We had begun to despise our enemy, and to prophecy safety without much hazard. We had laughed at his cowardice, and boasted of our superior prowess and skill. Is it strange that, while indulging such a temper, we ourselves should be made to turn our backs, and to become a jest to those whom we had jeered?

We had grown licentious, intemperate, and profane; is it strange that, in the midst of our security, God should teach us that sin is a reproach to any people? Is it strange that He should remind us of the moral conditions upon which alone we are authorized to hope for success?

The first lesson, therefore, is one of rebuke and repentance. It is a call to break off our sins by righteousness, and to turn our eyes to the real secret of national security and strength.

The second end may be one of trial. God has placed us in circumstances in which, if we show that we are equal to the emergency, all will acknowledge our right to the freedom which we have so signally vindicated.

We have now the opportunity for great exploits. We can now demonstrate to the world what manner of spirit we are of. If our courage and faith rise superior to the danger, we shall not only succeed, but we shall succeed with a moral influence and character that shall render our success doubly valuable.

Providence seems to be against us — disaster upon disaster has attended our arms — the enemy is in possession of three States, and beleaguers us in all our coasts. His resources and armaments are immense, and his energy and resolution desperate. His numbers are so much superior, that we are like a flock of kids before him.

We have nothing to stand on but the eternal principles of truth and right, and the protection and alliance of a just God. Can we look the danger unflinchingly in the face, and calmly resolve to meet it and subdue it?

Can we say, in reliance upon Providence, that, were his numbers and resources a thousand fold greater, the interests at stake are so momentous, that we will not be conquered? Do we feel the moral power of courage, of resolution, of heroic will, rising and swelling within us, until it towers above all the smoke and dust of the invasion? Then we are in a condition to do great deeds.

We are in the condition of Greece when Xerxes hung upon the borders of Attica with an army of five millions that had never been conquered, and to which State after State of Northern Greece had yielded in its progress.

Little Athens was the object of his vengeance. Leonidas had fallen — four days more would bring the destroyer to the walls of the devoted city. There the people were, a mere handful. Their first step had been to consult the gods, and the astounding reply which they received from Delphi would have driven any other people to despair.

'Wretched men!' said the oracle, which they believed to be infallible, 'why sit ye there? Quit your land and city, and flee afar! Head, body, feet, and hands are alike rotten; fire and sword, in the train of the Syrian chariot, shall overwhelm you; nor only your city, but other cities also as well as many even of the temples of the gods, which are now sweating and trembling with fear, and foreshadow, by drops of blood on their roofs, the hard calamities impending. Get ye away from the sanctuary, with your souls steeped in sorrow.'

We have had reverses, but no such oracle as this. It was afterwards modified so as to give a ray of hope, in an ambiguous allusion to wooden walls. But the soul of the Greek rose with the danger, and we have a succession of events, from the desertion of Athens to the final expulsion of the invader, which make that little spot of earth immortal.

Let us imitate, in Christian faith, this sublime example. Let our spirit be loftier than that of the pagan Greek, and we can succeed in making every pass a Thermopylae, every strait a Salamis, and every plain a Marathon.

We can conquer, and we must. We must not suffer any other thought to enter our minds. If we are overrun, we can at least die; and if our enemies get possession of our land, we can leave it a howling desert.

But, under God, we shall not fail. If we are true to Him, and true to ourselves, a glorious future is before us. We occupy a sublime position. The eyes of the world are upon us; we are a spectacle to God, to angels, and to men. Can our hearts grow faint, or our hands feeble, in a cause like this?

The spirits of our fathers call to us from their graves. The heroes of other ages and other countries are beckoning us on to glory. Let us seize the opportunity, and make to ourselves an immortal name, while we redeem a land from bondage, and a continent from ruin.

# Afterword

Letter from Lord Acton:

Bologna
November 4, 1866

Sir,

The very kind letter which Mrs. Lee wrote to my wife last winter encouraged me to hope that you will forgive my presuming to address you, and that you will not resent as an intrusion a letter from an earnest and passionate lover of the cause whose glory and whose strength you were.

I have been requested to furnish private counsel in American affairs for the guidance of the editors of a weekly Review which is to begin at the New Year, and which will be conducted by men who are followers of Mr. Gladstone. You are aware, no doubt, that Mr. Gladstone was in the minority of Lord Palmerston's cabinet who wished to accept the French Emperor's proposal to mediate in the American war.

The reason of the confidence shown in my advice is simply the fact that I formerly traveled in America, and that I afterwards followed the progress of the four years' contest as closely and as keenly as it was possible to do with the partial and unreliable information that reached us. In the momentous questions which have arisen since you sheathed the sword, I have endeavoured to conform my judgment to your own as well as I could ascertain it from the report of your evidence, from the few English travelers who enjoyed the privilege of speaking with you, and especially from General Beauregard, who spoke, as I understood, your sentiments as well as his own. My travels in America never led me south of Maryland, and the only friends to whom I can look for instruction, are Northerners, mostly of Webster's school.

In my emergency, urged by the importance of the questions at issue in the United States, and by the peril of misguided public opinion between our two countries, I therefore seek to appeal to southern authorities, and venture at once to proceed to Headquarters.

If, Sir, you will consent to entertain my request, and will inform me of the light in which you would wish the current politics of America to be understood, I can pledge myself that the new Review shall follow the course which you prescribe and that any communication with which you may honor me shall be kept in strictest confidence, and highly treasured by me. Even should you dismiss my request as unwarranted, I trust you will remember it only as an attempt to break through the barrier of false reports and false sympathies which encloses the views of my countrymen.

It cannot have escaped you that much of the good will felt in England towards the South, so far as it was not simply the tribute of astonishment and admiration won by your campaigns, was neither unselfish nor sincere. It sprang partly from an exultant belief in the hope that America would be weakened by the separation, and from terror at the remote prospect of Farragut appearing in the channel and Sherman landing in Ireland.

I am anxious that you should distinguish the feeling which drew me aware toward your cause and your career, and which now guides my pen, from that thankless and unworthy sympathy.

Without presuming to decide the purely legal question, on which it seems evident to me from Madison's and Hamilton's papers that the Fathers of the Constitution were not agreed, I saw in State Rights the only availing check upon the absolutism of the sovereign will, and secession filled me with hope, not as the destruction but as the redemption of Democracy. The institutions of your Republic have not exercised on the old world the salutary and liberating influence which ought to have belonged to them, by reason of those defects and abuses of principle which the Confederate Constitution was expressly and wisely calculated to remedy. I believed that the example of that great Reform would have blessed all the races of mankind by establishing true freedom purged of the native dangers and disorders of Republics. Therefore I deemed that you were fighting the battles of our liberty, our progress, and our civilization; and I mourn for the stake which was lost at Richmond more deeply than I rejoice over that which was saved at Waterloo.

General Beauregard confirmed to me a report which was in the papers, that you are preparing a narrative of your campaigns. I sincerely trust that it is true, and that the loss you were said to have sustained at the evacuation of Richmond has not deprived you of the requisite materials. European writers are trying to construct that terrible history with the information derived from one side only. I have before me an elaborate work by a Prussian officer named Sander. It is hardly possible that future publications can be more honorable to the reputation of your army and your own. His feelings are strongly Federal, his figures, especially in estimating your forces, are derived from Northern journals, and yet his book ends by becoming an enthusiastic panegyric on your military skill. It will impress you favourably towards the writer to know that he dwells with particular detail and pleasure on your operations against Meade when Longstreet was absent, in the autumn of 1863.

But I have heard the best Prussian military critics regret that they had not the exact data necessary for a scientific appreciation of your strategy, and certainly the credit due to the officers who served under you can be distributed and justified by no hand but your own.

If you will do me the honor to write to me, letters will reach me addressed Sir J. Acton, Hotel [Serry?], Rome. Meantime I remain, with sentiments stronger than respect, Sir,

~ Your faithful servant

John Dalberg Acton

Lexington, Vir.,

15 Dec. 1866

Sir,

Although your letter of the 4th ulto. has been before me some days unanswered, I hope you will not attribute it to a want of interest in the subject, but to my inability to keep pace with my correspondence. As a citizen of the South I feel deeply indebted to you for the sympathy you have evinced in its cause, and am conscious that I owe your kind consideration of myself to my connection with it. The influence of current opinion in Europe upon the current politics of America must always be salutary; and the importance of the questions now at issue the United States, involving not only constitutional freedom and constitutional government in this country, but the progress of universal liberty and civilization, invests your proposition with peculiar value, and will add to the obligation which every true American must owe you for your efforts to guide that opinion aright. Amid the conflicting statements and sentiments in both countries, it will be no easy task to discover the truth, or to relieve it from the mass of prejudice and passion, with which it has been covered by party spirit. I am conscious the compliment conveyed in your request for my opinion as to the light in which American politics should be viewed, and had I the ability, I have not the time to enter upon a discussion, which was commenced by the founders of the constitution and has been continued to the present day. I can only say that while I have considered the preservation of the constitutional power of the General Government to be the foundation of our peace and safety at home and abroad, I yet believe that the maintenance of the rights and authority reserved to the states and to the people, not only essential to the adjustment and balance of the general system, but the safeguard to the continuance of a free government. I consider it as the chief source of stability to our political system, whereas the consolidation of the states into one vast republic, sure to be aggressive abroad and despotic at home, will be the certain precursor of that ruin which has overwhelmed all those that have preceded it. I need not refer one so well acquainted as you are with American history, to the State papers of Washington and Jefferson, the representatives of the federal and democratic parties, denouncing consolidation and centralization of power, as tending to the subversion of State Governments, and to despotism. The New England states, whose citizens are the fiercest opponents of the Southern states, did not always avow the opinions they now advocate. Upon the purchase of Louisiana by Mr. Jefferson, they virtually asserted the right of secession through their prominent men; and in the convention which assembled at Hartford in 1814, they threatened the disruption of the Union unless the war should be discontinued. The assertion of this right has been repeatedly made by their politicians when their party was weak, and Massachusetts, the leading state in hostility to the South, declares in the preamble to her constitution, that the people of that commonwealth "have the sole and exclusive right of governing themselves as a free sovereign and independent state, and do, and forever hereafter shall, exercise and enjoy every power, jurisdiction, and right which is not, or may hereafter be by them expressly delegated to the United States of America in congress assembled." Such has been in substance the language of other State governments, and such the doctrine advocated by the leading men of the country for the last seventy years. Judge Chase, the present Chief Justice of the U.S., as late as 1850, is reported to have stated in the Senate, of which he was a member, that he "knew of no remedy in case of the refusal of a state to perform its stipulations," thereby acknowledging the sovereignty and independence of state action. But I will not weary you with this unprofitable discussion. Unprofitable because the judgment of reason has been displaced by the arbitrament of war, waged for the purpose as avowed of maintaining the union of the states. If, therefore, the result of the war is to be considered as having decided that the union of the states is inviolable and perpetual under the constitution, it naturally follows that it is as incompetent for the general government to impair its integrity by the exclusion of a state, as for the states to do so by secession; and that the existence and rights of a state by the constitution are as indestructible as the union itself. The legitimate consequence then must be the perfect equality of rights of all the states; the exclusive right of each to regulate its internal affairs under rules established by the Constitution, and the right of each state to prescribe for itself the qualifications of suffrage. The South has contended only for the supremacy of the constitution, and the just administration of the laws made in pursuance to it. Virginia to the last made great efforts to save the union, and urged harmony and compromise. Senator Douglass, in his remarks upon the compromise bill recommended by the committee of thirteen in 1861, stated that every member from the South, including Messrs. Toombs and Davis, expressed their willingness to accept the proposition of Senator Crittenden from Kentucky, as a final settlement of the controversy, if sustained by the republican party, and that the only difficulty in the way of an amicable adjustment was with the republican party. Who then is responsible for the war? Although the South would have preferred any honorable compromise to the fratricidal war which has taken place, she now accepts in good faith its constitutional results, and receives without reserve the amendment which has already been made to the constitution for the extinction of slavery. That is an event that has been long sought, though in a different way, and by none has it been more earnestly desired than by citizens of Virginia. In other respects I trust that the constitution may undergo no change, but that it may be handed down to succeeding generations in the form we received it from our forefathers. The desire I feel that the Southern states should possess the good opinion of one whom I esteem as highly as yourself, has caused me to extend my remarks farther than I intended, and I fear it has led me to exhaust your patience. If what I have said should serve to give any information as regards American politics, and enable you to enlighten public opinion as to the true interests of this distracted country, I hope you will pardon its prolixity.

In regard to your inquiry as to my being engaged in preparing a narrative of the campaigns in Virginia, I regret to state that I progress slowly in the collection of the necessary documents for its completion. I particularly feel the loss of the official returns showing the small numbers with which the battles were fought. I have not seen the work by the Prussian officer you mention and therefore cannot speak of his accuracy in this respect.– With sentiments of great respect, I remain your obt. servant,

~ R.E. Lee

Various Books Published By
# CONFEDERATE STATES PRINTING OFFICE[10]

You can find these fine books and others by C.S. Publishing Office at your favorite Bookseller, or at www.lulu.com

**The Confederate States of America in Prophecy**, by Rev. W.H. Seat, a Southern Methodist Minister, and is edited by Dr. William G. Peters. This work examines Daniel's prophecy of the of the Five Governments; with the United States as the Fifth Government and the Confederate States as the little stone cut from the mountain, as a revived Government of Judah.

The Eschatology of the United States as Restored Israel, and the Confederate States as a Restored Judah, is a secular prophecy of the people of North America as God's special chosen people.

In the heady days of Southern victories over Northern armies, Rev. Seat posits the future history of the Confederate States based upon the Prophet Daniel.

**Sermons of the Confederacy 1861-1862**, edited by Dr. William G. Peters, is a collection of sermons by Southern ministers, bishops, and priests, from 1861-1862.

These ministers cover, in their sermons and discourses, a wide range of subjects, from the cause of the War, differences between Yankees and Southerners, Negroes and their purpose among Southerners, the life and death of Confederate heroes, service to God, military service and Christian Faith, etc.

This is an excellent book for those who want to understand our Confederate ancestors, the C.S.A., and the South's Faith in God and victory in the face of implacable Northern invasion.

**Sermons of the Confederacy 1863-1865**, edited by Dr. William G. Peters, is a collection of sermons by Southern ministers, bishops, priests, and rabbi from 1863-1865, and a continuation from "Sermons of the Confederacy 1861-1862."

These men of God cover a wide range of subjects, from the cause of the War, differences between Yankees and Southerners, Negroes and their purpose among Southerners, the life and death of Confederate heroes, service to God, military service and Christian Faith, etc.

This is an excellent book for those who want to understand our Confederate ancestors, the C.S.A., and the South's Faith in God and victory in the face of death and destruction from Federal invasion.

---

[10] Also designated as C.S. Printing Office. A division of Confederate States of America, Inc.

**The True Church Indicated to the Inquirer**, by Bishop John McGill. Confederate Bishop of Richmond, Virginia, edited by Dr. William G. Peters.

Bp. McGill examines the claims of various and sundry groups to be the true Church. He examines these claims in the light of scripture, history, tradition and reason. Then he contrasts them against the claims of the Catholic Church to be the One, True Church, showing how the claims of all other groups fall short.

**The Confederate Army Navy Prayer Book** is the Episcopal Prayer Book for the Armed Services of the Confederacy, edited by Dr. William G. Peters. The Prayer Book went through annual editions from 1861-1865, and was the official military prayer book of the Confederate States.

Additional prayers have been included, including national calls to prayer by President Jefferson Davis throughout the War, and a sermon by Bp. Stephen Elliot delivered upon the Day of National Humiliation, Fasting and Prayer in 1861.

**The Catholic Devotional for Confederate Soldiers** was written by Bishop McGill for the Confederate soldiers to carry with them into battle, and for their encampments.

The work was published and registered by Bp. McGill in the Confederate States of America in 1861, and is edited by Dr. William G. Peters.

The Devotional contains many Catholic prayers, novenas, selections from the Mass, etc., which are appropriate to daily devotions, for Catholics and other Christians.

**Faith The Victory** by Bishop John McGill, Confederate Bishop of Richmond, Virginia, edited by Dr. William G. Peters.

Bp. McGill presents an explanation of Catholic doctrine for Catholics and non-Catholics who hold to the old orthodox Protestant beliefs and traditions, and want to know more about the development and meaning of Christian doctrine.

A non-polemical work, the Bishop provides a rational explanation of sometimes difficult subjects. It is a clear concise summary of doctrinal points of interest to all Christians, without being either too brief, or tedious.

www.ingramcontent.com/pod-product-compliance
Lightning Source LLC
Chambersburg PA
CBHW020349170426
43200CB00005B/110